"*Jewel of Heaven* is the rare book th while." **Rick Bundschuh**, author of

"In this equal parts harrowing and .... told with grace and unabashed honesty, Angie reminds us that when we surrender the things that mean the most to us only then can we begin to understand the power of God." **Grant Nieporte**, screenwriter of *Seven Pounds* and *Breakthrough*

"I can't get over how true and real, honest and raw, Angie's voice is in sharing her story about life, loss, faith, and hope. I encourage anyone who can to go grab this book and make it part of your life." **Rachael Lampa**, contemporary Christian music artist

"So thankful for who Angie is and her heart for people. What a remarkable and inspiring story she has to tell of God's goodness in her life!" **Brant Hansen**, radio personality and author of *Unoffendable* and *Life Is Hard, God Is Good, Let's Dance*

"In *Jewel of Heaven*, Angie shares her heart in a way that is both deeply personal and universally relatable. Her journey through life's messiness— marriages, children, faith, and self-doubt—is told with humor and raw emotion. This is a story that inspires courage, compassion, and the belief that even the hardest paths can lead to unexpected blessings." **Justin Narducci**, President and CEO, Cure International

"*Jewel of Heaven* is an extraordinarily authentic and faith-based narrative of personal transformation and overcoming challenges. It offers a unique perspective on motherhood, illness, and the power of belief. The story explores Angie's emotional journey as she grapples with guilt, grief, anger toward God, and despair. *Jewel of Heaven* will challenge you to explore your own views of faith, hope, redemption, overcoming adversity, and the power of prayer." **Gary Bellig**, Senior Regional Director of Donor Relations, Cure International

"From the first chapter I was riveted! I couldn't put *Jewel of Heaven* down until I finished the entire book in one day's read. More than anything, this story is authentic and vulnerable, which is why I know many will be touched by Angie and Jade's testimony! I feel edified and uplifted after reading Jewel of Heaven." **Rebekah Prager**, Director, Project Little Child

"*Jewel of Heaven* is an extraordinary story that will leave you feeling inspired and uplifted. Angie's courage and resilience in the face of adversity, combined with the miraculous events that unfold, make for a truly unforgettable read. Whether you're a believer or a skeptic, this book will touch your heart and leave you with a renewed sense of faith in the power of love. By the end, I was swept up in a whirlwind of emotions, torn between a standing ovation and the struggle to contain the tears welling up inside." **George Sisneros**, author and founder of Ordinary Missionaries

"*Jewel of Heaven* is a memoir that leads us into the tragic, hidden corners of our broken world. Nevertheless, we emerge from reading *Jewel of Heaven* awestruck by God's sovereignty and redemption. With vulnerable and vivid prose, Angie Howell pens a gem of a book you'll have trouble putting down." **Karlie Ruiter**, registered nurse and founder, Casa Tabito

"In my work in Mexico, I've witnessed the difference people can make in the lives of the helpless. After the extensive Job-like sufferings of Angie and Jade, as shared in this book, we saw and were impacted by how unfettered their compassion was! Theirs is a powerful, heart-wrenching, and triumphantly heartwarming story. It is well worth the time to read!" **Baja Bob Sanders**, Founder, Baja Christian Ministries

"*Jewel of Heaven* will break your heart and send your spirit soaring. Angie holds nothing back as she shares the good, bad, and ugly of her family's transformational journey with Jade. You will be drawn into the family as you experience their gut-wrenching pain and miraculous joy. In the end, you also will be transformed by knowing God is with you, He is madly in love with you, and He will never forsake you. Don't miss this opportunity to get to know the Jewel of Heaven and her Savior Jesus." **Vicki Sutter**, Founder, Winsome Ministries

"It's truly inspiring to witness how God works in stories like *Jewel of Heaven*. Not everyone has the privilege of sharing a story of a true miracle, but seeing the transformative power of prayer is profoundly moving. I was reminded of this the day Angie brought her sweet daughter into my home—a moment that exemplified faith in action. This story is a powerful testament to how faith can move mountains and transform lives. I encourage you to open your heart to this story. It has the potential to change your perspective and inspire your own journey in incredible ways." **Ray Carter**, cofounder of Eternal Brothers Ministry

Jewel *of* Heaven

A Beautiful Story of Brokenness, Redemption,
and the Power of a Biker's Prayer

ANGIE HOWELL

BROOKSTONE
PUBLISHING GROUP

Birmingham, Alabama

Jewel of Heaven

Brookstone Publishing Group
An imprint of Iron Stream Media
100 Missionary Ridge
Birmingham, AL 35242
IronStreamMedia.com

Library of Congress Control Number: 2025902010

Cover design by MindStir and Hannah Linder Designs

ISBN: 978-1-960814-14-2 (paperback)
ISBN: 978-1-960814-15-9 (ebook)

1 2 3 4 5—29 28 27 26 25

Dedication

Before Jade was even born, God orchestrated a symphony of beauty in the background of my life, bringing together a group of people who would forever hold a space in my heart. Each of these people has contributed to this story in their own way, and I am grateful for their presence in my life at exactly the right time and exactly the right place.

To my Lord and Savior, Jesus Christ. You were there with me on the floor when I thought all hope was lost. You were there with me when the diagnosis came. You were there with me in the garage when I didn't think I could go on. When I thought You had left me, it was You who held me close. You never left me. Not once. Thank you for a journey I never would have chosen on my own. Thank you for always working all things together for your good.

To the beloved biker group, Eternal Brothers Ministry. I am still in awe of who you are and all you did for a faithless woman and her dying baby more than seventeen years ago. I would like to specifically dedicate this book to Cousin Rich and his friends Ray and Russ for their persistence in making our meeting happen and showing me the power of prayer. You are humble and gracious men of God, and we should all serve and give to others the way you do.

To Tank. Although I never met you, your presence was felt that day at Ray's house as they used your anointing oil on my daughter. I've been told that you were a strong man of faith who loved the Lord deeply, and I believe you were with us that hot August day. I can't wait to meet you when I, too, become a citizen of heaven.

To my grandmother, Mamaw. You were steadfast in your prayers for Jade. Your letters of support and love for your sweet great-granddaughter meant everything to me during a time when nothing mattered anymore. I look forward to the day when I get to feel your soft, squishy hugs again and hear you call my name in your biscuits-and-gravy Arkansas twang.

To my mom, Marilyn. You were the reason I had a foundation of Jesus in my life and the only reason I let God back in when I lost my faith. You stood by me through my choices, let me steal your days off to watch my children, prayed for me, cried with me, and gave me a life of love I didn't deserve. I love you, Mom. I am who I am today because of you.

To all the Jades, Lillys, and Harpers of the world (and their warrior mommies and daddies). You did not ask for this road you are journeying on. But you travel it with grace and strength. Don't ever let yourselves get trapped in the dungeon or forget you were made for a time such as this. Jesus is with you. Don't ever lose sight of that.

To the misfits like me. You are the reason I wrote this book. To all the women at the well, addicts, church hurts, and anyone who has ever felt far from God, I see you. But most importantly, Jesus sees you and wants a relationship with you. I pray that you won't wait as long as I did to feel the freedom that comes with a walk with Jesus. He's waiting for you.

Contents

Foreword

Strap yourself in for a wild ride.

The true story that follows is one of those wondrous tales that is such a blend of the chaotic and miraculous that it seems more of a Hollywood creation with fictional characters than an account of actual events and real people.

I find in this story a common thread in many stories of those whom the "hound of heaven" is tracking: the rebel being taken to a point of hopeless darkness only to find God using unlikely people to deliver His loving and inexplicable touch.

By receiving this adventure into our hands, we have been invited not only to bounce along with the twists and turns of this family but also to find the encouragement for us not to give up and throw in the towel if (or when) our own lives become a soap opera of tragedy and disappointment. To find in these pages the promise that God is active, caring, and listening when the heavens seem to be made of brass.

It is also an opportunity to rejoice. To know that even our rebellion and frothing against what we perceive to be the injustices of God do not prevent Him from hearing the even deeper cry of our helpless hearts . . . and answering with kindness.

Especially fun to this reader is who God chooses to use as the delivery men of His miraculous plan: a crew of tough, tobacco-stained, chain-draped bikers.

Their role in this adventure rings with familiarity of all the other bottom dwellers whom our Lord tapped to do His bidding. Smelly fishermen; hot-headed rebels; disloyal, cheating tax collectors; pompous know-it-alls; fallen women; and those with innocent blood on their hands. And biker gangs.

Who of course give all those who are losers, failures, sin-stained, or think of themselves as such a burst of hope that they might, too, become useful in God's hands.

And there is the transformation of Angie, the central character who spares no raw, unpleasant memory of her actions and attitude.

Having spent time with Angie, I still find it hard to fathom that the diminutive, nimble, and upbeat woman I know was ever the tough, bitter, and tortured soul who inhabits these pages. It is obvious that the hand of God not only touched Jade, Angie's "Jewel of Heaven," but also has done a marvelous remodel job on her as well.

Which leads me to the reason I hope that this book finds its way into many hands: we need to hear these stories. True stories such as this can be a life ring for those drowning in some kind of misery. They can help those of us who feel all alone in our time of fear and frantic questioning know that God is at work in spite of our empty feelings.

We need these stories because, sooner or later, we or someone we know may need the encouragement and hope they give.

We need such stories to see that the expression "God works in mysterious ways" is not just a dusty saying but an actual reality.

So buckle up.

Angie will toss you in the passenger seat and take you on the wild ride of her life. She will take you precariously close to disaster and slosh through the swamps of despair. You will be with her as she spews disdain and doubt at God and accompany her as she rattles down roads of doubt and fear.

Many times, you may wish that you could step into her story and yank her hands off the wheel as you can see potential disaster looming ahead.

And I promise, by the end, you will also feel as if you are along in a victory parade riding with her as the ticker tape of God's blessings pours upon her . . . and you as well.

So, enjoy this ride.

And if you by chance know someone for whom the clouds have darkened in their life, someone for whom God is a thousand miles away, someone for whom hope is a long-shot lottery, perhaps you might pass this book along.

They too may find within these pages encouragement, hope, and perhaps the whisper of God telling them that they are not forgotten.

Rick Bundschuh
Author of *Soul Surfer*, The Bethany Hamilton Story
Kauai, Hawaii

Preface

Why I Wrote Jewel of Heaven

I didn't save her for you. I gave her back to you so her miracle story would lead others to Me." Those were the words whispered in my ear as I begged God to show me my purpose in this world during a difficult season of my life not long ago. After being not so gently nudged by the Holy Spirit, I surrendered my insecurities to God and began writing *Jewel of Heaven* in December 2022. In an effort of obedience, I semiretired from my company, Tender Hearts Home Healthcare, and wrote full time until I completed the manuscript in August 2023.

I have but one goal for writing this book. If just one person comes to know Jesus because of the story God wrote with Jade's life, then our time in the dungeon will have been worth every dark, grueling second.

Special Thanks

I would like to acknowledge and thank a team of incredible people who surrounded me before, during, and after the writing of this book.

To Rae Lynne Johnson, writing coach extraordinaire. I cannot thank you enough for the months and months of guidance you gave me while on this writing journey. You walked with me every step of the way, and I am so grateful for your expertise, your feedback, your humble redirection, and your friendship.

To my literary agents at Legacy LLC, D. J. Snell and Susan Andreone. In an ocean of ridiculously talented authors who wanted nothing more than to have an agent believe in them, I was no more than a guppy, a fledgling author who was convinced nobody would believe in me. But you did. Thank you for taking a chance on a broken woman with a promise of an extraordinary story.

To Joyce and John Smith. By being brave enough to tell your story, you became the inspiration for me to write my own. Thank you for taking my call. You are gifts from God.

To all the nurses, physicians, physical therapists, occupational therapists, and speech therapists who worked with Jade along the way. Each of you has touched our lives in your own special way. Thank you for making Jade work so hard even as you made her cry. Your efforts made the difference in her life.

To three incredible physicians whom Jade fell in love with and requested that I mention specifically: Dr. Alan Seay, Dr. John Guenther, and Dr. Max Elliott. You are angels sent from God who made our journey lighter. Your constant attention to my daughter in times of great stress and uncertainty was a beacon of light in the darkness that almost consumed me. You have served your profession with humility, grace, and brilliance.

To Jade's Dad

Oftentimes, the hero of a story is the one who works in the shadows while everyone else falls apart.

When Jade was born with such extraordinary medical needs, this was you. Our rock who worked tirelessly being both father and mother. The voice of reason when I couldn't think. The calm when our world became chaotic.

I owe you a thousand thank-yous for being our steady hand, for reminding me when to keep my mouth shut, and for loving on all of the children while I withered away in a dungeon I created all by myself.

I know now there were things I was wrong about back in those days, and for that I am sorry. Our road hasn't been easy, but despite our circumstances now, I will forever be grateful that it was you who was there.

There to guide us. There to help me. There to cook up your amazing spaghetti and meatballs while the rest of us waited to be served by you.

The struggle we faced was not just mine and Jade's. It was yours too. Thank you, Todd, for being the strength of our family during the hardest time of our lives.

1

John Travolta Good

I fumbled for the keyring and escaped through the side door into a dark and dirty garage. Someone might see, and I would be trapped again. I bolted for the car as I shushed the sound of my own breath. I was almost free.

Free from potty training and Disney movies. Free from temper tantrums and fruit snacks. Free from a messy life with my third husband and seven children.

A mess I created all on my own.

I gunned the accelerator and fishtailed down the washboard road toward the first stop sign on my way to freedom. I turned up the radio and sped onto the highway while I put on eyeliner and lipstick in the rearview mirror. My sweet escape was underway. My refuge lay ahead.

I arrived right on time as usual and Brooklyn Shuffled down the sterile white hall while the Bee Gees played "Stayin' Alive" in my head. The choreography of my day was sharper when I slid into work ready, confident, and cocky. Like Tony Manero in *Saturday Night Fever*. The club was his dance floor. The hospital was mine. Tony and I had one thing in common. We were both good at what we did.

John Travolta good.

A warm chocolate donut dangled from my teeth, and a cold Dr Pepper numbed my hand. I scanned my employee badge and hip-bumped the door into the postpartum unit at Poudre Valley Hospital. I flung the door wide in a dramatic display announcing the world's best nurse and lactation consultant had arrived. The other nurses would be relieved I was there to save the day and dry the eyes of new moms who cried all night.

I loved coming to this place where I could smooth-glide in and be who I couldn't be at home. Just like Tony at the club. When I was at the hospital, I was free. Put together. Self-assured and confident. I danced like Cinderella at a disco. Coveted. Needed. It was the place I escaped from my life. Life with a husband who I was certain didn't love me anymore. Life of mundane repetition. Life that was a failure of my own creation. The hospital was an intermission from loneliness and the mess I made at home. It was freedom I couldn't find anywhere else. I was untethered when I was there.

I had a hunger to fill an emptiness inside. Something that stalked me from childhood. Something I tried to fill with husbands. Children. Education. Work. Something was missing. I just didn't know what. That would take a lifetime of miracles to figure out.

As I slid my way to the nurse's desk, the Bee Gees continued in my head. I flipped my long, brown curls over my thin shoulders, cracked my knuckles, and rubbed the palms of my bony hands together as I prepared for the challenges of the day. A crowd of nurses waited for me, drained and desperate for my help. I could tell by the dark bags under their eyes and their tousled hair that anticipation of my arrival had been building for the past twelve hours of the endless night shift. I gulped down the chocolate donut whole and chugged the last few swallows of soda. Exhausted nurses clamored for my attention and interrupted the tune in my head. The Bee Gees stopped singing, and my Cinderella dance started again.

"506 has sore nipples."

"Baby in 518 is too sleepy to nurse."

"Mom in 512 has been up all night. She's about to snap."

The nurses of the night were weary and ready for me to take over. The breastfeeding struggles during their grueling hours had almost broken them. They passed the heavy weight of their flaming torches, knowing they could count on me. Their nurse backbends would end, and mine would start. They knew I could get any baby to breastfeed. Any baby. I would not be defeated by a newborn.

Not yet anyway.

I was good at what I was there to do.

John Travolta good.

The nurses knew it. I knew it. I had no humility.

I was the Picasso of breastfeeding. I created masterpieces for every new mom I helped, painting memories on a canvas of lofty expectations and lack of sleep. I was the heroine who came to save at least one of their dreams. Like Wonder Woman. Or Lara Croft. I gave them the confidence they needed to put a piranha back on their bloody nipples and try again. They would remember me for years to come as the one who made a difference the day they almost gave up.

I was unexpectedly joined to tag team the postpartum floor by the only lactation consultant who threatened my title and made me better at what I did. I was good, but she was good too. Lynel was my friend and colleague of the last decade and my dynamic duo partner. We fed off each other's knowledge and accomplishments in a synergistic blast of greatness. We leaned on each other when there was nothing to hold us up.

We never gave up.

We were there to save babies and nipples and the world. It was something that was part of our fabric as nurses, lactation consultants, and mothers. Neither of us was willing to concede when we knew we were right. Not even to doctors whom we rubbed raw with our aggressive patient advocacy. Together, we were a force to be reckoned with. We wouldn't back down if there was a baby in need. Everyone knew it. We danced the dance until our legs quivered.

We never gave up.

Like with Charlie. Charles Everett Sterling III was his given name. He was a peculiar-looking baby with a head the size of a small pumpkin. He looked like his mom, Jana, who was also a bit peculiar. Nobody took her seriously when she and Charlie went to the pediatrician repeatedly because he "did this funny thing." Every time she got him in front of a doctor, he wouldn't perform. Jana was the only one who ever saw the panting, the rapid breathing, the blue face. So she was discounted as an odd duck and told not to worry about him. Until Charlie showed up with Jana at our outpatient lactation clinic one Friday afternoon. Lynel and I had worked with Charlie many times, and we both knew something wasn't right with that peculiar boy. But every time we told Jana to take Charlie to the doctor, they sent her home with a shrug and a smirk. They dismissed her concerns. She gave up.

"Watch this," Jana said to Lynel and me. "He's so freaking cute. He's flying! Like Superman!" She held two-month-old Charlie away from her body while he stiffened into a tight plank, puffed out his chest, and lunged his arms behind him at his waist. "Isn't he just adorable?"

Lynel and I gasped so loud Jana's smile disappeared. This wasn't only abnormal, it was alarming. Charlie began to pant and struggle for air as his face turned progressive hues of blue, then purple. Lynel snatched him from Jana.

"Oh no. This is not OK." Lynel went straight into resuscitation mode. Charlie tried to fill his lungs but could only take wispy, labored breaths. His eyes were wide with fear. He needed help. Lynel sat him up and rubbed his back. One long, breathless pause later, and the pink filled his cheeks again. He looked at Lynel and smiled, thanking her for being the only person who noticed he was dying. "You need to take him to the emergency room. Like right now." Jana cried as she left us. A few hours later, Jana called Lynel to thank her for saving Charlie's life. He was life-flighted to a pediatric specialty hospital for open heart surgery that night. Charlie was later diagnosed with some obscure genetic syndrome neither of us had heard of. We knew something wasn't right with peculiar Charlie. We just didn't know what.

But we never gave up.

I stood at the nurse's desk when Lynel showed up minutes behind me wearing her favorite lactation consultant Crocs and "Got Milk?"

T-shirt. She was ready to run circles around the postpartum unit with me.

"Girrrl!" Lynel said when she saw me. "I didn't know I was working with you today! It's gonna be a good day here on the Mom-Baby floor. You ready to slay some nipples?"

I was always ready. Lynel energized me more. She made me better at what I did. We were on a mission when we worked together. We would not leave until every baby was breastfeeding. Eyes dried. Dreams restored.

"I'll take 512, and you can take Sleepy Baby. Then, let's tag team Sore Nips," I said. We walked like Thelma and Louise in scrubs as "Stayin' Alive" rebooted in my head. "See you in thirty," I said. Lynel laughed. Thirty minutes was never thirty minutes. Not on the postpartum unit. We would meet at the nurse's desk to share our stories of greatness as soon as we could.

Some days and some moms were like picking cotton in a cornfield, though. The strength required to be a new mom was herculean. Sarah in room 512 was almost over the edge before I got there. She was ready to snap like her nurse warned. I tiptoed in to avoid eggshells. One wrong word and she would jump off a thin postpartum ledge. Sarah realized the fantasy of giving birth to a cherub baby with rosy cheeks who naturally and easily nursed on cue was a dream.

I chose my words like a mental health therapist as I spoke a sweet lullaby to her. I pulled up a chair and listened to how hard it was to be a mother. Sarah was already broken by her newborn son. She cried and told me her mother left when she was two years old. She had nobody to teach her how to do this.

"I've never breastfed a baby before. He's never breastfed before. Who's supposed to help me figure this out? My dad?" Tears trailed down her face and landed on the cross tattoo below her collarbone. I was her absent mother's proxy. I spoke to her like she was one of my own daughters. I was there as long as she needed me. Her tears had nothing to do with breastfeeding.

My sole purpose in that room was to show her compassion.

Seeing Sarah in her newest role was a beautiful thing. A fledgling mama in her dirty hospital gown. Unshowered. Smelling like birth. Recovering from her steep hike into motherhood. It was a journey so quick that, in one breathless moment, her life changed forever. I couldn't imagine making that climb without my mom. For the next hour, Sarah was my daughter, and I was her mother. I reassured her that her baby was acting normally and that her boobs were perfect for the job.

Sarah's baby stirred in his tightly wrapped swaddle. I seized the moment to teach her things her mother should have. I unbundled her baby boy from his pink-and-blue-striped hospital blanket and placed him by her tattoo. He was a twig of a baby with a long, hairless, coned head and a crooked nose from his recent journey through the birth canal. He was one of those babies who made me wonder if it was possible to outgrow ugly. But to Sarah, he was the most beautiful creature in the world. There was nothing about him that wasn't perfect. She watched in disbelief when her baby snuggled in close. He bobbed his head up and down until he found his target. The tension in the room evaporated.

"Wow! You were right. He hasn't acted like this before." I let her bask in the moment as she held her baby boy. It took patience to breastfeed. Sarah understood. Her eyes grew wide when I told her I had some experience with my own seven babies I had breastfed.

"Seven? Did you say seven children?" Sarah exhaled a breath of anxiety and relief. She was with the world's best lactation consultant. She melted into her bed. She was strong now. Strong enough that she wouldn't fall apart every time her baby wanted to eat.

There were no more tears. She didn't snap. It was a win for the lactation consultant in 512.

I emerged from the eggshell battlefield of the hospital room and took a victory lap around the nurse's station. I pumped my fists above my head and declared triumphantly, "I can get any baby to breastfeed!" Lynel gave me a high five as I rounded the corner.

"Lactation—two points," she said. We traded stories about

the previous hour and chatted about how we loved being Boob Whisperers. Then, from nowhere as we finished charting our work, the chocolate donut and Dr Pepper crept up the back of my throat. I put my hand to my lips and threw up a sour taste in my mouth.

"Dang. That was way better going down than coming up. I need to slow down and let my food settle. That's the second time I've almost puked today." I held my stomach. But I didn't mention to Lynel that I had been nauseous all week.

And my period was late.

I continued charting my victory notes for room 512 while I ignored the obvious. But not Lynel. She came in with a sneak attack.

"Are you pregnant?" Lynel whispered behind her hand so nobody at the nurse's desk would hear.

"No! I am not pregnant!" I snapped. "Todd and I barely even see each other anymore. I'm pretty sure one time in three months doesn't even count." Lynel knew Todd and I were nearing the end of our marriage. She'd seen my tears and heard my heartbreak over the years. I often lamented another doomed marriage to her. We nervous-laughed and finished charting our breastfeeding victories while I buried another mess I wasn't ready to face.

"Hey, we should go fix Sore Nipples," I said. Lynel high-fived me again, and we headed down the hall to room 506 together. Two lactation consultants were better than one. We were armed and ready to save the day and a pair of nipples for another new mom.

I was distracted by nausea and the Bee Gees playing in my head the rest of the day. But I was thankful I worked alongside Lynel and that she covered for me when the donut and soda crept into my throat again. I wasn't good like usual. Lynel's question unsettled me. It followed me around like a shadow into every room. I didn't have time to address the accumulating small details in my life that Lynel noticed. It was easier to ignore the obvious all around me. I did anything I could to be distracted from my life. I had a third husband I saw occasionally. I had five young daughters at home. I had two more children living with my first ex-husband who were trying to become adults. And I had my refuge at the hospital, where I went to leave behind what I could not change.

I was a mother of eighteen years. Almost half my life. Soon all my children would be in school or living on their own. The thought of regaining a smidge of freedom made me think of the days before I became a mother. The days when the only responsibility I had in life was myself.

But those days disappeared when a child became a mother.

Having another baby was foolish. Reckless. Not in my plans. A salty gray streak of hair had formed on my left temple in the past year. Having a baby at my age was too risky. I didn't want to take a chance that I would have a disabled baby who would steal what was left of my freedom. I had no place in my life for a peculiar boy like Charlie. Somehow, I beat the odds with my seven children. Another baby was not in my future.

Even if I had been Catholic or Mormon.

I was not having another baby.

I couldn't possibly be pregnant. Todd and I kept ourselves busy. Busy at work. Busy with the kids. Busy anywhere but together. We learned how to live together without seeing each other. Neither of us wanted to confront the erosion of our marriage. It was too painful, so we avoided spending time together under the same roof.

Except that one night two months earlier.

That night we were under the same roof. Huddled up behind a locked bathroom door where we hid from the children. A bread crumb offering to quiet the tension between us. One time. Three minutes of our lives. Nothing more. Only memorable because my period was late, and I was nauseous.

I carried that three-minute memory in my gut the rest of the day. Beside it sat a partially digested chocolate donut and flat Dr Pepper seasoned with nausea. But nothing would stop me from the work that needed to be done on the postpartum unit. I did my best while barely standing up at times. Lynel and I went room to room, dancing the same dance from mom to mom. Drying tears. Helping them make memories they treasured.

I was, after all, John Travolta good. I could get any baby to breastfeed. But I was still human. Still tired at the end of the day. Still worried about Lynel's pesky question.

"Are you pregnant?"

The day of lactation champions closed, and I met Lynel at the time clock to punch out and limp to our cars at opposite ends of the employee lot. We clocked an impressive ten miles on our Fitbits and also on our strained backs. But we were smiling and proud of ourselves for a day of victories on the postpartum unit. We were the heroines in an exhausting dance nobody could do like us. I pulled my car out of the parking lot feeling anxiety and nausea. My phone flashed a text message from Lynel.

"You were good today."

I responded, "Ditto, my friend."

"Take a pregnancy test. It's gonna be OK."

The music in my head stopped. I gripped the steering wheel tight and hung my face in shame. A sigh from my lungs was the only sound I heard.

I turned my car around, drove to Walmart, and walk-of-shamed through the sliding doors, no longer confident and no longer cocky.

No longer John Travolta good.

2

Another Baby

The long drive home from a day of lactation gymnastics upheaved the nausea that churned in my gut. My back protested the bending, twisting, and stretching from my disco dance at the hospital. The Walmart bag mocked me from the passenger seat and threatened to steal every plan I had. I bounced down our rugged country road and scanned the dry, yellow stalks of grass surrounding the house for cats and children. Mom was there with Emmie, my three-year-old tornado and youngest daughter. Emmie enjoyed her Nana more than she did me. Nana was Play-Doh in her tiny hands. I wasn't as easy for Emmie to manipulate.

I felt a twinge in my bound-up stomach. I was the first parent home. Again. Todd's parking spot was empty. Again. Disappointment punctuated the twinge in my stomach because he wouldn't be home until I was asleep. I stopped asking what meetings kept him away so often and so late. I thought I had stopped caring long ago. I was wrong.

Four of the five cats who lived on our rural property darted in front of the car as I pulled up the dusty driveway. I slammed my foot on the brake and slid on the washboard road, trying to avoid a collision with one of them. *Stupid cats.*

My favorite, Matt the Girl Cat, was missing from the gang of five. Our kitties were defenseless enough to be a meal for the hawks and coyotes that stalked the grounds around our home. I worried when one of them didn't show up to greet me. But Todd reminded me often that The Five had one purpose, otherwise he never would have agreed to take the whole litter. The cats were there to rid the high, dense grass of rodents that lured the rattlesnakes to our backyard.

But that's not how my daughters saw them. The Five delighted in the girls, and the girls in them. My daughters were masters at taming wild felines, and they loved to silly-play with their cats for hours. They dressed them in doll clothes and twirled them around like meowing ballerinas. The girls thought they were pets. No matter how much I protested the attachments, The Five were part of our family.

Each of them was given a hand-picked name as if they would survive the perils of our property more than a few years. Star and Storm, our faded butterscotch vagabonds. Snowball, our snow-white cream puff. Sasha, our long-haired lover. And Mattie, Matt the Girl Cat, whom we presumed was a boy until she grew into her parts. Mattie was a striking tortoiseshell cat who didn't belong in the dangers of the country. Mattie belonged with an old, widowed woman who would stroke her back and feed her soft food from a can. She didn't deserve to be consumed by predators in the darkness of the night. Not Mattie. Naming them made it personal. Just like the girls wanted.

The cats would eventually fall victim to the elements around them, and the girls would learn a thing or two about death along the way. The Five served their purpose. They mostly kept the rattlesnakes from getting close to the house. Mostly.

A minefield of bikes, scooters, cats, Barbie dolls, and basketballs lay strewn about when I pulled into the driveway. Mattie was still missing. She was probably in the house. By the look of the mess left for me to clean up, Emmie had a good day with her nana.

One day a week for the past three years, Mom trekked the long drive down our dusty road to babysit Emmie while I escaped my children to work a superhero lactation job. A few months earlier, I learned a hard lesson—Mom was the only person besides Todd or me who could watch Emmie. I had been excited for Emmie's trial run at Auntie Jo's Hometown Daycare in the small town a few miles away from our house. It would give me the freedom to work more and focus on myself a little, things I hadn't been able to do for years. I dropped Emmie off with a kiss and a quick wave before her reality set in, and then I smiled every bump of the three miles home. I imagined the jetted tub tucked in the corner of our master bathroom that awaited me.

I sashayed into my childless, husbandless house and inhaled a deep breath of silence. I screamed. Nobody came to check on me. I undressed in the kitchen and ran naked up the stairs to the bathroom where I filled the tub with steaming-hot water. I dipped my toes into the bubble bath like Julia Roberts in *Pretty Woman*, ready to soak my worn-out mom bod for hours. I began my descent into the tub, skimming my backside in the hot water, when I was interrupted by the chime on my cell phone.

It was Auntie Jo's.

"Hi, um, Angie? Is this Emmie's mom?" The teacher was frazzled, and I could hear Emmie screaming in the background.

"Yes, this is Angie." There would be no bubble bath.

"This is Heather at Auntie Jo's. You need to pick Emmie up. She's having a meltdown and making the other children cry."

Despite my best attempt to enroll Emmie at Auntie Jo's, her first, and last, day was no more than thirty minutes. I had to get her. Right then. I put my clothes back on and picked Emmie up, trudging home defeated while she played with her Barbie doll in the back seat as if nothing had happened. Emmie followed me to my room like a shadow and slid into my still-warm bath, fully clothed, while I made my bed.

I had to call Mom and ask her to give me her day off from work again. It strangled me to have to ask Mom because she needed to rest on her day off. To kick her feet up on her recliner. To watch John Wayne reruns all day. I carried the guilt of stealing her time like an albatross around my neck. Retirement taunted her. She craved it like a bowl of fried okra. Only a few years stood in the way of doing whatever she wanted for the rest of her life. I hung my head and asked her for help again. She said yes. She always did. But sideways comments over the years told me Mom didn't expect I would have so many children. Or need so much help. Mom fretted about me a lot. She had a front-row seat to the drama of the impossible life I created. I understood because I had six daughters and a son. I fretted too.

I heard Emmie laughing through the garage door as I made my way up the steps. The Walmart bag was buried deep in my purse. Hidden from Mom and the girls. Four of my daughters sat at the kitchen table putting together a Lion King puzzle with Mom. The pregnancy test screamed from deep within my bag as it tried to expose a shameful secret like a tattletale. I wasn't ready to have that discussion with Mom yet. I wasn't ready to concern her more about my difficult and complicated life. I wasn't ready to hear her reaction. She would wonder who in the world was going to babysit this one. I could already hear her deep Southern twang response.

"Another baby?" Mom would be so disappointed in me.

I hobbled through the door and felt my twisted and shredded back muscles tighten with every step. I wasn't defeated yet, but the day left me black and blue. I would soon discover if my brilliantly planned future was about to vaporize after a three-minute marital tryst.

"Hi, guys. How was your day?" I dragged myself into the kitchen.

"Mommy! I missed you, Mommy!" Emmie encircled my legs with her nubby arms. My mumble turned to a smile, and Emmie got tangled up in my legs like one of the cats. I leaned down and picked her up while my back screamed.

"I missed you too, Em. Did you have fun with Nana today?" I pecked Emmie on her face and neck until she no longer missed me. She slid out of my arms to the floor and climbed on Mom's lap. She didn't want any more "I love you" kisses from her absent mother.

"She was good today. Weren't you, Em?" Mom pulled Emmie high onto her lap while I melted into the only empty chair and sat with them. My tween daughters, Brooke, Hope, and Kinnah, ignored me as usual.

"She only snuck out once while I was in the bathroom. I found her playing with the cats under the deck."

That was my Emmie. She had a penchant for ruleless flight. She was my free bird. Spirited. Headstrong. She loved her cats. She loved to run alone through the dry grass that towered over her. She loved the freedom she felt when she escaped like a stealth fighter jet. More than once I located a missing Emmie where she didn't belong. Running like a gazelle through rattlesnake dens and rabbit holes, so far beyond the deck out back that all I could see were bouncing blonde curls just above the tassels of tall, dry grass. She ran barefoot in the tattered blue gown she refused to take off for months at a time. Hardly protection from a snake bite. Emmie challenged me from the moment she was born. I was no match for her. She won almost every battle. The other kids were in school. But not Emmie. She discovered right away she had wings. My free bird couldn't be grounded within a cage.

And Auntie Jo's wanted nothing to do with her.

Sitting across the table covered in puzzle pieces, Mom glanced my way with that familiar sideways look.

She knew.

"Hey, Ang, I was thinking maybe the girls could go to church with me on Sunday." Mom was a regular at Summerside Baptist Church and taught Sunday school to third graders. She was first in line to enter the church every time the doors were open for any reason. She even volunteered to clean once a week after work.

"Yeah, sure. If they want to. I have to work. I mean, I have to work every Sunday, you know. Girls, you wanna go to church with Nana this weekend?" A small foot kicked me under the table. The tweens glared at me when Mom wasn't looking. But they agreed to go because they didn't want to hurt her feelings.

"Maybe you should take a Sunday off here and there so you and Todd can bring the kids to church."

The tweens laughed. Then another kick under the table.

"Mom, I don't think Todd will go to church with me. Anyway, I have to work weekends around his schedule since Emmie won't stay with anyone but you. We really can't afford for me to miss any work." Mom asked me to go to church with her a lot. Anxiety consumed me every time she suggested I go on a day I had to work. I wanted to respond with a crescendo. But I didn't. Todd and I lived under the same roof because neither of us could afford a separation. Mom knew this. I grew up in a Baptist-like church where divorce for any reason was cause for rebuke. If I walked into her church, I would catch fire before I made it past the greeters standing at the tall, white double doors. I knew all about religion. I grew up with it pummeled into my soul. Not by Mom, but by the people entrusted with teaching me about Jesus. I wasn't welcome as a two-time divorced woman with seven children from three different husbands. That was blasphemy.

I was offended Mom kept asking me to go to church. Triggered. My chest turned red as I shook my head side to side. I would burn that place down if I showed up. Mom surely knew this.

"No, Mom. I really can't. I have to work." I made a lot of reckless decisions in life. Church couldn't fix my kind of broken.

Emmie cried as Mom gathered her things and headed out the front door. Mom dodged four feral cats and most of Emmie's toys on the sidewalk.

"Tell Todd I'll pick the girls up Sunday morning at eight and bring them home after church." The car door slammed shut, and Mattie scampered from underneath. Mom waved goodbye as she backed her car down the driveway.

"Thank you, Mom!" I hollered from the front door. I had to hold Emmie back from running out with her. "We love you!"

I was glad Mom was driving down that dirt road, kicking up dust all the way to the stop sign. Not because I wanted to see her leave but because the Walmart bag was still in my purse. I needed to take a test I might fail. So I rounded up my posse of daughters for dinner and bed. I enforced their normal bedtime as groans ricocheted off the walls. My five-year-old daughter, Faith, conceded without resistance, though. Faith came home every day from her first year of kindergarten exhausted. She enjoyed the laziness of her evenings and didn't put up a fuss when it was time for bed.

Emmie, however, was different. Emmie required coercion and brute strength. I corralled her and carried her to bed with me. She knew how to delay her slumber and demanded four glasses of water before she agreed to close her eyes. She stroked my face with her small fingers and played with my hair to soothe herself to sleep. I sang her a lullaby about a rambunctious little girl named Emmie who was born with wings, liked to herd cats, ran away from her mama often, and danced with the rabbits and rattlesnakes under the moonlight. As soon as I heard her snoring as loud as her dad, I slid out of the bed we shared. The Walmart bag was still in my purse. It was calling to me.

What happened next remains a blur.

When my senses came to me, I found myself on the bathroom floor in the fetal position sobbing. Every plan I made was stolen. I wept and lamented my lost future. The pregnancy test dangled loosely from my hand. My pants and underwear wrapped around my ankles. I repeated over and over, "No. No. No." I held my knees tight to my chest and hyperventilated while I rocked back and forth.

"Damn it!" I screamed out as I held myself. I failed the test. It was positive. There was another baby growing inside me.

Shock and anger flooded my nauseous gut. I berated myself for not being responsible. For not learning a lesson from all the other pregnancies before. *You are so stupid, Angie.* I deserved every word.

The day bruised me, but the pregnancy test rendered me an emotional quadriplegic. I was numb from the heart down. Covered with a thick coat of desperation and hopelessness in what would be the most shameful moment of my life. Not because I was a married woman who was pregnant with her eighth baby.

Because I would ask God to take a life.

Not just any life.

The life of an innocent baby.

In Sunday school, I was taught that God was the Father of all creation. He said whoever causes a child harm would be better off drowned in the sea. The verse had been seared into my memory for a time such as this. The words were so profound I still remembered them after more than thirty years. But I was desperate. I needed to be rescued. So, as I lay curled up on the bathroom floor, I whispered a reprehensible prayer to a God I barely talked to anymore.

"God, please. I'm begging you. Please, take this from me. Make me miscarry. I can't do this again. I just can't do this."

I was despicable.

I lay on the floor defeated. Beaten into submission by a pregnancy test. I prayed God would take the life of my own child. I couldn't take it back. I couldn't believe the heartless words that came from my mouth. It wasn't a prayer. It was a death sentence. It was a twisted and humiliating compilation of egocentrism, selfishness, and shame. The orator of that unholy ejaculation was the most disgusting person I knew.

Todd arrived home while I was still on the bathroom floor. He heard me crying and found me naked from the waist down on the other side of the door.

"What's wrong with you, Ang?"

"You really don't want to know, Todd," I sobbed as snot ran down my chin. Then he saw the pregnancy test dangling from my hand.

"Oh wow. You OK?" I couldn't decide if he wanted to comfort me or make small talk. It didn't seem to bother him that I was pregnant.

"No, Todd. I'm not OK. Are you OK with this?" I paused then attacked. "Because this is bullshit. It's all your fault!"

"All right, Angie. Whatever. It's honestly not the end of the world. Pull yourself together, and act like a woman. Things could be way worse." He walked out of the bathroom and left me on the floor with my pants still around my ankles.

Things could be way worse. Neither of us knew the power of those foreboding words. They were a window to a future I couldn't fathom.

I lay there stunned. Stunned by his response. Stunned by my response. Stunned that Todd was the only rational adult during a mistake that would forever alter both our lives. His undisturbed reaction enraged me. He tried to be nice to me. *How dare he?* The disgust and shame I slathered on myself was too thick to acknowledge that he might be a decent man or that he still loved me. I was ashamed of myself. I was ashamed because I knew better. I was ashamed because I prayed for God to end my baby's life.

Everything changed. One moment I was John Travolta good getting high fives and back pats. Twelve hours later I was curled up on the bathroom floor drowning in a sea of shame and guilt. The glimpse of freedom I craved was gone. Stolen. Nothing would be the same again. This mess was my fault.

I was reckless.

I was irresponsible.

I was having another baby.

3

The Monster

The thought of another baby in my future diminished my confident Brooklyn Shuffle to a Sloppy Joe Line Dance. Five days had passed since I lay on the bathroom floor with my underwear around my ankles, screaming about all I lost. It was the day I prayed God would remove the burden of another baby. The Walmart pregnancy test choked me into humility. My dreams died beside me on the bathroom floor. The budding nausea transformed into a gargantuan monster, consuming every minute of the day. A monster that reminded me of what a bad person I was. A monster that fed on my weakness and despair. A monster that devoured my peace. Stole my plans. Took my freedom. I was tethered by the noose of raising another baby for the next eighteen years. Like the umbilical cord that tethered the tiny eight-week fetus to my uterus. It was more than I could handle. I tried not to think about it.

Except The Monster would not allow that.

Patients awaited me at the hospital that morning, so I finished getting ready in the bathroom where the mess started. A bathroom I had vomited in all day and night for five days. Mom would arrive soon to watch Emmie, and I was going to be late for work if I didn't get moving.

"Nana!" Emmie saw a car she recognized. "Mommy, Nana's here!" Emmie saw Mom through the front window as she drove down our road kicking up dust behind her again. I hid in the bedroom until she was preoccupied with Emmie. Then I slithered out of the house before she could see The Monster had returned. The truth was smeared on my face. I didn't have to tell Mom when I was pregnant.

She always knew.

Before anyone else and sometimes before me. But I wasn't ready for the dreaded "Another baby?" question. So I didn't stay home long enough for her to hear me puking up a breakfast I had not yet eaten. I slow-motion tiptoed out the garage door and yelled over my shoulder.

"Thank you, Mom. I'm running late. I'll see you this evening. Love you, Em. Love you, Mom!"

Emmie didn't care that I left her without a hug. Nana was with her. I no longer existed. Emmie was at home enjoying her favorite day of the week. Her sisters were at school enjoying a sunny, fall day. Todd was at work enjoying whatever it was Todd did. Everyone was enjoying life but me.

I made it to the hospital thirty minutes late after stopping twice to throw up. I crept through the shadows of the dim stairwell in the back corner of the postpartum unit and snuck in unnoticed. Only a handful of rooms were occupied by new moms and their babies, and the front desk was empty. The nurses were busy. They were in rooms with fragile new moms trying to do a job I was late for. They would be frustrated with me. I wasn't on time to save the day for them. *Thank God there wasn't a full moon last night.* A full moon always brought hordes of pregnant women in to deliver their babies. Those were hectic days. I couldn't handle a full postpartum unit. Not today. I had no energy to fight what followed me everywhere. I was weak and beaten down, and my stomach required an escape route. I needed to be able to retreat to the closest bathroom when I started to gag and retch again. The green hue on my face was only a shadow of the devastation in every cell of my body. A baby I didn't want grew in my belly. The omnipotent Monster hovered. With every step I took. With every breath I inhaled. With every word I spoke. It would only be a few weeks before everyone at work knew the truth. The reactions that were coming terrified me. The nurses chided me often about the number of children I had. It was the first thing they told the new hires about me during orientation on the unit.

"Good Lawdy, Angie," Rosalyn joked the day we first met. "I can't believe that little body has had seven babies, Sista. I mean, you might as well have a litter! Ten or twelve, right?" Rosalyn and everyone at the nurse's station bellowed like Ray Liotta in *Goodfellas*. Their generous laugh at my expense was so loud a patient slammed her door. Their ridicule plunged a knife between my shoulder blades.

"Real funny, ladies. I'm not having any more babies. Todd's going for a vasectomy as soon as he gets brave enough. Seven is definitely enough for me." They didn't know my marriage teetered on divorce. My failures were private. I just showed up to do a job I used to be John Travolta good at, not to gossip about what a mess I was.

But the conversation with Rosalyn was months before my trip to Walmart. Everything was different. I stood in the middle of the nurse's station alone, touching my stomach. Hoping nobody would notice I was about to throw up. *Where's Lynel when I need her?* I wished she was here so we could tag team the handful of new moms who needed us. But the day was mine. And The Monster was everywhere I was. Sharp and immediate. Reminding me of how my selfishness ransacked me. It stalked me. It was behind me. In front of me. All around me. I couldn't escape.

Marsha and Hannah snuck up behind me at the nurse's station with a desperate good morning greeting. They were relieved I had finally shown up. The nosy questions began immediately.

"We thought you weren't going to make it! I'm so glad you're finally here! Did you run into traffic?" Marsha was an elder on the nursing staff and had become a historic figure among our group. She often joked she would die on the postpartum unit while checking an episiotomy or hemorrhoids. She was incessantly concerned about the details of everyone's personal lives because she didn't have one of her own.

I lied and told her I was tardy because Mom was late to watch Emmie. The truth was too complicated. I turned to an open chart and pretended to read the night nurses' reports. An in-depth conversation would make the nausea worse. I gulped back acid in my scalded throat. *That one really burned.* Marsha and Hannah stood at the desk behind me and talked about things I would soon regret hearing.

"I have done ovulation kits. I have taken hormones until I'm a bawling mess. I had a hysterosalpingogram to see if there was something blocking my tubes. Everything. Literally everything but IVF. We just can't afford that." Hannah's voice cracked as she lamented her barren womb. "I thought this month was going to be different for us, and then I got up this morning and started my period."

"Oh, Honey. I'm so sorry. I know how much you and John want a baby. That just makes me so sad for you guys." Marsha put her arms around Hannah and hugged her like she was her own daughter.

"It's the same thing every month." Hannah choked back tears. "We have been dealing with this every month for more than five years. I'm about to give up."

I couldn't listen to Hannah anymore. I couldn't eavesdrop on their conversation for one more sentence. Hannah wanted a baby. Just one baby. I had seven babies. And an unwanted eighth on the way. A wave of guilt and shame overcame me like a tsunami and instigated an immediate need to rush to the bathroom. I speed-raced to the closest toilet and barely closed the door before a loud gush of nothing thrust from my empty stomach. The noise was so loud I was sure everyone heard the sonic boom under the door and through the halls. I waited as long as I could in the bathroom until the coast was clear. Then I snuck into room 508 and stayed until I couldn't manage The Monster anymore.

I made it to the bathroom just in time to faux-vomit again and rest my weary head on the seat of a dirty toilet. I tried to slip out of the bathroom and hide in another room, but Marsha accosted me. She was annoyed.

"If you're sick, Angie, you need to go home. You shouldn't be here if you're sick. Did you eat something bad? Do you have a fever? How long have you been throwing up? Have your kids been sick?"

Marsha was sure I brought the stomach flu to work with me and would infect everyone.

"I'm OK. None of the kids are sick. Nothing to worry about."

"Well, I know you have so many kids, and I'm sure one of them probably got you sick. You know there's some nasty stomach bug going around."

The Monster abruptly overcame me again, and I rushed to the bathroom. The pressure was more than my stomach could handle. I didn't know how to respond without giving up my secret. I emerged after fifteen minutes of retching, patted my mouth with the back of my hand, and gulped back the temptation to throw up again.

"You need to go home, Angie." Marsha was waiting outside the door for me. She followed me from the bathroom to the nurse's station, hovering over me like a nectar bat. "You can't stay at work if you're sick." She was more relentless than The Monster. "I can't afford to get sick, Angie! I don't have any more PTO. You have to go home!"

I spun on my shaky heels and met Marsha in the middle of the nurse's station.

"Marsha, what I have is not contagious. For crying out loud. Just leave it alone and let me work. Please." My secret was out. I immediately regretted those words.

Everyone would know now. Everyone I didn't want to know. Everyone who would judge me because I was pregnant with my husband's child.

Marsha's mouth gaped open. She knew what I meant by my cryptic response. She knew the only thing she wouldn't get from me was a pregnancy. Her female parts had shriveled up years before. She gasped and then lowered the volume of her voice before humiliating me.

"Are you? Are you pregnant? Again?" She whispered under her breath like it was a dirty secret. Her questions exposed my poor choices and decisions. I turned away and walked to the opposite side of the nurse's station.

"Oh, good grief, Angie. You have to be kidding me. Whatever you do, do not say a word to Hannah. She and John have been trying to have a baby for five years, and this will hurt her so much." She spoke as if I hadn't heard about Hannah's infertility a thousand times. Or as if I hadn't felt guilty a thousand times too.

Marsha didn't know what it felt like to be me. Shame and humiliation dripped like sweat from every pore of my skin. She had no regard for how I felt.

Marsha offered no opportunity to say anything during her rant of humiliating and demeaning words. And I didn't have the energy to defend myself or interrupt her.

"Don't you already have like ten kids, Angie? It's not fair. It's just not fair." Marsha shook her head back and forth in disgust. One last dig.

It was the worst thing that could have happened. At a place where I once found refuge from my life at home. Marsha thrashed me with truth that made me feel like a disgraced Martha Stewart on her way to prison. I cowered like a whipped dog. I retreated inside myself because I knew everyone would react like Marsha. My kids. My mom. My friends. Everyone. They would all think I was horrible.

Because I was horrible.

I was mortified by an unplanned pregnancy. I was degraded by a nurse who validated all the horrible things I thought about myself. A nurse who turned my devastation into humiliation. A nurse whom I had helped many times before with any need she had. There would be no "congratulations" that day or any other day from Marsha. Only shame.

I bolted for the bathroom again. This time to sob and ponder what the next seven months were going to be like. I sat on the toilet and buried my face in my hands.

There was a streak of pink blood in my underwear. *God might answer my prayer.*

Marsha might choke on words meant to shame and embarrass me. A shallow concern for the life growing inside my womb gave me pause. This might be the beginning of the end for a baby who deserved more than me. A baby who didn't even get a chance at life.

But The Monster took over again. In my selfishness, I tried to remember what it was like to not be pregnant. To not be sick day and night. To not rewrite all the plans I made for a future that didn't include another baby.

Marsha, The Monster, and the blood were more than I could take. I clocked out and left the hospital. I drove home wondering if I would ever meet the baby whom I hadn't felt move inside me yet. Any amount of blood was abnormal in pregnancy. I might have a miscarriage. My emotions confused me. My prayer might be answered. A single tear made its way down my face.

My secret was about to be revealed again. I didn't know if I could handle the disappointment. Mom wouldn't need an explanation for why I was home early, crying and walking with the limp of a fallen heroine. She would know the moment she looked at me.

She always knew.

Mom was surprised when I arrived home early. I startled her as the side door slammed shut. She sat on the living room floor playing with Emmie, baby dolls, and Sasha. I didn't remind Mom and Emmie that Sasha was an outdoor cat. It seemed trivial.

"Oh! What are you doing home so early?" I hung my head and tried to hide my tears. "Angie, what's wrong?" Mom stood and walked toward me. Emmie cried because the attention was no longer hers and she was left alone with her babies and Sasha.

"Oh, Mom. I've really done it this time." I prepared myself to hear the daunting question she would certainly ask. "Another baby?" But she didn't. Mom started to cry with me.

She knew.

"Angie, it's going to be OK. I knew last week when I left that you were pregnant. I could see it on your face. I can read you like a book, my sweet daughter. It's all going to be OK." She held my face in her hands. "When are you going to believe me that God has a plan for you and every baby He gives you? You have to stop crying because it's not good for my grandbaby."

Emmie continued to wail on the floor. As she kicked and

screamed, I was reminded of what I would experience again in three years. But only if the bleeding that started at work stopped before it was too late.

"Mom, I'm bleeding." My body shook as I sobbed in her arms. Mom pulled away and looked at me straight on.

"You need to call the doctor. Right now. Stop crying and call your doctor."

A call to the doctor wouldn't save my baby. There was nothing that could be done about the bleeding, but I called anyway. The doctor told me I would probably have a miscarriage. There would be no extraordinary measures to save the tiny baby growing inside me. We scheduled an ultrasound for the next morning, but it would only tell us if the baby was alive. I was scared. I was sad. I was nauseous. I was confused. My shame had metamorphosed into fear for my baby's life.

Mom hugged me and started to leave while Emmie continued to cry for her.

"I'm praying for you, Angie. You need to pray too. Ask God to give you peace so you can see that His way is always *The Way*, even though you might not understand it now. I just know God has big plans for this baby. Everything is going to be OK." The screen door slammed behind her.

But Mom didn't know about my prayer five days before. Nobody but God and me would ever know about that prayer.

I wasn't convinced God had big plans for me or my baby. But I sat in my favorite recliner in the living room and talked to God like I did during other difficult times of my life. I prayed God would unhear the prayer I spoke on the bathroom floor. I prayed He would remove all the monsters from my life. The Monster that followed me everywhere all the time and The Monster I left behind at the hospital.

Then I prayed God would transform the selfish woman I was into one who didn't speak prayers that stole innocent lives. And though it wasn't possible, I prayed I would be able to look at myself in the mirror and no longer see a monster staring back at me.

4

Finding Nemo

ornings came too early at our house of children, noise, and monsters. I hadn't slept well. I could feel my stomach consuming itself while I worried about the bleeding. I awoke to the sound of my identical twin daughters fighting over the last blueberry muffin in the kitchen. And a heavy pad filled with blood. I felt no pain except that of the noise of two pre-teen girls screaming at each other. Their loud squeals permeated the ceiling from the first to the second floor and jolted through my body.

"It's mine! You had one yesterday!" Brooke screamed then slammed the refrigerator door shut. The glass condiments rattled the house like a San Andreas earthquake.

"You do this every time!" Hope yelled back as she closed a cabinet door with fury. "You *always* take the last one. Mom! Brooke took the last blueberry muffin again!"

I left The Monster in my room and stumbled down the stairs. I wasn't strong enough to intervene during a world war. I would probably have to separate Brooke and Hope like I did almost every morning. They were identical twins but, in every way possible, they were different.

Except when a blueberry muffin was involved.

"Girls! Knock it off! Hope, there's a box of muffins in the freezer. Just throw one in the microwave." I descended the stairs while they screamed profanities at each other until I rounded the corner to the kitchen. Hope conceded and retreated to the freezer to find her breakfast. I would not be forced to throw my almost lifeless body between them.

"You two, I swear. This is so insignificant. You have to stop acting like this. It's ridiculous. It really is. Oh, and you both smell like teenagers, so go take a shower when you're done eating. And shave your armpits. You look like bush women." The moisture in my underwear reminded me of the ultrasound appointment I needed to get ready for, so I finished my scolding. After I made sure they weren't going to hurt each other, I rushed up the stairs to get dressed. In the same bathroom where a Walmart pregnancy test had shattered my world just a week before.

Todd and I met at the top of the stairs like two strangers in the subway.

"Hey. I'm bleeding. Just thought you might wanna know," I said as our shoulders grazed past each other. "I have an appointment at nine today for an ultrasound to see if I'm miscarrying."

Todd's body shifted, and he stalked me through the hall to the bedroom. "What do you mean, you're bleeding? Isn't that a big deal?"

I started to close the door, but he stepped in the way. "Yes, Todd. It's a big deal. I don't know if you noticed, but I've been throwing up almost nonstop for a week, and yesterday I started bleeding. The doctor said I'm probably going to miscarry, but they are going to look for a heartbeat today."

"Well, I'm going." Todd acted like he was a requisite participant in my medical care. "I'm going to be there. I'll go into work late."

I didn't have time to be touched by Todd's heroic gesture because The Monster overcame me again as soon as Todd finished his sentence. I scrambled to the toilet to throw up an entire teaspoon of stomach acid that burned my throat and mouth. I wretched again as acid slid into the water below my face. I noticed a few drops of dried blood on the toilet seat and remembered I had a blood-soaked pad on.

My heart began to ache. Something had changed. I didn't see it coming. I didn't want to say goodbye to my baby. I didn't want to have a miscarriage anymore. I didn't want to lose the life growing inside me. But it was too late. I was losing my baby. There was nothing I could do to stop the answer to my unholy prayer.

I looked at myself in the mirror and saw a woman I was ashamed of. The lingering taste on my tongue reminded me how foul I was. I brushed my teeth until I couldn't taste it anymore. I put my thinning hair in a messy bun. It would have to do because I was running late and needed to change my pad before we left. There was no time for makeup, and the top of my baggy jeans had to stay unbuttoned. The pressure on my gut made the nausea worse.

Emmie sat cross-legged on the living room floor eating a bowl of Froot Loops and watching *Finding Nemo* on our big-screen TV when I returned downstairs. Pink milk dripped off her dirty chin, and her blonde curls were matted into a perfect bird's nest on the back of her head. Tears and patience were needed to comb through her knotted mess, and I didn't have the energy or the time to deal with her this morning.

"Emmie, you need to get dressed." I tossed Emmie's clothes to the floor beside her feet. She ignored me. She was fixated on Nemo, the bright orange fish swimming in front of her. Then Dory joined in, and I knew my life had gotten more difficult.

"Dus keep svimming. Dus keep svimming. Svimming, svimming." Emmie imitated Dory while the two fish darted back and forth across the TV.

"Emmie, please get dressed, Sweets. Mommy and Daddy need to leave, and you're going with us."

"I'm watching Nemo, Mommy!" Emmie was headstrong and defiant. More so than most three-year-olds.

There was no time to negotiate with Emmie. I snatched her up and dressed her while she screamed and arched her back. Her wad of matted blonde hair went into a loose, messy bun like mine. I wrangled her into her clothes in a WWE wrestling match and came out on top this one time in a surprising win.

Todd helped the older girls out the front door to the waiting school bus while I finished with Emmie. He snuck in from behind and carried Emmie under his arm to the garage. She kicked and writhed in protest of being removed from her perch in front of

Nemo. But Todd won his battle, too, and loaded her into the car seat while The Five clambered to join her.

"I want to watch Nemo, Daddy!" Emmie squealed as Todd began shooing cats out of the car.

"Damn cats. Get the hell out of the car. Why did we have to get all of these stupid cats? They're just a nuisance." Then he whispered under his breath just loud enough for Emmie and I to hear. "I freaking hate cats."

Emmie screamed for ten minutes because she was denied her heart's desire to watch her favorite movie. Then she demanded that all five cats travel with us into town. The Five stayed behind despite Emmie's loud protests.

No doubt whose daughter she is. Emmie was Todd's clone in a little girl's body. She sang a nerve-racking song of defiance that rang through the car like the Liberty Bell for the fifteen-mile drive to the doctor's office.

For once, we arrived early. We waited uncomfortably next to each other while Emmie commanded the waiting room with her overbearing personality. We were called to the check-in desk to answer a slew of necessary but mundane questions about my pregnancy. Those were always interesting conversations for me.

"OK, so you have been pregnant six times but have seven living children?" I confused the nonthinkers every time.

"Yes, I have a set of identical twins."

"Oh, of course. Yes. I see. Are they boy-girl twins?"

"Um, no. They are identical. Both girls." I slapped myself on the forehead in the privacy of my mind.

The receptionist offered us a standard "congratulations." She had no idea how out of place her words were. Someone would be with us shortly. Emmie blazed through the waiting room, bouncing, climbing, and twirling about like she was at home. The Monster returned and crept up on me like a pouncing black panther. I choked back a throat full of vomit as a gangly woman named Phyllis sauntered to the end of the hall and called my name.

"Come on, Em. Let's go find Nemo." Emmie squealed with joy and skipped down the hall in front of us. I was barely able to see the knotted hair underneath her bouncing blonde bun. She ran ahead, eager to find her favorite fish before anyone else.

Phyllis was our ultrasound technician. She would tell us if the baby had a heartbeat. She escorted us to the last door at the end of the hall where I undressed in front of Todd for the first time in more than two months.

"Undress from the waist down. Take your underwear off. Just crack the door when you're done, and I'll come back in." We were left alone in the ultrasound room while Emmie searched for her favorite fish on the screen beside the ultrasound bed. I let my pants fall to the floor.

"Ang! You're so skinny. What the hell is going on with you?"

"I've been throwing up day and night for a week, Todd. That's what's wrong with me. I've lost ten pounds. Maybe if you didn't work so late every night, you would have noticed. Crack the door so Phyllis will come back in."

Phyllis returned to the ultrasound room and assisted me onto a table lined with a thin, white paper sheet that crackled underneath me. I reclined on the table and waited for the ultrasound to begin. I stared at the ceiling above me and noticed every flaw in the texture and paint. But I was alone in a room the size of a walk-in closet with three other people. Close enough I could smell their breath. A tear ran down the side of my face as I waited to hear that my baby was dead. I would be sent home to miscarry alone in the toilet of my bathroom. Todd saw the tear land on the thin strip of white paper and blotted my temple with a tissue he pulled from a box of Kleenex on the table beside us. It felt like the first time in months he had expressed any care or concern for me. *It was probably a show for Phyllis.*

I was still confused about everything. I didn't know what to feel. Should I be happy or sad that I was on the ultrasound bed while someone searched for the heartbeat of a baby I had not wanted? I didn't know if my tears were for me or for my baby.

So I prayed again. In the only silence to be found in the room, I escaped into my mind alone with Jesus and prayed again. But this time, I asked forgiveness for my unholy prayer. This time I asked for the bleeding to stop and for a heartbeat to be found. This time I asked God to save my baby's life.

Emmie continued to be a distraction as she interrupted the aloneness of my mind. She crawled up and down Todd's lap like the egocentric three-year-old she was. She was convinced we were only there so she could watch *Finding Nemo* on the ultrasound screen. As Phyllis began, I cocked my head sideways to see what would appear on the screen. It wasn't Nemo. Phyllis moved the ultrasound wand and tried to find the source of the bleeding. A pear-shaped image became clear and then distorted and then clear again as she located my uterus in the lower part of the screen. I had seen many of these images as a nurse, so I knew what Phyllis found.

"Is that Nemo?" Emmie climbed over Todd to see the screen above my shoulder.

"Yes, Em. That's Nemo." I wasn't ready to share the truth with Emmie or my other kids. She would have to believe we were watching her favorite movie instead.

As the wand moved back and forth, I saw Baby Nemo appear in my uterus. A small sac and a tiny baby with no definition lay still inside of me. It was so small. But it was there. A disproportionately big head, four short nubs, and a bump for a tail. No bigger than an almond. Its chest fluttered. There was a beating heart. My baby was still alive.

"Eight weeks and three days," Phyllis said as Emmie ignored her and continued to stare at Nemo. "Your baby is eight weeks and three days along. The heartbeat is 178 beats per minute. The paperwork says you came in for a threatened miscarriage, but I don't see anything unusual. I'm not supposed to tell you that, but I can see you're upset."

She paused then whispered to Todd and me, "Everything looks very good." Phyllis finished with her measurements while I fell in love with Baby Nemo on the screen, a baby I had asked God to take from me. Todd seemed confused that I was still crying.

"Aren't you happy?" He didn't know what I had prayed the week before. I cried harder.

"I'm happy. Just overwhelmed."

My baby was a perfect little person with a beating heart who cried out to me. "Mommy! I see you, Mommy! I can't wait for you to hold me, Mommy!"

I was no longer unsure about my feelings or the future. But shame took hold of me, and I remembered what a selfish woman I was.

Todd put my hand in his and squeezed. For a second, I liked him again. The doctor came in and reviewed the ultrasound report with us. She explained that the retching had most likely caused the bleeding. Then she sent me home with a prescription for nausea and a pat on the back for the dubious honor of being her only advanced-maternal-age, grand-multiparous, vaginal-birth-after-C-section, high-risk pregnancy for the past three years.

"Our liability insurance bill just doubled." She laughed. But it wasn't funny to me. This was an honor I preferred to pass to someone else. She cautioned us that there was no guarantee I wouldn't miscarry. But the baby looked strong.

I breathed a trepid sigh of thanks that God heard my prayer atop a crackling sheet of white paper in a closet-sized ultrasound room. My baby still had a heartbeat. I was hopeful but not sure I would allow Jesus to walk through this unplanned season of life with me. I didn't like surprises. I didn't understand why Jesus let this happen. I didn't trust Him much anymore.

As we made our way out the doors of the clinic, Emmie held hands with Todd. She looked up at him puzzled and shook her head in the sweetest disappointment of a three-year-old windstorm.

"Daddy, that wasn't Nemo."

5

Bombs

*T*he disappointment of a strong-willed three-year-old echoed through our car the entire drive home like the sound of a vacuum bomb. Emmie experienced a delayed but cataclysmic shock to her system. She didn't realize she had been duped until we got to the car. There was no consoling her. I had cheated her out of a life experience so grand she would never be the same. She thrashed and hit the back of her head on her car seat.

She was devastated.

I had taunted her with a false promise that Nemo would be waiting for her in the tiny ultrasound closet so she wouldn't throw a fit and embarrass me. But I was lying, and she was not happy about it. Her wails sucked the last few ounces of energy out of me after The Monster took its share. I hoped Emmie's tantrum and her memory of the morning's ultrasound would be forgotten before her sisters arrived home from school. It was a temporary catastrophe. *Surely she would forget.* I didn't have strength left in my body to tackle a conversation about another baby and face the disappointment of my children. They didn't have enough of me already. They craved my attention like chocolate cake. But the pieces could only be cut so thin, and a beating heart in my belly meant each slice would be much smaller in a few months.

As a young child, I created my own Barbie doll family and played with them for hours atop the green shag carpet in my bedroom. I created a perfect family. One that I dreamed of having someday. Ken, Barbie, and their ten children. The parents never argued. The tweens never fought over the last blueberry muffin. The toddlers never threw temper tantrums. I created a family where nothing went wrong. Ever. It was an escape from my own childhood. A place I could go and be a perfect Mommy and Daddy to my ten perfect children. The reality of having so many children was something I didn't consider as a little girl.

Todd dropped Emmie and me off at home and offered me what felt like an awkward, disingenuous hug of reassurance. Emmie flew through the house and bounced from room to room as usual. Her stamina never ended. She forgot about the tragedy she experienced at the doctor's office as I expected she would and then carried on like it was just another day at our house.

But nothing would be the same again.

The medicine the doctor gave me to fight The Monster made my eyes heavy. The bleeding slowed enough to calm my worries, so I let myself nod off to a shallow sleep while Emmie blew back and forth by me like a Tasmanian devil. All I had to offer the best escape artist I knew was scant supervision. As long as the doors were locked, she wouldn't die while I slept. But if she figured out the top lock on the door, Emmie would fly away from me unnoticed. After lunch, she settled in on the floor in front of the TV and picked up where she left *Nemo* earlier in the day. She was in a trance and dozed off to a much-needed nap. She curled up like one of The Five on the floor, tangled in her favorite pink blanket. The house was quiet except for the sound of Nemo and Dory "svimming" in the background of my light sleep.

I enjoyed two sacred hours of peace while Emmie slept on the floor. But the raging bulls arrived home, and the beautiful silence was interrupted. My three pre-teen hurricanes stormed through the front door exactly on time. They raced one another to get to the refrigerator first in case there was only one Dr Pepper left. Backpacks and shoes flew through the hall. Explosions startled Emmie and me. We were both jolted awake from our naps.

"I call the last Dr Pepper!" Ten-year-old Kinnah scrambled to the refrigerator, trying to get there first. But the twins pushed past her. They were only slightly bigger than her but stronger and faster.

"You jerk!" Brooke yelled at her. "You know I wanted it."

"You two both suck," Hope shouted as she sped past Brooke. "I'm getting it first."

Hope slid around the corner to the finish line in the kitchen. She arrived at the refrigerator first to the disappointment of her sisters. They didn't know there was an entire case of soda waiting for them. *Would it have mattered if they had known?* They always found something to argue about. Even in the presence of complete calm. Brooke and Hope were twelve, and Kinnah was born only eighteen months later. The three were so close in age that people sometimes assumed they were triplets. Every day since Kinnah learned to speak full, clear sentences before she even turned two years old, the three girls bantered back and forth in an exhausting circle about one thing or another. Clothes, shoes, food, or anything of minuscule value was a point of contention among them. They agreed on nothing except the brutality of a chick fight.

"Girls! Good grief. Just stop!" I dragged myself off the couch from a Zofran-induced coma and went to the kitchen to intervene. "I can't keep doing this with you girls. There are enough sodas in there for all three of you. Come on girls. I don't feel well. Can you please try to get along? Please?" I pleaded with them to change the unchangeable. Faith skipped in the front door without a worry and was giddy to be home. Emmie screamed in the background. She had been awakened before she was ready. We all knew the consequences of disturbing her sleep.

"Sorry, Mom." Hope spoke up for her sisters as usual. "We'll stop fighting."

The girls sat on the living room floor and watched *Finding Nemo* with an almost calm Emmie. They each had a Dr Pepper in one hand and a Nutty Bar in the other. They knew snacks had to stay in the dining room. It was a rule. But I didn't have the energy to enforce my own directive, and they didn't abide by it unless I did. They knew when I was vulnerable or weak or unable to take on three tweens at once. I gave up on the fight before it even began, and I returned to my favorite chair in the living room. I leaned way back and raised the footrest on my recliner while Emmie lay in front of the TV. She was still trying to recover from the trauma of being woken up by her sisters.

"Dus keep svimming. Dus keep svimming." Emmie chanted to herself as she lay on her side on the living room floor. Her cheek was buried in her blanket, and she stared with one eye at the screen in front of her. Nemo and Dory swam across the TV while I tried to nod off again. Without warning, the ultimate of all thermobaric explosions detonated.

Emmie remembered our trip to the doctor.

She sprung up from her place on the floor and dropped a truth bomb on her unsuspecting sisters. And me.

"Mommy and Daddy took me to see Nemo today, Faith!" Faith joined Emmie on the floor to watch the movie. "It wasn't Nemo, Faith. But Mommy showed me a little bitty, teeny tiny fishy in her tummy. Dus keep svimming. Dus keep svimming!" Emmie made a motion with her hands like she was swimming through the ocean with Nemo and Dory as she freestyled through the living room.

I jumped to my feet. An attack was imminent. I scooped Emmie up in my arms and shushed her mouth with my fingers.

"Let's get you a snack, Em. I know you must be starving. Wanna Nutty Bar?" Emmie squealed as I lifted her from the ground and pushed my fingers away.

"Stopppppp, Mommy! I'm not hungry! I want to watch Nemo!" Emmie writhed and screeched. I tried to change the subject hoping nobody heard her.

But they all heard.

Not even Emmie's screams were a big enough distraction from the truth. The girls started asking questions I wasn't ready to answer.

"Emmie, what do you mean you saw a fish in Mommy's tummy?" Kinnah questioned Emmie first. Then the others joined in.

"Where did you go today, Emmie?" Brooke asked in a whiny voice, afraid she might have missed a fun outing.

Hope turned sharply and looked at me.

"Are you freaking kidding me, Mom?"

"Can I have a Dr Pepper, too?" Faith asked as her older sisters interrogated Emmie and me.

The messy truth was revealed in a percussion bomb thrown by a three-year-old. I had no choice. I had to explain to the girls how their piece of the cake was going to be much smaller.

"Wow, Mom. Becky is almost nineteen, and you're having another baby?" Hope asked the same question I already pondered in my own mind. I knew why she was asking. "You're already so busy with work. Now you'll be even busier." She shook her head in disappointment. She knew she was losing a part of me. I knew it too. I put my arms around her.

"I know, Hope. I wasn't expecting this either. But we're having another baby, and I need you on my team. Maybe this time you'll get a little brother." I pulled her in close and gave her a tight squeeze. Hope's demeanor changed when she thought of having a little brother. But she was wise beyond her years—not easily fooled into thinking everything was going to be OK. She was hopeful but hesitant.

Each of the girls took the news in their own way, and I was surprised there weren't any more explosions. I needed to tell my two oldest kids, Becky and AJ, whom I shared with my first ex-husband. They were my only children not living with me anymore. I knew they wouldn't be ecstatic about another baby in the family. Becky was my first born and had moved in with her boyfriend at the end of the summer just before her first semester of college. She was one of the smartest people I knew and had razor-wire wit that almost always went unchallenged by others. She would discover the truth soon enough, and I didn't want her to hear it from anyone but me.

AJ, who was the only boy among a sea of sisters, was my sweet, sensitive, big-hearted Rico Suave who didn't move with us to our country home a few months earlier. He instead chose to break my heart and live with his father. AJ was finally anchored in a school he enjoyed after moving thirteen times since he was born. I didn't see him enough. He was sixteen and behaved like a typical teenage boy. He had a girlfriend, so I was no longer important to him. He was completely uninterested in me. That was a hard blow for me to take. I had not forgotten the days when I was the only person AJ needed. We were bonded like mamas and baby boys are. Until baby boys become teenage boys.

The girls returned to their activities almost unfazed by Emmie's shocking revelation. I found my phone, then paused for a while before I dialed the numbers. I was forced into a corner by a three-year-old to tell Becky and AJ a truth I wasn't ready to share with them. They deserved to hear it from me. I had no choice. I dreaded the conversation because I worried they would feel even more squeezed out of my life. Neither would get to grow up in the same home with the baby. I was sad they would miss out on being a big brother and sister to Nemo. I wondered if that's how other families felt when the older children moved on and their mother kept having children beyond the years she should.

I balanced the cell phone in my quivering hand as I fumbled the numbers to call Becky first. I didn't expect her to answer since she was busy in college now. I hoped she would be in the middle of class or something far more important than taking my call.

"Whaaaaaat?" Becky knew it was me.

"Hey Beck, I need to tell you something." My words disappeared into the phone as I explained my life was turned upside down because I was having another baby in April. I was startled from my rambling stupor by her usual but unexpected response.

"What the hell, Mom!" She laughed a loud belly laugh. "You're not serious, are you? I'm not watching it, just so you know. But that's kind of cool. How does it feel to be an old woman having a baby?" *Razor wire.*

"I've been so sick. I've been puking up my guts for over a week now, and it's not going to get any better for a while. Don't say anything to anyone yet, though. I'm bleeding, but the doctor says the baby looks good. I just don't want to tell everyone and then have a miscarriage. I didn't want to tell you guys yet, but Emmie told the girls this afternoon."

She laughed again.

"Leave it to Emmie. She can't keep her mouth shut. I love that girl. I'm just glad it's you and not me." She ended the conversation on a cackling high note that elicited a small grin on my lips.

AJ was next. I wasn't sure how to tell him. He and I had grown distant when we moved, and I didn't see him much. It didn't seem right to have another baby when my son didn't live with me. But I had to tell him. I dialed his number with trepidation.

"Hello." I heard my son's voice for the first time in a month.

"Hey, it's Mom. How are you doing?"

"I'm OK. But I'm working right now. What's going on? Becky just tried to call me."

"Oh, that's nice since I told her not to tell anyone. Son, I need to tell you something. I just found out that I'm having another baby, and I wanted to be the one to tell you."

"Oh, I guess that's cool. But I'm at work right now, so I'll call you later, OK? I love you, Mom."

AJ hung up before I could tell him how much I loved him too. I got to hear his voice, and I would have to be content. But I didn't know why he hung up so fast. I wanted to tell him he would never lose me. That I missed him. That I was proud of him. It would have to wait until he wasn't too busy to talk to his mother. But he didn't call back.

The truth was out to everyone. We hadn't experienced Hiroshima or Pearl Harbor. It wasn't a war zone or complete annihilation. But I knew our lives were changed. Now everyone who mattered to me and some who didn't knew I tangled things up. Again. I was very good at complicating what could have been a richly boring life.

But it wasn't as simple as just having another baby. I had altered the course of my children's lives by this one thing. I was relieved to get through the conversations and come out mostly unscathed. They all still loved me, and we would get through this together.

The hardest part was over.

6

So Small

J ust as the bleeding started, it also stopped. But the days in
between were heavy. Heavy with blood. Heavy with worry.
Heavy with regret. I carried the guilt of a shameful prayer with me
like a clamp on my throat. The constant whisper from a dark place
in my soul told me I didn't deserve to be a mother to this baby. I
believed it. I knew it. I felt it deep inside my aching gut every time I
remembered how I pleaded with God to take my baby from me. But
five weeks had passed since I thought I was losing the baby, and I was
still pregnant. Somehow, I was still pregnant. My baby was growing
inside my rapidly expanding belly, and I was almost two weeks into
my second trimester. It was a milestone I didn't expect to reach. The
threat of miscarriage was fading. My mind could rest at ease. As my
abdomen grew, so did my confidence that everything was going to
be OK.

Though the nausea had waned slightly, it was still ever present.
Even in the middle of the night. The distraction of work and children
simply dulled The Monster that clung to me weeks longer than I
expected. But life didn't stop for monsters. I still showed up to do a
John Travolta good job at the hospital. I still took care of a houseful
of daughters who did not even attempt to get along. And I was still
married to a man who I thought didn't love me anymore.

Everything and nothing had changed.

Another Monday morning made its way into our home, and
I heard the girls scampering downstairs to get ready in time for the
school bus. The arguments ensued in the kitchen below my room just
like they did every morning before the sun even had a chance to rise.

But I didn't have the energy to intervene after such a long shift at work the day before. The sound of unparented children fretting over donuts rang through the house until the school bus thundered down the road. I stumbled from my bed and made it to the front porch just in time to wave goodbye to my family as Todd backed out of the garage.

"Didn't want to wake you!" Todd yelled through the passenger window as he drove down the driveway. "Faith got herself dressed. She's on the bus." I waved back at Todd and thought about Faith's morning hair. The tangles of her thick, naturally curly hair had to be combed through with precision and deliberation. It was a job that required time and patience. It was a task that went undone while I slept through my alarm. I had lain in bed too long trying to ignore the bustle below me.

Faith sat three rows behind the bus driver with her nose and mouth pressed against the dirty glass window. She tried to catch a glimpse of her lazy mother before she left for school. Her hair was uncombed. Her face was covered in strawberry toaster strudel. Her blue sweater peeked out the top of her zipped coat. It was the same sweater she wore to school three days earlier. The same one I didn't have time to launder. Faith's kindergarten teacher would have to understand I had nothing to do with getting her ready for school this morning.

Faith had breakfast. She was wearing a coat. *At least Todd tried.*

"I love you girls!" I yelled through the bitter-cold morning dew that hung heavy in the air. I tightened my grip on the robe that covered me to my ankles. I shivered as I stood barefoot on the frost-covered concrete porch. As I waved goodbye to the girls, there was a familiar strain in my pelvis. The same tug had come and gone a few times over the past several days. It had only gotten my attention. Nothing more. Pregnancy at my age was like carrying iron weight plates around my waist. It was a workout.

Todd followed close behind the school bus until I could no longer see them through the thick fog. Most of my family left for the day. Emmie and I would spend this Monday at home together. Just like every Monday. I stood a little longer. The cold, dense air stung my throat as I breathed deeply. It was thick. Choking. Foreboding. There was a storm front that would blow across the mountains in just two days. We would get the taste of a Colorado storm in October, bringing with it a season of early darkness.

Not just over our home and our land.

But also over our lives.

I made my way back up the stairs and peeked at Emmie who had fallen asleep in Faith's room the night before. She lay sprawled out across the bed wearing her usual blue gown. Her head was tipped back, and her mouth was wide open as she snored loudly. She slept through the commotion in the kitchen, and I knew better than to wake her from her Monday morning sleep. I didn't want to start and end the day with an ill-tempered three-year-old. Instead, I would enjoy precious minutes alone as I tiptoed to my room, hoping Emmie would sleep just a little longer. As I walked down the hall, I felt a discomfort in my abdomen again. Not unlike the tug of the previous few days. Except this time I stopped and held my right side. I was grateful the nausea hadn't kept me completely captive over the past week. But for several days I felt like a baseball was in my pelvis. *This is why old women shouldn't get pregnant.* Becky's sarcastic words of congratulation just a few weeks earlier punctuated my thoughts. She was right. Old women shouldn't have babies.

I made my way to the master bathroom. The same place I found out I was pregnant again. The same place Todd learned he would be a father again. The same place I prayed a despicable prayer. I looked in the mirror and smiled back at myself. I didn't feel any nausea. It was the first time in months I didn't have an urge to throw up. I turned sideways and admired the growing bump in my belly. I ran my hand over my abdomen and wondered who this baby would look like. If I was having a boy or a girl. What life would be like in six months. I forgot how incredible it was to feel normal and to have hope. It was a turning point I had been craving for a while.

But my smile and sense of normal evaporated just as fast as they appeared. I leaned over the sink to brush my teeth and felt something wet in my underwear. I continued brushing until I felt something run down the inside of my right thigh. The toothbrush dangled from my mouth. I lowered myself to the toilet and felt another tug in my abdomen. I rested on the toilet seat. *What's happening?* Maybe it was just a cramp. Maybe it was just a leak of urine that's common during pregnancy. Maybe I was imagining things.

But then . . . a gush.

A gush of warmth exited my body and splashed into the cold toilet water below me. I looked between my knees into the bowl. The clear water had turned thick red.

I was bleeding. Not just bleeding.

I was hemorrhaging.

I was in a frenzy. I took rapid, shallow breaths. The toothbrush fell from my mouth to the floor as I tried to regain my senses. Then I understood.

I was losing my baby.

There was no way a baby so small could survive a blood loss so great. I saw something in the toilet the size of a small tangerine and sobbed loudly. I fell to my knees in front of the toilet as blood poured from me.

"Oh, God, please! Father, please. Don't take my baby! I'm sorry. I'm so sorry." I began to plead with purpose and desperation. "Please don't let this baby die, God. Please!" I yelled out to Jesus in an agonizing prayer. He had to hear me and intervene.

There was blood in the toilet. On the toilet. On my legs. On the bathroom floor. Blood was everywhere. I didn't know what to do, so I cried out to God even louder. My words were agonizing. I lay on the bathroom floor for what felt like hours. Alone. Pleading for God to save my baby's life.

I got back onto the toilet and wept bitterly. I was sure I had just miscarried or was going to bleed to death right there in my bathroom. I found my phone on the counter and called the only person I was sure would answer. Lynel.

"Hey, girl! Whatcha doing?"

"Lynel, I'm bleeding. I'm bleeding a lot. I think I'm losing the baby. I don't know what to do. What should I do?" I cried out to Lynel for help only she could give me.

"Angie, what do you see in the toilet? Do you see any evidence that the baby was lost? If you're bleeding too much, you need to be seen right away."

I looked into the toilet and gasped. My heart sank as I stared at what was in the water. There were so many pieces of things I had passed. I couldn't tell what I was looking at through the red water.

"If I lose this baby, it's my fault." The only thing that eclipsed my sorrow was the shame that gripped my throat.

"Angie, this is not your fault. Call Todd and get to the doctor's office. I will call them and let them know you're on your way. Go lay down and wait for Todd."

I didn't want to lose my baby. But it was probably too late. There was so much blood. So. Much. Blood. My baby was only about the size of a peach, and there were clots in the toilet at least that big. There was no way a tiny baby could make it out of that blood bath. I had to call Todd.

"Todd! Todd! I'm hemorrhaging! I need help!" I screamed into the phone before he even said hello.

"I'll be there in fifteen minutes. Lay down until I get there."

As I waited for Todd to arrive, I knew my unholy prayer was answered. I was shaken by the disgusting woman I was.

I was so ashamed.

Emmie woke up amid the weeping from my bedroom and walked around the corner where I lay crying on the bed.

"What's a matter, Mommy?" Emmie climbed up beside me.

"I'm not sure, Em." I didn't think the baby was still alive in my belly. "Daddy is on his way to pick us up so Mommy can go to the doctor."

"OK, Mommy." Emmie was surprisingly cooperative for being disturbed from her Monday morning sleep. "Let's go find Baby

Nemo again, Mommy." She patted my arm gently and smiled at me. Then she rested her head on my abdomen and whispered. "Hi, baby. I wuv you, baby. Dus keep svimming."

I cried softly as Emmie moved in close to me. I had been looking forward to snuggling and middle-of-the-night cuddles. Hushed newborn sounds. The smell of milky kisses. I would breastfeed for years. I would immerse myself in this baby. I would correct past parenting mistakes. I would take advantage of the patience that comes with being an older mom. Todd and I would reconnect and be the power couple we once longed to be. This was my last chance to be a near-flawless mother and wife. My last chance.

God, please let me raise this baby.

I continued talking to God. But it was very unlikely a baby would live through a catastrophic hemorrhage. I didn't want to consider it, but I assumed my womb was empty already. The thought of my baby drowning in bloody toilet water evoked an emotion I couldn't handle. I couldn't flush the toilet until I knew. I couldn't flush the toilet without retrieving the baby. No matter how small it was.

The back door opened and Todd ran up the stairs to the bedroom. Emmie was still curled up next to me. She consoled me in the only way she knew how.

"What's going on? Are you OK?" Todd asked as he rounded the corner.

I cried while I explained what happened in the bathroom. Todd handed me a pair of sweatpants from on top of the dresser.

"Where are your shoes? We need to leave." I motioned toward the bathroom and stood at the side of the bed.

"Don't flush the toilet!" I screamed. "Don't flush the baby, Todd!" I sobbed loudly as I pulled on the sweatpants Todd handed me.

"Oh, dear God," Todd said as he walked into the bathroom. "Dear God, what happened in here?" The tone in Todd's voice said he also knew our baby had died. He was shocked by the grisly scene and quickly came to help me to the car.

"We need to go now," he said. He was shaken too.

Todd scooped Emmie up even after she consented to get in the car on her own. It was a habit. He belted her into the car seat still dressed in a thin blue nightgown and winter coat. No socks. No shoes. No breakfast. Her blonde curls were matted to the sides of her head. She sat quietly in the back seat as Todd pulled out of the garage. The temperature outside was below freezing, and the fog infiltrated the countryside all around us. The impending snowstorm brewed just beyond the mountains, and the wind blew the clouds in a swirl of winter. I sat in the front seat wearing a pair of Todd's sweatpants, a pink pajama top, socks that didn't match, and tennis shoes stained with smears of blood.

"This is my fault. This is all my fault," I whispered into the palms of my hands as I covered my face.

Todd just drove.

Lynel alerted the clinic that I would be arriving, and I was whisked back for an ultrasound without even checking in at the front desk. Gangly Phyllis met us at the end of a familiar hall and took us to the same room I visited just weeks before.

"Dr. Warren will be in to watch the ultrasound with us," Phyllis said. "He wants to see what's going on with all this bleeding." Phyllis feigned a smile. Different from the last time we were there. Her eyes were void of hope.

I laid back on the same ultrasound bed atop a thin sheet of crispy white paper that crackled when I moved. Emmie sat next to me in her thin worn-out gown and winter coat in a remarkable show of compliance that was unlike her. Todd sat dazed trying to understand what was happening.

"Here." Phyllis handed me a wet diaper wipe. "You can clean your hands with this." I looked down and saw dried blood on my fingers. As I cleaned my hands, the wipes turned brown. I thought about the bloody bathroom at home. I hovered over myself in my memory as I looked at such a pathetic woman having a miscarriage. Alone. Surrounded only by tears, guilt, and shame.

I thanked Phyllis for her kindness then heard the hallmark stride of one of the greatest physicians I had ever worked beside. Dr. Warren walked down the hall toward our ultrasound room in size 15 cowboy boots. I had never seen him in scrub pants without them. Each step he took sounded like a small earthquake as he made his way to our room. Dr. Warren was a tall, broad man with a beautiful, white beard and thick, white hair. His hands were so big the hospital had to order specialty gloves for him. His voice was deep and smooth. He was frugal with his words and never said anything that wasn't exquisite and brilliant. I was grateful Dr. Warren showed up in our room. There wasn't any other doctor I wanted to be there.

"Hi, I'm Dr. Warren." He looked at Todd. Then he turned to me. "Hey, kiddo. You doing OK?"

"Not really," I replied.

Dr. Warren shook Todd's hand and then asked Phyllis to start the ultrasound. Phyllis squeezed a generous glob of cold gel onto my abdomen and looked for the baby. I wept quietly as I waited to be told what they saw on the screen just over my right shoulder. I couldn't look this time. I knew what was happening. I couldn't bear to see an image of my hollow uterus.

The room was silent while Phyllis moved the ultrasound over my lower abdomen. Even Emmie sat quietly between Todd and me. I looked at Todd. One hand covered his face.

He was still shaken from the bloody scene in the bathroom.

"Well," Dr. Warren crooned. "It appears that you're having a fairly significant subchorionic hemorrhage."

"What exactly is that?" Todd asked.

"It's when the chorion pulls away from the uterus and bleeds," I responded.

"Phyllis, can you look for a heartbeat again, please?" Dr. Warren asked.

It took a moment for Dr. Warren's request to sink into my heart. But then I realized they saw the baby. It was still in my uterus. I didn't know how, but it was still there.

Phyllis again moved the ultrasound device around trying to find my baby's heartbeat. It seemed like hours while she searched for a sign the baby was still alive. But the blood pocket was so big Phyllis had difficulty finding her way through it. She kept scanning for a window into my uterus that wasn't clouded by blood. Then she saw what she was looking for. She reached over my head and turned up the volume on the ultrasound machine.

Swoosh. Swoosh. Swoosh. Swoosh.

The most beautiful sound of an angel's song echoed through our tiny room.

A heartbeat.

It was the sound of a baby who was so small but so strong.

My baby was alive.

"The baby is highly active, and strong cardiac activity is present," Dr. Warren said. "However, there is a pocket of blood between the chorion and the uterus that needs to be absorbed by your body. If you continue bleeding beyond the next two days, you will probably miscarry. You should go home, rest, and take it easy. Were it not for the large amount of blood, I would tell you not to worry because you have a very busy little baby."

I was stunned by what Dr. Warren told us. My baby was alive. It was busy too. I didn't understand how this was possible after experiencing such devastation just an hour before. I knew God heard my cries for help on the bloody bathroom floor. The baby had survived a catastrophic hemorrhage. Not unlike a sparrow caught in a tornado. I remembered Mom's words when she told me God had big plans for this baby. I just didn't know then what that would mean.

We left the clinic in a haze of trepidation and fragile emotion. Todd drove the four of us home through the unusually thick fog that had settled all around us. I was reminded of the coming fall snowstorm. The days that followed would be cold and hard again. The clamp returned to my throat. The whisper from that dark place in my soul once again reminded me I didn't deserve to be this baby's mother.

I was given transient peace while looking at myself in the mirror earlier in the day. A peace that was short-lived. A peace that was stolen as soon as the grooves in my wrinkled face finally settled into an upward curve. A peace I craved would return. Despite the storms that brewed inside my body and outside our car, I clung to an unfamiliar faith. One I learned about from Mom and Sunday school. One that told me God had a plan so great for this baby so small.

7

The Calm

There was always a calm before the storms of my life. A time and place where I quietly gathered strength to take on adversity. A restful pause that deceived me into believing nothing lay ahead that was too difficult for me to handle. A place where illusive peace lulled me into a dream that everything would be OK. Where I escaped the reality of a coming that couldn't be stopped. An almost utopian place.

If only it were real.

In the months following The Great Hemorrhage, The Calm did not surround me as usual. The only peace for the rest of my pregnancy, real or deceitful, had already visited me when I gazed at myself in the bathroom mirror mere seconds before a gush of blood threatened to answer a shameful prayer. It was a fleeting moment of peace. One I wouldn't reclaim for many years. Hearing life beating in my womb after such a catastrophic blood loss should have been the bridge to peace. But every second after my baby's heartbeat echoed through the tiny ultrasound room was consumed by dread. Dread of the future. Dread of the coming moment when everything was *not* OK. The moment when *the thing* that was wrong would finally be revealed and prove more than I could handle.

I couldn't stop it. It was coming.

Right on time and as predicted, the October 2006 storm blew in and dropped three feet of thick, heavy, wet snow on the countryside surrounding our home. It went on record as the fourth-largest snowstorm in Colorado's history. I rested inside, safe from the cold, while my body worked to absorb the large pocket of blood that threatened to end my pregnancy. The bleeding stopped about the same time the last snowflake fell, but the fear of losing my baby did not. I lingered in perpetual anxiety with every step, twist, and movement I made. One wrong move and I would cause a miscarriage and stillbirth. Even though I didn't see one more drop of blood. Even though I was still pregnant with a lively baby at every prenatal appointment. Even though everyone told me everything was going to be just fine. Something wasn't right.

Another storm was coming. And The Calm eluded me.

Hypervigilance became a substitute for my utopian peace. I consented to every medical test pregnant mothers were offered at my age. But there could be nothing so wrong with my baby that I would choose to end my pregnancy.

Nothing.

Despite my egocentric world that did not have room for a disabled child. Despite my John Travolta good cockiness at the hospital. Despite being in a marriage that could not endure the challenges of a baby with extraordinary needs.

Nothing could be wrong enough with my baby to electively end a life.

There was a smorgasbord of syndromes and peculiar problems that could be detected in utero. I needed time to prepare myself for the worst that was coming. So a short three weeks after I lay on my bathroom floor begging God to save my baby, I visited Dr. Warren again. I was scheduled to have another ultrasound, but this time I would also watch him insert an instrument the length of a knitting needle into my abdomen. Then he would go through my uterus and remove amniotic fluid for genetic testing. A test that would do nothing more than upheave my fears to a peak I hadn't yet summited and provide no useful answers in the end. I had to know what was coming. Knowing was easier than guessing.

Todd and I arrived at the clinic early and sat together in the waiting room while I nervously anticipated a painful procedure I had never been through. All my other pregnancies were routine, even with the twins, whom I carried full term. I tried not to think about the needle or how it would pierce my abdomen and my uterus. It was too much. But Dr. Warren needed to get a small sample of fluid that would tell us if the baby had Down syndrome or some incompatible-with-life abnormality.

Todd held my hand, and I could feel anxiety tremble through his palms. Beads of sweat formed on his forehead and then ran down the sides of his face while we waited to be called to a room. He tried to be strong, but he was scared. Scared for his wife and scared for his baby. He reminded me of the man I fell in love with. The one who whisked me away from loneliness. The one who held me in his arms while we danced together all night. The one who promised me forever. I laid my head on his shoulder and sunk into the safety of his chest while we waited.

Young, pregnant women smiled and talked to one another in the waiting room as if nothing in life ever went wrong. They didn't talk to me though. I was too old. I assumed not one of them was there to have a needle plunged into her uterus. They were going through the motions of normal pregnancies. They celebrated every prenatal visit with a bougie Grande Decaf Creme Frappuccino while they giggled with their friends. They had no idea what it was like to know a storm was coming and be powerless to change its course. They were so naive to think everything was just going to be OK.

Gangly Phyllis appeared in the waiting room with a smile and a clipboard and called my name. "Angie, we're ready for you."

I stood and walked toward her, still holding Todd's shaking hand.

"Hi, Angie. Are you ready? I'm so happy to see you. A few weeks ago I didn't think we would be doing this today." The truth was out.

"I'm as ready as I can be." My voice trembled with anxiety. "Considering I'm about to have a needle puncture my uterus." Fear took over.

Phyllis walked us to an ultrasound room further down the hall from the one we visited a few weeks earlier. It was bigger and had more surgical instruments and a more sophisticated ultrasound machine.

"You can go in there and change into a gown. Empty your bladder then undress from the waist down." She pointed toward the adjoining bathroom. When I returned to the ultrasound room, Phyllis and Todd were chatting about how deep the needle would go into my uterus. Phyllis quickly changed the subject when she saw the distress on my face.

"OK, first I'm going to do the ultrasound and look at the baby's heart, palate, brain, and spine anatomy. I'll do some measurements to verify your due date, and then I'll look for a pocket of fluid for Dr. Warren to do the amniocentesis. Would you like to know your baby's gender today?"

"Yes. Yes, we would." I was sure this was the boy I promised Hope. It wasn't statistically possible that I was having a seventh girl. We would have better luck winning the lottery. It was for sure a boy.

I laid back on the bed as the crinkle of the white paper reminded me of the two other times I was there for ultrasounds. Phyllis applied a generous amount of gel to my abdomen and moved the wand over my pelvic area like she did just a few weeks before. I looked at the screen and saw my baby moving and rolling around like Nadia Comaneci at the 1976 Summer Olympics. Phyllis explored the contents of my uterus for a few minutes then suddenly stopped.

"I need to get Dr. Warren. I'll be back in a minute." Phyllis offered no explanation for the abrupt end to the ultrasound. Something was wrong. I sat straight up.

"Wait! What's going on?" Phyllis closed the door behind her. I looked at Todd. His face was buried in his hands again. "Something's not right. She saw something on that ultrasound, Todd. Something's not right with the baby." I started to cry and imagine all the things that could be wrong. There was a cocktail of things she may have seen. My mind dove deep into a dark pit of abnormalities our baby could be afflicted with.

A familiar series of miniature earthquakes walked toward our room, and Dr. Warren appeared at the door with Phyllis.

"What did you see?" I asked Phyllis before Dr. Warren could greet us.

"Hey, Angie. Hi, Todd," Dr. Warren said in his deep, molasses-smooth voice. "I'm going to take over from here. Phyllis just wants a second opinion."

Dr. Warren stood at the side of the bed where I was lying, cowboy boots peeking from under his green scrub pants and stethoscope dangling from his neck. His thick, white hair was combed with precision in place. His short, boxed beard grew handsomely on his face. He held the ultrasound wand in his right hand and moved it slowly over the top of my abdomen. Through tears I tried to see what they were looking at on the ultrasound screen above my shoulder.

"There it is." Phyllis pointed to an area that was not the baby, circling her finger around a distinct anomaly I couldn't name. Dr. Warren continued to move the device to see different angles of the abnormality he saw.

He removed the ultrasound wand and carefully returned it to its place on the machine as he turned and looked at Todd and me.

"OK, so first of all what I'm seeing is there's not a good pocket of amniotic fluid to aspirate. Your placenta is right out front. It's anterior, and it's right in the way. I'll have to go through it to get a sample. But more concerning is that you have a complete separation of the amnion and chorion. If I penetrate the sac surrounding the baby, you will most likely lose all of your fluid and miscarry. It's just not safe." Dr. Warren explained we could wait a few weeks and complete the amniocentesis, but a complete amnion separation diagnosed before twenty-four weeks increased the rate of stillbirth. Significantly. I was only sixteen weeks pregnant. I might not even be pregnant in a few weeks if Dr. Warren was right. He was always right.

No matter what we did, there was a much higher risk I would deliver a stillborn baby.

That restful, undisturbed place where I went to escape the reality of what was coming remained hidden. I knew I was powerless to change anything that lay ahead. *Something was wrong.* I had known since the first episode of bleeding. The Great Hemorrhage reinforced my fears. The ultrasound confirmed it.

"Before coming in to see you, I called and spoke with Dr. Wexler out of Denver who specializes in Genetics and Obstetrics. I'm going to recommend we wait to do the amnio. You can return in a few weeks for a more complete ultrasound if that sounds good to you both," Dr. Warren said.

"Yes, of course. I don't want to do anything to hurt the baby." I was relieved I would be spared the torture of a needle being pushed through my abdomen. "But, before you go, do you know the baby's gender? My kids are really excited to know if they're having a baby brother."

"Yes, I saw the gender," Dr. Warren replied. "You're having a girl."

A girl.

Todd started laughing, and then I did too. Neither of us was unhappy. Just surprised for some reason.

I was having a girl.

When we considered the totality of our visit, there was no disappointment in having a girl. Our baby girl was alive and active and fighting through everything my body was doing to betray her. I spent no time even trying to calculate the probability I would have seven daughters and one son. It was beyond my comprehension. But nonetheless, I was having another girl. A sweet baby girl who would join her gang of sisters and fill our home with more estrogen than Ladies Night at a country bar. We would need to add tampons as their own line item on our monthly budget. That seemed to be Todd's biggest and most pressing worry anyway.

"I need to call Becky," I said to Todd as we left the clinic and climbed into the car. "I bet her I was having a boy. I owe her fifty bucks."

I dialed Becky's number, smiling about the loss of fifty dollars and knowing she would have one more thing to chide me about. The phone rang until I thought it would go to voicemail, then Becky answered.

"Hello." Becky cried intermittent, hushed tears and tried to hide them from me.

"Hey, what's wrong? Why are you crying?"

"I'm not crying. How did the amnio go?"

"Well, you won the bet. I owe you fifty bucks."

Becky continued to cry under her breath. Then she burst into tears. She couldn't take it anymore.

"Mom! I can't believe this, Mom. I have to tell you something. Remember when I said I was glad it was you and not me? Remember that? Well, Mom, it's me, too. I'm pregnant. And I'm due three months after you are," Becky blurted between snotty snubs.

I dropped the phone then balanced it on my open palm as I sorted through what Becky had just told me. It was not unlike what I told Mom seven times. I had to be purposeful with my words. Like Mom. Todd stared at the phone in my hand. But I couldn't talk. I wanted to shake Becky and tell her she just made college and the rest of her life harder. But that wouldn't help her. She needed me to be supportive. She needed me to love her through this.

My nineteen-year-old daughter and I will be pregnant at the same time for almost six months.

It couldn't get any better than this.

"Beck, it's going to be OK. I'm so happy for you guys! My baby will be your baby's auntie! Can you believe we are pregnant at the same time?" Todd was eavesdropping on my call and stared more intently at me. Now he understood. I didn't tell Becky about the complete amnion separation. I didn't know if I was telling her the truth about being pregnant at the same time. But I had to be there for her and walk with her through her first pregnancy while I trudged through my last.

"Mom, how am I going to get through school with a baby?"

"Oh, girl, if I can go to nursing school as a single mom with five kids, you can do this. You're way stronger and smarter than I ever was. Everything is going to be OK. I promise. God has big plans for your baby." The same words Mom said to me.

I'm going to be a grandmother when I'm thirty-eight.

It was mind twisting.

I still didn't know if my own baby was going to make it through the next twenty-four weeks. But I was going to be a grandmother. It was a beautiful distraction from the coming storm I wouldn't be able to handle.

It was an escape from reality. Something to look forward to. A light on the unknown horizon.

I turned and looked at Todd who was barely able to contain himself. He rudely pointed out something I already knew.

"You're going to be a grandmother," he said as he shook his head from side to side and laughed out loud. "And this baby is going to be an aunt when she is three months old. Unbelievable." He said it again. "Unbelievable."

It was the first time in a long time I agreed with Todd.

I was excited Becky and I would have the next five or six months to bond over pregnancy things and compare swollen feet, heartburn, stretch marks, and weight gain. But it was a distraction only. It was time that temporarily diverted my attention away from the worries of what was coming. It was time of a miniscule distance from the thing that would defeat me. It was time that gave me reprieve from the darkness of the unknown storm. But moments only. I still didn't know what was coming for my baby. The guessing ravaged me.

I spent the remaining months of my pregnancy circling my life like a hawk, acutely aware something wasn't right without being able to identify what that meant. It was more than a feeling. It was a truth from the DNA of my cells that told me something was wrong with my baby. I told everyone. Todd. Lynel. Mom. The doctors and midwife. Everyone. But they didn't believe me.

There would be no restful pause for me. There would be no elusive peace. I tiptoed on eggshells to the last days of my pregnancy, guarded and apprehensive about the thing I would not be strong enough to handle. It was more than foreboding.

It was ominous.

8

Jewel of Heaven

Nervous laughter echoed through the kitchen as I descended the stairs for the last time with my baby girl tucked safely inside my belly. The girls would meet their sister soon. They could barely contain their eagerness to increase the size of their chick gang by one. Todd was outnumbered before. Now he didn't stand a chance. He was the only male in our home, except for a few feral boy cats he couldn't stand. Four new stretch marks appeared on my lower abdomen overnight as my belly grew to an impressive size. My baby girl was folded in a tight contortion and couldn't stay that way any longer.

She was ripe.

It was time.

A neatly packed suitcase covered in tropical flowers sat beside the back door waiting for me to join it on an unexotic trip to the hospital. This was the day I would meet the last baby who would ever grow in my womb. The day my eighth baby traveled a perilous six-inch journey from the darkness of her home into the blinding lights of a birthing room. The day I finally exhaled a sigh of relief almost nine months in the making.

I rounded the corner to the kitchen and paused in a breathless moment. I saw my family in a way I never would again. By the end of the day, we would grow by one and leave behind the picture I saw giggling in the kitchen. The birth and life of another baby would forever change the fabric of who we were together.

"Good morning, girls." I peeked in the kitchen at five of my children. "Does anyone know what today is?"

"Mommy!" A choir of children sang in unison as they clamored to be the first one to surround my massive waist with a tight hug.

"Just think, girls. Our baby will be here in just a few hours!" An anxious tremble in my voice reminded me I would soon be the mother of eight.

The girls happy-jumped as they anticipated the change coming to our family. I couldn't jump with them, but I was excited too. Mostly because I wouldn't be pregnant much longer. My fingers were swollen like Jimmy Dean sausage rolls, and I could barely fit my feet into my shoes. Pregnancy at my age was hard. Hard like open-heart surgery. Hard like running a marathon in flip-flops.

Just as the girls released me from their grip, the front door swung open. Becky waddled into the kitchen with her own swollen hands and feet and a six-month pregnant abdomen leading her way.

"Hey, brats!" Becky said as she popped Brooke on the back of the head. "Hey, Mom. You ready to get this party started?" Becky was there to keep Emmie safe from herself and her adventurous wanderings in the tall grass outside our home while I was away at the hospital. An induction was planned because I always had fast-moving, intense, and overwhelming precipitous labors. Labors that took me by surprise and peaked without warning. Like the ones on the news where the baby is born on the front lawn or in the toilet or in the checkout line at Walmart. They were stealthy. Brutal. They brought immediate and mind-blowing pain rather than a slow and steady culmination of contractions over hours. I could deliver a baby in minutes. I had plenty of experience. Enough that none of us wanted a delivery on the side of a dusty, washboard road after the Great Hemorrhage and risky pregnancy. The upside to a scheduled induction was that I could plan. Plan for a babysitter. Plan my labor and delivery. Plan to get my baby girl safely into my arms.

"Make sure someone calls me when she's born." Becky slung her backpack full of textbooks on the kitchen counter. "Wanna go look for baby rattlesnakes this afternoon, Emmie?" Emmie's attention piqued. "Just kidding. I was just trying to get Mom to go into labor already. Oh, and are you for sure going to name the baby Jade?"

"Rebekah Lynne! Stay away from the snakes," I snapped back as if Becky were a child herself. Her pregnant belly reminded me that while still young, she was no longer a child. "I'll have Todd call as soon as I'm in active labor. It won't be long after that when I have her. Oh, yes. Her name is Jade. I just love that name."

"I've never even heard of a baby named Jade. But I guess I like it. It's pretty."

"I think the jade gemstone is so beautiful. She will be our sweet little Jadey Bug." I gushed and felt a tickle in my stomach just thinking about her.

"I almost forgot to tell you. AJ said he has to work all weekend so he can't see you guys for a few days. But call him after Jade is born." Becky broke the news that broke my heart.

All my girls were with me, but my only son wasn't there. I wasn't complete without him. Teenage boys have agendas that don't usually fit their mamas' needs. My son was acting as he should.

Todd appeared at the back door and snatched my suitcase while I hugged everyone goodbye. "Hey, we need to go. You're supposed to be there in thirty minutes," he said. Todd was only ever on time for work, Nebraska Husker football games, and Catholic Mass. He just added having babies to that very short list.

We drove down our bumpy road as the April rain sang a hymn of expectancy over us. There was still a possibility I was wrong the whole time and everything was going to be OK. Perhaps I had spent day after day in useless worry over things that would not come to pass. Perhaps I squandered my time anxiously fretting for no reason.

Or maybe I was right all along. Maybe I was only a few hours away from paying the price for a prayer I had spoken seven months earlier. Either way, it wouldn't be long before the guessing would be over and the knowing would start.

We arrived at the hospital right on time for a momentous delivery that would come quickly. All the requisite procedures were completed, and I found myself bouncing and rolling around on a large, pink birthing ball in no time at all. I was given a blue, oversized, hospital gown that tied in front to wrap around my protuberant abdomen. Then I started to feel the pain of the contractions tighten and release around Jade. Pain that would steal my composure and my thoughts. Pain that would allow the profanities that lived in my head to slip off my tongue. Pain that would ebb and flow like a violent ocean riptide. Pain that would imprint on my heart a memory so tangible I would never forget it.

My midwife, Leslie, stopped by occasionally to check on me and hide from the other laboring mothers who were whining about how much they hurt. She knew I was an expert at this. All I needed was a little time. Once my uterus remembered its purpose, it would take over like an athlete and do a job worthy of an Olympic gold medal.

A few hours passed as I walked through my birthing room and the halls of the Labor and Delivery unit. I chatted with my nurse friends and took bets on who would be screaming for an epidural first. Todd sat quietly on the sidelines on a slick, dark green, blood-proof couch and read the newspaper while I labored through not-yet seismic pain. He didn't provide the counter pressure to my lower back the nursing staff recommended. He knew better. He knew a point would come when even looking my way would irritate me. He was wise to wait it out. I didn't want anyone's hands on me when the crescendo of birth arrived. Todd played it safe and minded his own business on the couch while my uterus and I worked.

The afternoon passed in an instant. The sun went down and the room became dimly lit. Anxiety found its way into my birthing room sometime just before the contractions overwhelmed me, and I had Todd turn on a playlist of soothing songs to ease my fear and pain. As my uterus found its rhythm, Amy Grant sang "Breath of Heaven" throughout the room from Todd's iPod.

It was time. Jade was coming.

I summoned my tribe to the birthing room so I would have a crowd of onlookers present to cheer me on. Todd called Becky and

AJ and let them know Jade would be born soon. Lynel was working just down the hall, so she joined us in the room and helped me climb onto the birthing bed. Mom was parking her car and would be there on cue. Everything was going just as I had planned it in a meticulous design of organization. All I needed was for everyone to simply follow the instructions I spelled out in a well-written birth plan and not deviate from a single word.

As expected, my contractions escalated from annoying to unbearable in only minutes. Like a light switched on, the rapid process of a precipitous delivery started. A tremendous pressure between my legs took me by surprise. When I planned the day's events, I overlooked the possibility that my body might take over without my assistance. I cried out in a loud scream and grunt.

"She's coming! Todd! Push the call light now!"

"What the hell?" Todd stood up and tossed the newspaper to the floor. "Why didn't you tell me you were hurting that bad?"

"I've been hurting for a freaking hour! Now push that damn light, Todd!" I was getting louder.

The familiar beep of an emergency call light echoed through the hall outside our room. Leslie hurried in with Mom close behind as I felt the uncontrollable pressure of Jade's head pushing its way out on its own.

I grunted some more. "I can't stop her!" I startled Mom with my scream as she walked past the foot of the bed where my feet were firmly placed in stirrups.

"Angie, I don't even see her head." Mom looked between my legs for a baby. "Don't scream, honey. That's not going to help." Mom was sedated with general anesthesia when she was in labor decades earlier. I had no patience for her experienceless words of advice while I was readying to blow a baby across the room unmedicated.

"Mom! That's not helpful!" I grunted back at her. "Can I push, Leslie? I need to push!"

Leslie checked to ensure it was safe for me to assist Jade with her journey into the world.

"Yes, Angie. Your cervix is completely dilated. Go ahead and push." Todd stood near my left shoulder while Lynel held my right knee back to my chest.

I pushed once.

There was a pause between the mountainous contractions. I was overwhelmed. Frightened during the brief duration between my pain peaks. Now that I was given permission to push, I was afraid to.

"Lynel," I said in a whisper. "I'm so scared. What if something is wrong with her?" I wanted to hold onto Jade forever. I was terrified that as soon as she was untethered from my body, she would die.

"Angie, she's going to be just fine. Focus on pushing her out and into your arms. She can't wait anymore." The orderly procession of nursery nurses and a pediatrician swarmed just in time to care for Jade and make sure she was safe and healthy.

I pushed again. With purpose. Like a champion.

With a loud grunt and scream, Jade's head was delivered. A thick head of dark hair and the porcelain doll face of an angel protruded between my legs for what felt like hours.

"Dad, would you like to help deliver your baby?" Leslie summoned Todd to the foot of the bed. He put on blue gloves and waited like the catcher in a World Series game.

A third push. Jade's body slid into Todd's hands.

"Give her to me! Give me my baby!" Leslie quickly placed Jade on my naked belly. The protuberance that occupied my waist only seconds before had metamorphosed into a flabby abdomen where Jade lay on her back on my bare skin. A hushed cry came from under the blankets placed over her wet and blood-streaked body.

I released an emphatic sob that could be heard in the hall as I cried out, "Thank you, Jesus. Thank you for this baby."

Jade began to cry more vigorously in a small, hushed tone under the warmth of the blankets. I pulled her close and kissed her goopy, wet head.

"I love you, baby girl. Mommy loves you so much."

Nine months of tears of relief poured down my cheeks. The

ominous feeling of doom that had followed me since the first hemorrhage finally lost its grip on me. I sank back into the hospital bed with Jade lying in my arms. I sobbed as I looked at her pink, round cheeks and thick, dark hair. She was here. She was healthy. She was perfect.

I was wrong about everything.

The guilt and shame I carried since finding out I was pregnant was magnified briefly as I gazed at the beautiful baby God had given me. I did not deserve Jade or the peace her birth brought to my heart. A lone tear rolled down my cheek.

Will I ever be able to forgive myself?

I took in a deep breath of unfamiliar calm and thanked God again that Baby Jade was resting safe in my arms. And for offering me a forgiveness I couldn't give myself.

Jade lay against my bare chest waiting to fulfill her instinct to nurse. Her pink tongue danced on her lips and told me she was ready. There was no working at it. She knew what to do. She did it skillfully. I cried tears of relief as Jade rested in my arms, tired from her travels and a few short minutes of feeding.

I didn't want to, but I reluctantly handed Jade to her pediatrician who examined every part of her body. I never wanted to let her go.

"Congratulations, you guys. She's perfect," Dr. Hall said as she handed Jade back to me. I held Jade close while Leslie repaired the deep laceration left behind from a rapid delivery, not even aware that it took twelve stitches to put me back together. When Leslie finished the repair and the nursing staff was satisfied I would not hemorrhage, we were ushered to a different room for postpartum moms and babies. This was my dance floor. The place where I spent my time on John Travolta good days as the world's greatest lactation consultant. The refuge from my life at home. I readied myself to breastfeed Jade again when I heard a light knock on our door.

"Surprise!" Becky marched her sisters in like the cavalry.

"Baby Jade!" The girls pushed their way to the side of the bed to see their baby sister.

"I told Emmie she had to stay by herself if she didn't wear something besides that stupid blue gown." Becky laughed. It didn't affect Emmie that she was required to change her clothes this time. It was the first time in weeks I saw her in something besides her tattered, blue gown.

"Girls, come see your baby sister. Isn't she so sweet?" The girls fawned over Jade.

"Get over there so I can get a picture. Todd, you too," Becky ordered. She was taking photography classes at college and pulled out a camera to capture the first photo of the eight of us together. It was a picture that would rescue me months later. A paper salvation on the darkest night of my life.

"When are you coming home, Mommy?" Faith whined. "We miss you already."

"We will be home in a day or so. Jade has some tests they need to do tomorrow afternoon. I'm sorry, sweetie. I miss you too." I hugged her tight.

The girls took turns staring at their baby sister. They were all smitten with her. Especially Brooke, who kissed every finger and every toe at least twice. Emmie climbed on the bed and put her head next to Jade's.

"I wuv you, Baby Jade," she whispered in her ear. She looked up at me with her chocolate-brown eyes and blonde curls.

"She's *my* baby sister, Mommy." She was right.

A combination of weariness and adrenaline made me feel euphoric. An unexpected concoction of relief, exhaustion, and peace poured over me. All my daughters surrounded me. Baby Jade was safe in my arms. I could finally rest because the imaginary nightmare I had created in my mind was behind me.

I was never so happy to be so wrong.

The girls stayed past visiting hours, and my nurse had to nudge them to head home for the night so Jade and I could get some rest.

"Well, she's pretty damn cute," Becky said as she gathered her herd of sisters. "I'll get them home and into bed and see you guys when you get home." She hugged me and kissed Jade on the forehead. "Yeah, I guess you're kinda cute," she whispered to Jade. "Let's go, brats." A choir of tears spilled on my shoulders with every goodbye hug I got.

The girls were crushed to go home without Baby Jade. They hung their heads low and reluctantly followed Becky's command to leave.

My eyelids fell heavy when the room was still, and my body jerked from exhaustion with Jade in my arms. I didn't want to surrender her to the bassinet even though my ravaged body needed rest. We spent the night in perpetual awakeness as my nurse friends did their jobs and watched over us. The morning came with little sleep.

This is just what it feels like for an old woman to have a new baby.

I heard a knock on the door, and Dr. Hall smiled as she approached the bed where Jade lay in my arms.

"Good morning. How is our little Jewel of Heaven this morning?"

"Jewel of Heaven?" I said.

"Yes. Jewel of Heaven. That's what Jade means." She smiled as she snatched Jade from me and unwrapped her tight swaddle. "I assumed that's why you named her Jade."

"Oh wow! No, I didn't know that at all. I just like the name. But that's even better. You're my Jewel of Heaven, Jadey Bug." I admired her through the clear plastic sides of the hospital bassinet where Dr. Hall examined her. "She had a pretty good night, except she's a puny eater, and she's kind of floppy today. She was strong when she was born. Quiet, but she definitely had better tone. I assume she will pick up when my milk comes in. Other than that, she seems to be doing pretty good."

"Her bilirubin is slightly elevated, so we're going to have to watch her for another day. She has her dad's blood type, so she's considered a set up for jaundice," Dr. Hall explained. "And since you had to receive antibiotics during labor, we need to make sure she doesn't have or get an infection."

The excitement of going home dissolved. I was disappointed to spend another day away from the girls. But it was best for Jade. We had to make sure she was healthy. There was a whole checklist of tasks to complete anyway. She had to pass her hearing screen. She had to have blood drawn every few hours to make sure the bilirubin didn't go up. And she had to get a professional newborn picture before we left. There was much to do. I already felt beat up from lack of sleep. I closed my eyes later that day while Jade rested in her bassinet and Todd went home to check on the girls. When I awoke from my quick nap, three hours had passed and there was a note sitting at the foot of Jade's bassinet from the photographer. It read:

"Dear Mommy and Daddy, they tried to get my picture, but I was much too tired to open my eyes for even a minute. We can try again another day if you want to bring me back to the hospital. The photo you will receive in the mail is the best they could get. Love, Your Sleepy Baby."

The note wasn't cute. It offended me. Jade and I would not be coming back to the hospital once we went home. I craved my own bed and my other children. Under no circumstance was I coming back.

Jade was still asleep in her bassinet. She would have slept through all feelings of hunger and a train steaming through the room. I had to work my lactation magic and coax her to eat. After placing her against my skin, Jade reluctantly awoke and pacified my worry by breastfeeding for a few minutes. Nobody was concerned she was so sleepy or that her tone was low. But the ominous feeling of doom started to return. I quickly slapped it away like a buzzing fly. I refused to live in that dark place again.

The next morning came as sweet relief. It was time to pack our room and take Jade home. We stayed until she was forty-eight hours old to ensure she was stable. To make sure nothing was wrong. I spent the day either napping or working harder than Jade did on breastfeeding. The clock ticked down until it was time to leave. *It will be easier at home.* Todd and I loaded our things like pack mules and exited the hospital as a family. I would, of course, follow their strict instructions to call if I had any concerns. There was no obvious reason why she should stay a second longer in the hospital. Todd scooped Jade up in his nervous new-father hands and placed her in the car seat in the back of the car. I sat next to her while Todd drove us home. I wanted to be as close to her as I was only two days before when her gentle kicks tickled my insides. She was beautiful. Her lips and cheeks were full and pink. Her hair was thick and dark with tiny blonde streaks. I lingered in my mind about how I was so wrong for so many months. Todd was right all along. I was crazy.

Jade was perfect.

We bounced down the washboard road to our house, and I diverted my eyes from Jade long enough to see the sun begin its descent behind the majestic Rocky Mountains. A spectacular sunset spread across the horizon as a dazzle of colors splashed together across the peaks. I looked at Jade again, sensing a calm rush over my body with a promise of tomorrow. Everything was going to be OK.

My Jewel of Heaven survived the journey.

All was right in my world.

9

Something Is Wrong

The euphoria of bringing home our Jewel of Heaven brought with it a genesis of our family. Jade joined five of her sisters under a roof of estrogen and tweenie drama. It felt like there was never life before her. We were now a family of eight. Everything changed. She was our completion. The piece of our jigsaw puzzle we didn't know was missing. She was a remarkable stillness within the chaos of our home. More than calm. More than quiet. More than a good baby. She was inexplicable.

She was ours and ours alone.

Jade and I settled into her new home amid the ramblings of five older sisters who behaved like I wasn't up most of the night with a new baby. Nobody noticed that I stayed with Jade in the living room on our first night home. I was awakened from a shallow nap by the usual sounds ringing through our house early on a school day. Arguments from the kitchen pierced the silence as they did every Monday morning before Jade's arrival. Brooke and Hope chastised each other for staking a claim to the last blueberry muffin.

Some things didn't change even as everything else did.

"The bus is coming!" Kinnah yelled from the front door. The girls grabbed their backpacks and jackets, then paused at the recliner to say goodbye to Jade. Each one kissed her on the top of her head. I was lucky enough to get a hug before they ran toward the door to cut the line and climb on the school bus.

"I love you girls!" I yelled from my place in the chair where I held Jade. "I'll see you this afternoon!" The door slammed without a response. Todd appeared from the garage as the girls sprinted for the school bus. He had taken the week off to help me at home with Emmie and to get some work done around the yard. I was glad he was there to help me.

I needed him.

The night before was sleepless. I closed my eyes only a few times between futile attempts to get Jade to nurse. The quiet left in the house by the girls' absence would be spent trying to remember how to mother a newborn. I had only eight hours to get over the feeding hump with Jade while Todd tended to Emmie. Pandemonium would return soon. Seven other babies had accompanied me home from the hospital over nineteen years of motherhood. I was used to screaming newborns who demanded to be fed the moment their bellies started to empty. They were ravenous and had no patience for a mother who might keep them waiting more than a few seconds. I was controlled by the needs of my newborns. When I ate. When I showered. When I slept. My life was theirs from their first breath.

But not Jade. She was lazy and content to starve. She acted a bit peculiar. I couldn't compare her to my other newborns because she was so different. She cried less. She moved less. She did everything less. Her belly never stirred her to fuss, and she was satisfied to sleep all the time. When I put Jade to my bare chest and tried to arouse her with skin-to-skin contact, she fell back asleep with no interest in me or nursing. Her heavy eyelids slammed shut every time she found enough energy to look at the world six inches in front of her. That was all she could do. I pushed worry and anxiety away as often as I could. If something was wrong with Jade, it would destroy me.

It would be my fault.

I didn't want to admit defeat. Todd already seemed annoyed with me for talking so much about something being wrong with Jade while I was pregnant. I didn't want to confront the reality of what I was living. I tried harder, then blamed myself for every feeding failure. I was older. More tired. Overly emotional after a hard pregnancy. But as the hours dragged on, nothing changed. Jade did not get better.

Life carried on as usual for everyone else in our house while I labored over trying to feed her. The girls and Todd were oblivious to the fear that had taken up residence in my heart. Before I knew it, Jade was four days old and my milk was trying to come in. My breasts were perplexed. Confused. Never before had they been so ostracized by one of my babies. I had no explanation for Jade's laziness or her droopy mouth and protruding tongue. The first two days home from the hospital, I felt like a workhorse that accomplished nothing. The worry became so intense that even the alarm clock set to wake me every three hours was worthless. I didn't sleep a minute. There was no reason why I had to work so hard to get just a few drops of milk into her. There was no reason why her head flopped from side to side and her body felt like a limp, rag doll in my arms. There was no reason why she didn't act like other babies who were four days old.

Unless there was something wrong with her.

I had never worked with a baby who was so difficult. Not at home or at the hospital or in the lactation clinic.

For two days and nights, I struggled to feed my helpless baby. Tuesday night marked Jade's fourth full day of life. I was exhausted in every way I could be. I rested my head on the pillow of our king-size bed while Jade lay beside me wrapped in a tight swaddle and a stretchy, pink newborn hat. The darkness of the middle of the night offered no comfort to my exhaustion. I couldn't go to sleep even after four days and nights of almost no rest. I lay awake worrying about her. She wasn't getting enough to eat. I was working harder than she was.

I didn't know what to do.

If I let myself believe something was wrong with her, I would have to go back to the paralyzing fear I carried through my pregnancy. I couldn't go to that place. A place of wondering and not knowing. The brutality of the relentless uncertainty was more than my fragile postpartum mind could handle. I pulled Jade close to warm her body with mine. It would be time soon to try to nurse again. Breastfeeding had become Everest, and we had yet to climb even a few feet. I stared at Jade in the dim light of the cracked bathroom door. The same bathroom where I lay begging God to save my baby seven months before. The light shone across her face, and I was stunned at what a beautiful baby she was. There was something extraordinary about her. Something unique. Something special. Her thick hair grew close to her temples. Her forehead was long and prominent like mine. Her cheeks were round, and her eyelashes were long. Her hands were delicate and soft with a single crease down the middle of her palms. Everything about her was beautiful.

My admiration was interrupted by reality. If Jade didn't eat, she would die. I was gutted. I didn't know what to do. So I prayed.

"God, I need you. Please let Jade start eating. I don't know what else to do. Please help me." I only prayed when I couldn't figure things out on my own, and I couldn't figure this out. I didn't understand why Jade wouldn't wake up and nurse. I went through all the steps I had taught new moms a thousand times. I unwrapped her from her thin, pink blanket and changed her diaper. She didn't move. I picked her up and put her on my bare chest while I stroked her back and shoulders. I kissed her on the forehead. Nothing.

"I love you, Jadey. Mommy loves you so much." She still didn't move. "Baby girl," I whispered. "Why won't you wake up and nurse for Mommy? You need to eat, my sweet girl. Mommy is worried about you." Tears fell down my cheeks and onto her bare skin. It didn't make a difference. She still didn't move.

I had to start pumping or my milk supply would go away before it even had a chance to be established. I laid Jade next to me and wrapped her in her pink blanket. I hooked up the Hoover suction of a breast pump and placed the cups on my despondent breasts. If she wasn't strong enough to get it herself, I would get it for her. I was tired. Emotional. Overwhelmed. But it was a delusion to think those were the reasons Jade wouldn't eat. It was a lie. One that protected my heart from the obvious. But one that left Jade vulnerable and unguarded. The voice of the ominous foreboding I slapped away in the hospital was getting louder and louder. I had ignored it the past four days. But now it screamed at me like a howler monkey. Begging me to listen.

Begging me to open my eyes. Begging me to see that if I didn't do something, the fifth day of Jade's life would be the last day of her life.

The long night was pierced with anxiety and fear. There was no sleep. The sun came up and reminded me that a new day had begun whether I was strong enough to face it or not. I gathered Jade in my arms and went to the living room where the older girls were watching TV.

"Why aren't you getting ready for school?" I was puzzled. They were still in their pajamas on a Wednesday morning at the end of April.

"No school today, Mom. Remember? I told you already forty times." Hope spoke up to remind me. "Teacher in-service day." She slurped her cereal and watched *Hannah Montana*. I had forgotten most of what went on since Jade came home. I hadn't slept. I was nauseous with worry. I had barely eaten. I tried every tool I knew to get milk into Jade. I was a frazzled wad of nerves. I didn't want to cry in front of the girls, so I asked them to tend to The Five on the back deck. They would get distracted outside, and I would have a few quiet minutes to figure out what else I could do to get Jade to nurse. She had to eat. Somehow I had to get milk into my baby. I was desperate. Terrified. Broken.

I studied the coffee table in front of my trembling knees and hovered over every piece of lactation paraphernalia I had at my disposal. The monkey continued to screech in my head. Every trick I ever used to get someone else's baby to eat glared at me. I stared past the undeniable. There was a baby scale and a breast pump. There was a bottle used to feed premature babies. There was a syringe and a feeding cup. There was a small tube for finger feeding. Everything I used to coax a baby to breastfeed was strewn about the table. Nothing worked. Jade wouldn't wake up. She wouldn't nurse. She had lost almost a pound in three days. She didn't even have enough strength to suck from a bottle or swallow the milk I dripped on her tongue. I picked up the syringe and put a few drops of milk inside her cheek. My gut ached. The milk spilled out through the corner of her mouth and ran down her chin. She couldn't even swallow a drop. The reality of failure sunk its claws into my throat and twisted until I couldn't breathe.

"Something's wrong," I whispered. I stared at the table that rocked me into reality.

"Something is wrong with Jade!" I screamed.

I was John Travolta good. I could get any baby to breastfeed. I had never been defeated by a newborn.

Until then.

My arrogance had blinded me from the truth in front of me. My head dove in a death spiral. Nine months of worry rushed into my soul, drowning me with truth. I choked on my own ignorance. Suffocated on my own pride. Collapsed under the weight of the ominous foreboding I thought I surrendered in the hospital the day Jade was born.

Jade wasn't lazy at all.

She was dying.

I was watching my baby slowly die right in front of me. I was powerless to stop whatever was trying to steal Jade.

I rushed to the kitchen and found my nursing school bag stashed in a drawer. I listened to Jade's heart. It beat with a pace so rapid I couldn't keep count. I placed a thermometer probe in her tiny armpit until it beeped. She didn't flinch. Her temperature was dangerously low: 94.4 degrees. Something was wrong with Jade. Something I couldn't explain. Something I couldn't fix. Something I couldn't control. The wrenching in my gut stabbed me over and over. I tried to determine what I would do if I were Jade's nurse. But I didn't know how to separate myself from being her mother and allow the experienced pediatric nurse to take over.

"Jesus, please. Please help me! What should I do? I don't know what to do!" I pleaded as I tried to stop the death spiral in my head. I found my cell phone and dialed the only number I could remember. It was the direct line to the on-call pediatrician's phone at the hospital's Neonatal Intensive Care Unit.

It rang once, and Dr. Hall answered. "This is Lori Hall."

"Dr. Hall, this is Angie." I spoke so fast I tripped over my words. "I brought Jade home three days ago, but there's something wrong. There's something very wrong with her. Her temperature is critically low. She won't wake up to eat. She's lost a pound. She can't suck or swallow. Dr. Hall, I have eight children. I have been a pediatric nurse and lactation consultant for almost ten years. There's something wrong with her. I don't know what to do." I was frantic.

"OK, Angie. I trust your judgment. I want you to take her straight to the Peds Floor. Dr. Smith is working Peds today. I'll let him know you're coming. How far away are you?"

I told Dr. Hall we would be there in fifteen minutes, and I gathered Jade's things before we even hung up.

I ran to the front door sobbing with Jade in my arms. I found Todd mowing the yard in athletic shorts, tennis shoes stained the color of wet grass, and a Nebraska Huskers ball cap turned awkwardly backward on his head.

"Todd!" I screamed over the sound of the mower. He didn't hear me, so I held Jade in one arm while I waved the other to get his attention. "Todd!" I screamed even louder. He stopped the mower and removed the sunglasses from his sweaty, red face. Jade lay floppy in my arms, unresponsive to my screams.

"What's up?" Todd responded as he saw me flailing on the front porch.

"Something's wrong with Jade! We have to take her to the hospital. I can't get her to wake up. We need to go now!"

"Can I finish mowing?" He didn't hear the urgency in my voice.

"No, Todd! We have to go now!" I screamed with punctuated fear that Jade would die in my arms on the front porch.

I was sure Todd thought I was crazy again. He had listened to my fears for almost seven months. I had created an imaginary drama in my own head for reasons nobody could understand. By the time he came into the house, Jade was in her car seat, and I was walking to the garage with her diaper bag on my shoulder. He was frustrated that I interrupted him and looked at me with a scowl on his face.

"Can I at least shower and change my clothes first?"

"No, Todd. You don't understand. Her temperature is too low. She won't wake up. She won't eat. Something is wrong. Oh, Todd. Something is wrong with her." Deep sobs shook the core of who I was as a mother. Todd pulled the blanket away from Jade's tiny body, and his face turned white. He was stunned. She was ashen and gray.

She looked dead.

"What the hell is going on?" Todd screamed. "Oh my God! Is she alive?"

"Todd, we have to go. I already talked to Dr. Hall, and she wants her at the PICU right now! Dr. Smith is waiting for us. We have to go, Todd. We have to go now!" I lost all sense of reason or calm. The girls slipped in the door and stood in the background of my frenzied panic. They were confused. They wanted to know what was wrong with Baby Jade. They were shaken. I couldn't help them. Jade had to go to the hospital. Right then. There was no time to comfort my girls. I couldn't take my eyes off Jade in case I needed to become her nurse again and resuscitate her. My head spun in senseless disorientation. Somewhere in the room I heard my five young daughters weeping in fear, confusion, and sadness. They were inconsolable and begged to know if Jade was going to be OK. I squatted down and held them briefly.

"Girls, pray for Baby Jade and take care of one another until I come home. Call Becky or Nana and see if one of them will come out." Brooke and Hope were forced to mature at a moment's notice and babysit the younger girls. I couldn't wait for an adult to arrive. I had no choice but to leave my daughters behind.

I sat in the back seat of the car and hovered over Jade. I was ready to snatch her out of her car seat if she needed me. "You didn't believe me. All those months I told you something was wrong. You didn't believe me. Nobody believed me." I scolded Todd from the back seat. My words were harsh. I saw the regret on his face in the rearview mirror as I drove a stake through his daddy heart.

We bounced down our bumpy, dusty road as fast as Todd could safely drive. I felt the jarring in my fresh episiotomy but demanded he drive faster. My words were the only ones spoken for the next fifteen miles. The only sounds in the car except for the tears I could not control and an agonizing prayer. "God, please. Please save my baby. Don't let Jade die." I was desperate. Willing to give my life for hers. Ready to take my last breath if He would spare her.

On Jade's fifth day of life, a darkness overcame our family. It was the day that had tormented me for the past seven months. The ominous foreboding that dwelled somewhere deep in the DNA of my cells. The unfathomable abyss of knowing what nobody else did and what nobody else believed.

But I knew. I knew all along. There was something wrong with Jade, and nobody believed me. Not Todd. Not the doctors. Not Lynel. Not Mom. Nobody.

But they would all believe me now. The ominous foreboding had come for Jade. It returned in the form of an evil I had never met. An evil so dark I couldn't possibly understand its insatiable thirst for death. An evil holding a scythe that dripped the blood of an innocent baby.

10

The Fishbowl

I left my tears in the car, and we rushed Jade to the visitor's entrance at Poudre Valley Hospital. The same place we left three days before. The same place I swore I wouldn't bring Jade back to. The automatic doors at the front of the hospital slid open as my matted curls blew across my face. I was still wearing sweatpants from the day before. I hadn't showered for three days. Jade was limp. She was dying in my arms. The episiotomy between my legs burned like a wildfire as I power walked next to Todd. Jade was a rag doll under her blanket. Her head bobbled from side to side on her shoulders like a bowl of Jell-O. We bypassed the emergency room entrance where all the sick and injured patients waited for help. Jade needed more than they could give her there. I wasn't willing to waste precious minutes. Jade needed a pediatrician. She needed Dr. Smith. He was her only hope.

We jogged past the security guard and volunteer greeter, whom I passed every day on my way to work. The elevators were just ahead of us, but the line snaked down the hall beyond the gift shop. I didn't stop. Neither did Todd. We cut the back of the line and hurried toward the front. Past a long stretch of elderly men and women in wheelchairs waiting their turn. Past families who held beautiful bouquets of flowers for their loved ones. Past children who screamed with impatience. Past nurses and doctors who tried to get to work on time. No one would get in our way. No one was as important as Jade.

A familiar face challenged me as we moved toward our place in front of the doors.

"You'll have to wait at the back of the line." It was the Elevator Security Volunteer. I knew her well. She was a wrinkled old woman who flexed her atrophied muscles in a pathetic display of control. A crotchety hag I avoided. She was the reason I would climb five flights of stairs on any other day. But today was different. My postpartum body wasn't nimble. The stairs were a delay.

I walked straight to the front of the line with Todd close on my heels. I didn't make eye contact with her. "I'm not waiting."

She glared at me through her thick glasses and snarled her face at Todd. She hesitated before stepping in front of us, then retreated when our eyes met in the middle of the hall. She knew. She recognized the look of a frightened lioness protecting her cub while backed into a corner, slashing her claws at every threat. She knew I would devour her or anyone who stood in the way of getting Jade help.

Then I roared, "Get out of my way! I'm taking my baby to the PICU. She's very sick!"

She did not challenge me again as Todd and I rushed past her and the others. I had barely closed my eyes the past five days. The person who simmered just below my skin was serrated. Frightened. Exhausted.

Todd knew how I acted when I was filled with anxiety and anger. He saw it coming. "Try not to say anything rude. I know you're scared but don't take it out on her." Todd gave mostly wise advice but never at the right time. I ignored him. I was entrenched deep in fear and anxiety. I held Jade close. The ashen gray color on her cheeks was darker. Her mouth hung open even more than before. I put her on my chest and rubbed her back. I gripped her head with one hand to keep it from dangling between her shoulders.

The elevator doors opened, and we stepped in first, no longer challenged by the elevator guard or anyone else. Jade flopped in my arms and inhaled shallow, listless breaths.

Ding. Ding. It was an eternity. We stopped on the third floor.

Hurry up people. Get out of here! We still have two more floors!

I wanted to scream at the top of my lungs. Nobody believed

me when I told them something was wrong with Jade. Todd didn't believe me either. He thought I was crazy and said it often.

I told you. I told you for months something was wrong. I wasn't paranoid. I was right.

I knew I had already hurt Todd in the car with my words, so he remained oblivious to my thoughts. I didn't want to prove his point and make a scene in front of an elevator of strangers. My postpartum hormones rose and fell like a roller coaster. Frightened then angry. Angry then despondent. It was a ride that made me unhinged.

Ding. One more floor.

The two-minute ride tested me. I was about to snap. I was angry Todd didn't believe me when I cried about my fears for Jade. I was angry he chastised me like I was a child. But I had to still my anger at him because Jade was dying in my arms. Any strength I could muster was for her.

Jade was slipping away from me. I was powerless and impotent to stop whatever was happening inside of her. For the first time in almost twenty years, there was nothing I could do to help one of my children. I stood in a pile of ashes. Jade's fire was almost burned out. I was defeated. I couldn't help her. I couldn't get her to eat. Or cry. Or wake up.

I failed during a time when failure came with a price too high to pay.

I was a worthless mother. A worthless nurse. A worthless wife.

I stood alone in my mind, consumed with how pathetic I was.

Where are you, Jesus? Where are you? I need you.

I was barely holding on. I was deep in my head now.

Oh, Jesus. Where are you? Have you left me?

The roller-coaster ride of emotions peaked as the elevator climbed to the fifth floor.

Jade's mouth was gravely downturned. The tone in her face was gone. Her tongue protruded through her parted lips. I berated myself for taking the elevator.

This is taking too long. We should have taken the stairs.

Jade was breathing. And her heart was beating. But that was it. She looked like a stillborn baby. One of those beautiful, expressionless babies who went to be with Jesus before taking a breath of life. Jade reminded me of those babies. But her chest still moved up and down as shallow breaths of air entered and exited her lungs. It was the only sign she hadn't joined those stillborns in heaven. Yet.

Jade was changed. Her body was under massive pressure. Something was shifting like a tectonic plate inside her. A devastating transformation was happening in front of me. She did not look like the baby I left the hospital with three days before. She had given up.

Ding. The elevator opened on the fifth floor.

I slid through the open crack in the doors like Harry Houdini and raced to the Pediatric Unit with Jade in my arms while Todd trailed close behind me. Dr. Smith and his team of nurses waited for Jade in the Pediatric Intensive Care Unit. As soon as they saw her, their eyes told a story their mouths did not have to speak. She was critical. They hurried us into the waiting PICU room and told me to put Jade on the bed. I couldn't. I couldn't let go of her. I was afraid it would be the last time I would feel her living body in my arms.

"Put her on the bed, Angie. You have to lay her down so we can start an IV." I heard a familiar voice from a faraway place in Jade's closet-sized intensive care unit room. It was Dr. Smith. He was the kindest physician I had ever worked with. He was a man who cried with his patients. He cared. The urgency of his voice echoed through my ears. It was a blow to my head.

"Lay her down, Angie! And step back from the bed. Please." Jade's nurse spoke sharply to me. She was the best pediatric nurse I knew. I looked around at an army of medical personnel. They believed me. I wasn't crazy. I put Jade on the bed in front of me and took one step backward in compliance with her orders.

Someone shuffled me to the back of Jade's room. Someone else guided me to the door. I stumbled my way through the crowd and stood alone at the entrance to her room.

"Get me a nasal cannula stat. Call the lab and get them up here.

Now! Have radiology on standby." Dr. Smith listened to Jade's heart while her nurse attached a pulse oximeter probe and applied oxygen. Alarms sounded. "Turn her oxygen up. I want her at 90 or greater." I had never heard Dr. Smith bark orders like that.

I didn't understand what was happening. I crumpled in the doorway. Lynel appeared from nowhere and helped me to a seat by the nurse's station. She was working on the postpartum unit and clocked out when she heard we were there.

I could still see Jade lying on the bed. Alone.

"I'll go see what I can find out." Lynel hugged me and told me to wait for her. I turned my gaze from Jade's unmoving body to the stranger sitting next to me. It was a man I barely recognized. He wore a Nebraska baseball cap turned awkwardly backward on his head. My husband. We were both motionless. Paralyzed with fear. Stunned. Silent. He started to sob. Then I did too. He held me as we both shook. We were forever bound together by that moment. The moment we knew our daughter might not live past that day.

I turned back to Jade in her PICU room and overheard Dr. Smith request lab tests, bags of IV fluids, and records from Jade's birth. But I didn't hear cries as Jade was poked with sharp needles. Not a whimper. I had started many IVs on many babies. The only ones who didn't cry were the ones who were critically ill. I peered into The Fishbowl of her PICU room. I was outside looking in on something I should be present for. Jade needed me. I stood on wobbly feet and approached the door while the team worked on Jade. Todd wiped his face and followed me. Lynel met us at the door. She put her arm around my shoulder and led us a few feet away.

"They want to run her newborn genetic screen again. Something about PKU or some other metabolic problem. Dr. Smith is worried that she's septic." She paused. "Angie, they think she might have Down syndrome."

Septic? Down syndrome? PKU? What is going on?

I felt like I was hit by the ungloved fists of Muhammad Ali. Todd's knees buckled. He dropped to the floor.

"What do you mean?" I pulled my arm from Lynel's hand. "What are you talking about, Lynel? What do you mean? All everyone has told me for months is 'Stop worrying. Everything is OK. Jade is OK.' And now this? Now you're telling us something is seriously wrong with our baby?" The volume of my voice increased with every word that escaped my mouth. My anger was aimed at the closest victim. Lynel was my friend. My tag team partner. The only nurse who always had my back. But that didn't stop my tirade. My words hit a crescendo so loud someone closed the door to Jade's room.

"I know, Angie. You were right. You were right all along. You knew." Lynel's voice cracked. She was ashamed she was part of the false reassurance I was fed for so many months. I tried to press past her to get to Jade. She lost my attention but tried to pray with us before I went to Jade. She put her hands on our shoulders and started to speak.

"I already asked God to help me, Lynel. He's not here," I said as I yanked away from her.

I was angry. In disbelief. On the wrong side of my career. A PICU parent. This was unnatural. It was inconceivable. The hospital was my refuge. Not my prison. The place where I was the heroine. I wasn't supposed to be here like that. I was the helper. Not the helped. I was a nurse. Not a patient's mother. I was a fish out of water flopping on the outside of The Fishbowl. Peering in. Gasping to be with Jade. In a level just above a whisper, I let my guard down and begged for help.

"Where are you, Jesus? I need you."

I was interrupted by Dr. Smith, who walked straight to Todd and me.

"Hi, I'm Dr. Smith," he said, shaking Todd's hand. "She's real sick, Angie. She's not responding to pain or stimulation. I've ordered a PKU and metabolic studies. We almost didn't get the IV, and we had a hard time getting any blood. I think she may be septic or have meningitis. Her ammonia levels are elevated. She's on oxygen now, and she's stable. But she's a very sick little girl."

His words punched me in the heart with a right, then a left, another right, then another left. I could barely stand up. I knew what he was going to say next. Dr. Smith needed to do a lumbar puncture on Jade. One of the most painful procedures an unsedated newborn could endure. A torturous invasion of the spinal column perpetrated by a needle so big and so long I wondered how it would possibly fit in that tiny space. I had assisted on a handful of these procedures with other babies. I dreaded it every time. It was the most difficult procedure I ever helped with. All I had to do was hold the baby in place. But the writhing beneath my hands and the mind-piercing screams haunted me. It was a brutal but necessary procedure to retrieve cerebrospinal fluid.

I was nauseous. My knees buckled. Todd caught me before I fell to the floor.

"I need to do a lumbar puncture to rule out meningitis." The words I knew were coming. I cried out in a heartbreaking sound that reverberated throughout the PICU halls.

"Where are you, Jesus?"

It was more than I could handle. I was already teetering on that thin postpartum ledge. This could be the pendulum that swung me over the cliff to the jagged rocks below. The serrated, frightened, exhausted woman simmering just below my skin was about to fulminate. I didn't want Dr. Smith to see an explosion. He was a good man. My favorite of all the pediatricians. I acknowledged him with a nod and slid past him to be with Jade while he talked to Todd.

I pushed through the bodies in the room and stood beside the bed where Jade rested. Her eyes were closed. She was still. Her color was an astounding, dull gray like the ashes of death. Her fire smoldered. An IV dripped fluids that filled her cells. She was stable. For now.

I leaned over the side of the bed and cradled Jade's head in the palm of my hand. Her thick, dark hair weaved between my fingers. I whispered in her ear as tears collected on the white sheet beneath her.

"I'm sorry. I'm so sorry, baby girl. This is my fault. Please forgive me. Please forgive Mommy."

The words I spoke on the bathroom floor when the Walmart test stole my future rang through my head.

"Take this from me."

I was disgusting. I didn't deserve forgiveness for the darkness I had cast on Jade's innocent life. This was my fault.

Jade was paying for the sins and selfishness of her mother. I could barely raise my head from the weight of shame. I felt the others in the room staring through me with the same disgust. They couldn't possibly know about my unholy prayer, but I knew they loathed me as much as I loathed myself.

They knew.

I lay my head on the bed next to Jade. Defeated. I prayed once more because it was all I could do. This time, though, I would offer my life as a sacrifice.

"God, please take me. Take me now. My life for hers. Take my breath and give it to Jade, Lord. You have given me a burden too great to bear. It's too much. I just . . . can't . . . do . . . this."

As I waited for the last breath I would ever take to leave my lungs, there was a small shift in the palm of my hand. Jade turned her head toward me, opened her eyes and looked for me. Her tongue protruded only slightly from her mouth. Her cheeks were pale pink. The IV fluids were working. Jade was coming back to me. I was still breathing. So was she.

God did not accept my deal. There would be no trade that day.

I lay my head on the bed next to Jade's. I stroked her hair and whispered in her ear again.

"I'm sorry, baby girl. Mommy loves you so much. I'm here, Jade. Mommy is here. I'll never leave again."

I had a choice to make. I could drown in self-loathing inside The Fishbowl. I could jump off the cliff to the jagged rocks below. Or I could summon a supernatural strength for Jade and fight to save her life. She needed me. She needed her Mommy. Even though I was broken and destroyed, she needed me. I took a deep breath and put guilt and shame away for another day.

It didn't leave me. It just hid in a superficial but dark place.

Simmering and ready to be released in a scream.

I stayed with Jade as Dr. Smith completed the lumbar puncture. I held her body still in my hands in case she flinched. The needle was inserted into her spinal column and clear fluid was aspirated. No movement. No cry that would haunt me. Nothing.

I stayed with Jade as more blood was drawn and tests were run.

I stayed with Jade when a nasogastric tube was inserted through her nose and into her stomach to feed her my breast milk.

I stayed with Jade for everything she went through from that day forward.

Never again would I be ushered away from her or be found anywhere but with her. That day was the last I would be on the outside looking in for anything Jade had to suffer.

She deserved for me to be completely present with her for everything we would face. Together.

Jade needed me for this dreaded, cursed journey I could only blame on myself.

I didn't know how I would walk this road. I wasn't sure Jesus would be there to accompany us on our journey. I asked Him many times that day where He was and heard no response. Simmering in a hidden place were shame and guilt that I carried on my heart like a mountaineer's backpack. Reminding me of the weight of my sinful prayer. Reminding me how heavy a load carried alone is. Reminding me Jesus wasn't there. Jade would have me. The girls would have Todd. But who would I have?

Where are you, Jesus? Where are you? Have you forgotten about us?

There was still no response. I was forsaken. This was the beginning of unbearable sadness. Hopelessness. Darkness. Tragedy for Jade. Tragedy for her parents. Tragedy for my other children.

In the silence of my mind where I crawled beside Jade, I unwillingly accepted that Jesus wasn't going to join us on this journey. I was on a road I had not chosen, and I would have to find a way to walk it alone.

11

Hostile Territory

Four agonizing slow-motion days in the PICU of Poudre Valley Hospital ground me down to a raw, open wound. Everything was a blur again. Like the moments frozen in time when the pregnancy test dangled from my hand while I writhed on the bathroom floor. The consequence of my unholy prayer lay clinging to life on a hospital bed in front of me.

Those four days with Jade in the PICU took me back to the two months I spent as a young child in the hospital. It was exactly thirty years, to the month, before Jade was born. My tiny seven-year-old body had been catapulted down a busy street by the hard impact of a chromium-plated steel bumper. Children walking home from school with me screamed in horror. Mom was only a few minutes late to pick me up. She arrived just in time to see a small body slam to the black asphalt road. And to recognize my bell-bottom blue jeans and white Kmart tennis shoes lying in front of a 1975 station wagon. My chin, elbows, and knees were bloodied. My right femur broken in two.

I lay on the ground surrounded by children screaming, my mother crying, and a strange man holding my leg in a makeshift traction until the paramedics arrived. Our local newspaper managed to beat emergency responders to the scene and took a photo of the stranger holding my leg as Mom hovered, completely powerless to save me. I understood the gut punch Mom felt that day as I hovered over my own daughter while she was poked and drained of blood in a quest to save her life. I wondered how Mom held on to her faith in God as she watched me lying motionless on the ground in front of her. But I wasn't Mom, and Jesus wasn't with me. My own faith dwindled to a frayed strand of hope with every vial of blood they removed from Jade.

But she was finally stable, which only meant she wasn't going to die. Not soon anyway. Though her cheeks were pink again, her body warm, her blood free of infection, and her spinal fluid clear, there was still something wrong with her. Something that kept her from thriving and eating. Something not a single physician, procedure, or blood test could explain.

At the end of the fourth day back at the hospital, we were moved just down the hall from The Fishbowl to a room for stable patients. But the tests continued. There were so many blood tests that I couldn't remember what they were all for. We stayed in the hospital hoping to get answers. Hoping Jade would start to nurse. Hoping she would have a sudden turn in the right direction. But none of that happened. The nurses looked in on us every two hours, but Jesus didn't. I still talked to Him often in the silence of my mind those first days in the hospital as I loosely hung to the hope that He had not abandoned us.

But He didn't answer me. And He didn't heal Jade.

By the time we moved to Jade's new room, I had mostly given up on Jesus. Jade still wouldn't eat, and I no longer wasted my breath or thoughts on unanswered prayers.

The haven of Jade's new room brought minimal comfort. Everything was dark in my life and in our room—despite the large corner window with a parking lot view that let sunlight creep in every morning before I was ready to face another day. Sleep eluded me, and I kept to a strict two-hour schedule to pump breast milk for Jade. It was the only thing I could control. I pumped so much milk that the staff asked Todd to take some home because there was no room left in their freezer. Sometimes I daydreamed about throwing the breast pump out the window while I imagined Jade nursing like my other babies did. But I always startled awake from those short naps by an alarm that reminded me my sleep was over and it was time to pump again.

I isolated myself from friends and family, even my children.

Anyone who meant anything to me. I only took a few calls and turned away most visitors. Including Lynel. The darkness of every day was blinding.

The girls were home without me. They missed me and worried about Jade. But the five of them didn't fit into the two-visitor policy on the Peds floor. Phone calls would have to do because I would not leave Jade. Todd let the girls call to hear my voice and check on Jade every morning. Otherwise I pumped or napped or took care of Jade.

On one of those dark days, the phone startled me awake from one of my unintentional naps.

"Hello." I was in a confused haze when I heard the sweet sound of Emmie's voice.

"Hi, Mommy!" Emmie smiled through the phone when she heard me. "I miss you, Mommy. When are you coming home?"

"Mommy's not sure, Sweets. Jade still doesn't feel good."

Without pausing, Emmie said something so matter-of-fact and painful I couldn't speak.

"Mommy, did Baby Jade die?" From the innocence of a three-year-old mouth came a dark foreboding of the life I didn't want to live. We had all at least thought it at some point since we rushed Jade back to the hospital. But to say it made it possible. To say it made it real. I understood what was happening only slightly better than Emmie did. But I couldn't bear to hear those words.

The phone slid from my hand and fell to the sterile floor below me. I inhaled small, shallow, rapid breaths. I was afraid I would start to cry and never stop. It was too much. The brutal reality was just too much. I couldn't face it. I abandoned the phone on the floor hoping Todd answered Emmie's question. I stood above Jade in her bassinet, taking in every warm and beautiful part of her. Every alive part of her.

I tried to erase Emmie's question from my mind. But I couldn't. I could never unhear those words. I hovered over Jade and stared at her. Every second of her life had been a struggle to stay alive. She was the only comfort I could find in this prison room. When I looked at her and ran my fingers through her beautiful curls, I saw perfection. Ten perfect fingers. Ten perfect toes. I stroked the curls on her head again. They were perfect too. I wondered how Jesus could make her curls so flawless and then forget the most important parts of her. There was a small tube hanging from her left nostril. It was the only way she could be fed. The only hint Jade wasn't perfect. I dreamed about days when Jade and I would be at home with her sisters and Todd. No tubes. No feeding pumps. No doctors or tests.

The door swung open without a knock or warning. Another daydream was interrupted. A tall, lanky man dressed in all black entered our room uninvited. He carried a black leather case in one hand and held a black ball cap in the other. There was a large red cross on the left side of his black leather vest. He wore tattered jeans and leather biker chaps and boots that were weathered from riding his Harley. His long, brown hair, peppered with tiny streaks of coarse gray, was pulled in a tight braid down the middle of his back. The chains on his belt clank, clank, clanked as they announced his presence in our room. I knew this man well. He was Cousin Rich. We had grown up together and were more like brother and sister than cousins. I hadn't seen Rich for years, and I barely recognized him when he sauntered in.

Rich's timing had never been great. Like Todd's. It was at best awkward. Despite the years and choices that distanced us from each other, that one thing stayed the same. Rich had given his life to Jesus a couple of years before and was one of those Bible thumpers we swore as kids we'd never be. Rich had found his place in a Christian biker group shortly before Jade was born. Not in prison or a cemetery like I expected. He was tight with Jesus. But I wasn't like Rich. I was never like Rich. We just happened to end up in the same family only one year apart. Jesus wasn't with me anymore, and I didn't have time for a family reunion. It was all too big to sort through in a place I was not supposed to be, and I wasn't ready for Cousin Rich to lash me with his Bible verses.

"Hey, Ang. Your mom's been telling me about Jade. I tried to call you a few times, but you didn't answer. So I decided to stop by." I knew Rich tried to call. I avoided his calls on purpose. I wanted to be alone. I wasn't ready to talk about God.

"Yeah, it's been really hard, Richard. I'm not doing good. We don't know what's going on with her. There's really never a good time."

A heavy odor followed Rich into the room. Warm, sweaty leather soaked in cigarettes. I was offended he would show up like that. I hadn't seen Rich in years. I didn't want him to sit down or stay. I was still shaken by Emmie's question and torn up there might be truth in her words.

Not today, Richard. I can't do this today.

I was tired. But mostly annoyed. Rich wasn't invited, and I didn't have the strength to argue with him about anything having to do with the Bible or God or Jesus. There was nothing left of me after pumping and taking care of Jade. I was weary from the weight of doing everything alone. I wasn't ready to talk about Jesus or figure out why He left me. Maybe it was because I was on my third husband. Maybe it was because I prayed for a miscarriage. Maybe it was because I was just a terrible person. It was my fault He allowed Jade to be born broken. But He didn't show up when I needed Him most.

Cousin Rich's surprise visit fell on the day Todd planned to have his priest come to our room. A visit I only reluctantly allowed at Todd's request. Since Jesus had forgotten us, perhaps the priest would bring a miracle with him for Jade. I knew what Rich thought of priests and anyone whose beliefs differed from his own. Mom told me Rich was "on fire for Jesus." I also knew Rich would argue with anyone about Jesus and the Bible. Anyone.

Even a priest.

We didn't exchange many words when Rich arrived. I tried to hide in the corner by Jade's bed, hoping he would leave. I yawned. He didn't leave. I yawned again. Rich sat down. Then he unzipped the black leather case he held in his hand and pulled out a book I was familiar with. It was his Bible. A special gift to Rich. One his mother, my aunt Margaret, gave him before she suddenly passed away the year Emmie was born. Rich opened his Bible and read a passage to me. His timing was not stellar for a second time. I was exhausted and annoyed. I didn't hear anything he said.

"Richard, I'm pretty beat. I really need a shower before Todd's priest gets here."

He kept reading. I saw a mischievous smirk form in the corner of his mouth as he looked up from the pages. Some things had not changed. His chest puffed out underneath his leather vest. Rich was readying himself to challenge the priest. He was scheming ways to have a hearty discussion about the Bible and prove the priest wrong.

"I know what you're thinking, Richard. Don't even go there. This isn't the time or the place. Everything is upside down. So if you can't keep your mouth shut, just leave now." He scoffed at me with the familiar side grin still on his lips then laughed nervously because he knew me. He knew me longer than even Todd. He knew I had my limits. He saw that I was teetering on a thin postpartum ledge, so he retreated for my sake. After all, he was there because he loved me. Because he was my first and oldest friend. Because he thought of me like a sister and wanted to give me words of comfort. Not to rub salt in my gaping wounds. Mom told him I gave up on Jesus in The Fishbowl, so he wanted to talk to me about putting my faith in God again. But Rich had no idea what he had walked into that day. He had stumbled across enemy lines.

Our room was Hostile Territory, a war zone of anger and uncertainty. Definitely no place for him or Jesus. I was wrecked. Confused. Broken. Sleep-deprived. Any filter I once had was decimated. Gone. Adrenaline induced by fear flooded my veins, and it was the one thing that kept me going for Jade. It fueled my sleepless days and nights so I could care for Jade. It was cruel and ironic. The only thing that kept me alive was the thing that would ravage my body from the inside out.

I stood in the corner of Jade's hospital room, gently stroking her thick, curly, dark hair while she slept. She was unaware of everything around her. I tried to ignore Rich, but it was hard not to hear nails on a chalkboard. His words teased that God was my protector and my refuge. That I would be covered under His wings. Rich stared at the words on the page of his Bible and kept reading even though I tried not to listen.

> Whoever dwells in the shelter of the Most High
>> will rest in the shadow of the Almighty.
> I will say of the LORD, "He is my refuge and my fortress,
>> my God, in whom I trust."
> Surely he will save you
>> from the fowler's snare
>> and from the deadly pestilence.
> He will cover you with his feathers,
>> and under his wings you will find refuge.

My heart beat mercilessly beneath my sternum as Rich kept reading. He wouldn't shut up.

"His faithfulness will be your shield and rampart. You will not fear the terror of night . . ." As those words rolled off his tongue, the relentless, consecutive, sleepless nights of worry, medical tests, needles, tubes, blood, puke, feeds, and pumps passed in front of my eyes.

"Do you even know what you're saying, Richard? All I have done since Jade was born is fear the terror of the night. Have you gone weeks without sleep? Do you have a baby who almost died? Who still might die? You are a liar, Richard. And so is everything in that Bible." Rich was sent to torment me with words from a book I didn't know if I believed in anymore. I suddenly found my face in Rich's face, close enough to smell the cigarette he smoked on his way to the hospital still lingering on his breath like a stale ashtray.

"You need to leave, Richard. You need to leave and take that book your mom gave you and don't come back. God isn't here. He forgot me, OK? God turned His back on me, and I got everything I deserve." My words were harsh, painful, and loud. Loud enough that

Jade awoke with a startle and began to whimper. Rich hung his head. His chest was no longer puffed up. I hurt him in a way I never had before. Not even as teenagers when we were both terrible to each other. He looked down so I couldn't see his eyes turn red from tears that choked him. My forked tongue plunged sharp and jagged words deep into Rich like a dagger. He didn't deserve it.

"Just go, Richard." I shook my head side to side. I was disgusted with myself for hurting him. "Just go."

Rich gently closed his Bible and zipped it back into its black leather case. "OK, Ang. I was just trying to help." He turned from me and walked out of Jade's room holding his ball cap and his Bible. His eyes were on the floor. He gripped the black leather case close to his heart. The chains that hung from his waist once again clanked with every step he took. The eerie sound faded in the distance as Rich continued down the hall and out of the Peds Unit. I looked out the corner window of our room to make sure he was leaving. His Harley sat in the rain in the parking lot below us. Rich emerged from the hospital, put his ball cap backward on his head, straddled the Harley but didn't move. He raised his hands above his head in the pouring rain and cried out. I couldn't hear the words he said, but I knew he was praying for a cruel woman and her broken baby. He skillfully lit a cigarette as the rain drenched him then drove off with it hanging from the corner of his mouth. Nothing would stop Rich from doing all he could to help me. All he could to help Jade.

I didn't deserve him.

But our room was Hostile Territory. A war zone. Rich had no idea that he was behind enemy lines until it was too late for him. It was not a place Jesus would visit. Especially after the way I behaved.

The priest didn't fare so well either. When he showed up without the miracle I was counting on, it solidified that Jesus didn't love me or Jade. The priest had nothing to offer. Not even one miracle. He spoke endless ritualistic words I didn't understand over Jade, crossing and crossing and crossing his chest. I held her close as he dabbed holy water on her forehead and signaled his hands in one last cross in front of his chest. He was my last chance, but he also failed me. He restored none of my hope.

I didn't understand the God Rich and I learned about as children in Sunday school. The God our Mamaw and our mothers put so much faith in. Trusted. Prayed to. Sang to. Cried out to. I could not remember the Jesus I asked to come into my heart when I was eight years old as I sat beside Mom in her sewing room late one evening. The same Jesus who loved all the little children, red and yellow, black and white, because they are precious in his sight.

All the little children except my sweet baby.

He gave Jade to me floppy and broken and fighting to stay alive. I didn't understand why the God I believed in and the Jesus I welcomed into my heart as a child would do something like that. When I needed them most, the Father and the Son were nowhere to be found. There was never a time in my life I felt so forsaken as I did at that moment. Even in the company of the priest, a guy who was closer to God than Rich or I ever could be.

There were no miracles performed that day in Jade's hospital room. She still wouldn't eat. I still had to pump. We still didn't know what was wrong with her. Any crumbs of remaining hope were swallowed up by the priest. Any lingering faith I had trailed close behind him like a shadow as he disappeared around the corner the same way Rich did. I was more alone and abandoned than at any other time of my life. Rich was gone. The priest was gone. Jesus was gone.

I was fighting for Jade's life in Hostile Territory. And I was doing it alone.

12

Stormy

Jade and I lived in Hostile Territory for almost three weeks in a stormy Colorado May. In typical Rocky Mountain form, every season passed over us during our stay in the Pediatric Unit. Four thunder-and-lightning storms. A windstorm. Two tornado warnings. Three hours of light snow. I watched the seasons change from the window of our corner room from spring to early summer with a gentle dusting of winter and fall. We were safe there from God and Mother Nature. Until the sunny Saturday morning on our nineteenth day when Dr. Stewart gruffly entered the room to examine Jade. Dr. Stewart was a tall, blonde pediatrician who could bulldoze anyone. Like the Rocky Mountain climate, she, too, was a force of nature. She visited us wearing flip-flops and knee-length shorts—like she had lake plans with her family once her hospital duties were over. I hadn't seen her since before Jade was born, and I was happy she was there. Despite her abrasive demeanor at times, I trusted her with Jade.

"Hey, Angie. How are you doing? How is Jade doing today?" She was inquisitive and irritated about something. Dr. Stewart was bold. She had a reputation for diverging from well-made plans designed by the other pediatricians she practiced with. She was professional. Not maternal. But she was one of the doctors I wanted to be on-call if Jade got caught in the undertow again.

"Hey, Beth. She's no better and no worse than yesterday, I guess. She's gaining weight but barely breastfeeding at all. Pretty much all my milk is going through the tube. I think she finally got back to her birth weight a few days ago." Dr. Stewart's cheeks were pink. I was jealous of the sun on her face. "It looks so nice outside today."

"Why are you still here?" She ignored my chitchat. She was sharp and insinuated I should also be out in the sun. She didn't understand why Jade was still in the hospital. She trusted my nursing skills and knew Jade would be better off at home. I wondered if she thought I was afraid to leave. Maybe I didn't think I was competent to care for Jade at home. Maybe the pediatricians didn't think I was competent to care for Jade without the nursing staff. Or maybe they saw that I still teetered on the thin postpartum emotional ledge and were afraid I would jump off at home.

I couldn't answer her question. For more than a week, I had begged for someone to let me take Jade home. But the response was always the same with every physician who made rounds on Jade. It wasn't safe for a newborn to be at home with an NG tube. Even though I was a pediatric nurse. Dr. Stewart flipped her blonde bangs to the side while she read Jade's chart. She looked up from the binder, tilted her head, and looked at me with raised eyebrows.

"The nurses tell me you haven't left this room since Jade moved out of the PICU." I had no defense. She and the nurses were right. "And they tell me you're barely sleeping or eating."

She was correct again. The nurses, my friends, did not lie to her.

"Well, I guess they're being honest about all the above. I just want to go home. I have seven other kids. Five live at home with me. My oldest daughter is pregnant. I haven't seen my son in months since he moved in with his dad. And my three-year-old just asked me if Baby Jade died. This room is about to get to me. But I'm not leaving Jade. I won't leave her." She listened but didn't respond. She continued reading Jade's medical record while I talked.

"I've asked all of Jade's pediatricians every day when they round to discharge us, but they say it's not safe for Jade to go home with a feeding tube in her nose. Aspiration risk. Choking risk. I get it. I'm a nurse." I paused. "I just want to go home and be with my children."

Dr. Stewart softened. I had made it through the eye of the storm with Jade. She had been stable for over two weeks and was gaining weight with the NG tube. I weathered nineteen long days and nights with Jade at the hospital. Pumping. Tube feedings. Keeping eyes on her like a lighthouse keeper. Dr. Stewart knew this. She saw it. She trusted my ability to take care of Jade at home.

"If you agree to let a home health nurse come to your house a couple of times a week, I will discharge Jade. You can follow up in the clinic and with The Pediatric Hospital." Her words gave me strength to face a sunny day outside of those hospital walls. If I could be with my children. If I could take Jade home and be with Todd. I was ready.

"That's fine with me. When can we leave?" I dialed Todd to pick us up before Dr. Stewart changed her mind. I looked forward to feeling the sun on my face again.

Dr. Stewart signed off on Jade's discharge and arranged for a home health agency to send a nurse to visit us twice a week. But a twinge of fear and trepidation came over me. I wanted to leave our haven, but I didn't know if I was strong enough to face the walls where everything started. I didn't know if I could return home without knowing what was wrong with Jade. She spent the last nineteen days not just under my lighthouse keeper's watch. She was also under the watchful eye of my colleagues and the umbrella of a hospital I trusted. Going home meant freedom from the constraints of a hospital room. It also meant I would return to a place where the memories were almost unbearable. My home was the last place I felt Jesus. I was worried He wasn't there anymore. Like in The Fishbowl.

But I had to go home. I needed to be with my daughters. They needed me too.

Todd arrived at the hospital and loaded our car with everything we accumulated over the previous nineteen days. The car was full. Suitcases. Medical bag. Breast pump. Diaper bag. Frozen breast milk. Much more than when we left the first time. He drove Jade and me home, and the three of us pulled up to a place that was changed. Weeks before, I left dry stalks of tall, yellow grass behind when we hurried Jade back to the hospital. But the landscape was different. It was lush and green from the rain that fell while I huddled inside our hospital room. I carried Jade through the garage door in my arms and stared at the place I ran from to save her life. The table in the living room was wiped clean. The same table where the howler monkeys screamed until I saw the truth in front of me. Todd tried to erase a memory I might not be able to handle. He knew I was still teetering. He would have to be the strong one. Let my bullet words bounce off him. Be our rock.

But even though he tried to expunge the scene to spare me the trauma, I remembered. I remembered arriving home when Jade was two days old with a false sense of peace that she was healthy. I remembered lying in bed with Jade, trying desperately to wake her and get her to nurse. I remembered being frantic and overwhelmed with fear and guilt and shame all at once when I realized something was wrong with her. I remembered the moment I knew Jade would die if we didn't take her back to the hospital. I remembered the Nebraska Huskers slippers I had on my feet that were sitting on the floor beside my recliner. I remembered the breast pad that fell from my nursing bra, now hardened and stiff and tucked into the cushions of the couch. Were it not for the girls and how they needed me, too, or for Todd who took care of everyone but himself and Jade, I might have found somewhere else to take Jade. But this was our home. I had to find strength to put aside the fear of drowning inside this place. The girls deserved to enjoy the comfort of their home with their mother under the same roof. Todd deserved to have his wife back.

I was apprehensive though. I tried in vain to settle in. We had left the safety net at the hospital. Pandemonium was normal at home. The girls expected their lives would return to that normal. They also hadn't forgotten what life was like before that rainy April day when Jade was born.

My home was disorganized. Loud. Overstimulating. I shushed the girls constantly like a nag. They just wanted to be children. There were new rules in our house that came with the new life we didn't plan. Rules that children couldn't possibly follow. Rules that were unfair. Restrictive. Unflattering to the parent I wanted to be. But Jade was sensitive to sound. All sounds. Quiet or loud. She flinched every time someone laughed. Every time one of the girls ran through the house. Every time one of us tiptoed through the kitchen. I kept the lights dim at night. Blinds were closed during the day. Activity was still. Sounds muted. It was a miserable home for five young girls who were hungry to be with their mother and baby sister. They craved time and affection too. Jade and I were home, but we might as well be back at the hospital. I still wasn't there for them like I should have been.

Nothing was the same. It never would be again.

Dark clouds settled in on our first warm and sunny day at home. The lifeline of a home health nurse was the only reason we were released from the hospital. I looked forward to having another nurse keep eyes on Jade since my judgment had been so poor before. The home health agency called to let me know they would send a nurse to visit Jade in two days.

"We will have our best pediatric nurse come to your home. Just have your insurance card ready, and Stormy will take a picture of it while she's there."

I shook my head in disbelief. *You've got to be freaking kidding me.*

The nurse who was supposed to have my back was named Stormy.

Of course our nurse is named Stormy. Why would it be anything different?

Monday morning blew in like a spring tornado. It was 10:30, and Stormy the nurse was late. I had just finished pumping when I saw a cloud of dust headed down our road. I presumed it was Stormy. An unfamiliar vehicle whipped into our driveway. The girls and The Five played on the front porch on their first day of summer break.

"Mom! Someone's here." They played for another ten minutes before Stormy emerged from a battered, gray pickup. As I peered through a crack in the blinds, the driver's-side door opened. I went to the front porch with the girls and the cats and waited for our nurse to round the front of her Dodge. A small woman dressed in ripped blue jeans, dirty tennis shoes, and a slightly cropped lavender tank top walked toward the front of our house. She held a cigarette between two fingers. A blue medical bag hung from her shoulder. A plume of cigarette smoke disappeared into the air above her. She leaned down and crushed the butt on our driveway. Then she tried to pet one of The Five.

"Hi, young ladies. I'm Stormy. I'm Jade's home health nurse." She greeted us with a smile stained by years of nicotine and dark sodas. "They're wild, aren't they?" Stormy spoke with a scratchy, deep voice. She tried again to pet one of our feral cats.

"The girls or the cats? Because the answer is yes to both. I'm Angie, Jade's mom." I tried not to show my aggravation with the smoke. The cigarette butt. The unprofessional nurse attire. The tardiness of a woman who had been trusted to ensure Jade was stable at home. She was my life buoy. But I already couldn't trust her.

This is the best pediatric nurse they have?

"Jade's asleep inside. You can wash your hands in the kitchen." Stormy followed me inside, and I motioned to the kitchen sink. She might not wash her hands unless I asked.

"You've got a nice house here. It's kind of in the boonies, but it's nice." Stormy dried her hands on a used, crumpled up dish towel that sat on the counter beside a new roll of crisp, clean paper towels.

She approached us while I held Jade in the safety of my arms. Stormy the Nurse would not be allowed to hold Jade. The stench of cigarette smoke invaded the sterility of my home. I was dumbfounded that a professional nurse would present herself in such an unprofessional way. Just when I thought it couldn't get worse, Stormy sat down in a chair next to us. She unpacked her nursing bag and noticed my bright-yellow, Symphony breast pump.

"They didn't tell me she was on oxygen." She pointed at the Symphony.

"That's my breast pump." I remembered Todd's advice from the hospital elevators and bit my tongue.

The meeting with Stormy didn't go well. Our nurse thought a breast pump was an oxygen concentrator. She smelled like cigarettes.

And her name was Stormy. Why couldn't it have been Grace? Or Ruth? Or Esther?

Anything but Stormy.

Stormy the Nurse chatted for the next hour. She talked more than she helped but told me at least ten times how beautiful Jade was. She was personable. Polite. She gushed words of affirmation over me and the great job I was doing with Jade. She didn't tell me anything I didn't already know. I hoped we would be given a nurse who had taken care of many babies like Jade. So did Dr. Stewart. Instead, I was given a chain-smoking home health nurse named Stormy. A sweet woman who offered kind words and not much more.

When Stormy ran out of things to talk about, she packed her nursing bag, coughed a deep Marlboro cough into the air of the living room, and turned toward the front door.

"Thanks for letting me see Jade. She's a real sweetheart. You're doing a good job, Mama. Don't you let anyone tell you no different." Stormy offered more accolades for my work with Jade. She wanted to come back, but we both knew she wouldn't be invited to return.

"Thank you, Stormy. I'll call the office tomorrow and make another appointment. Drive safe."

I had no intention of calling.

Stormy passed the girls and The Five on the front porch and tried for a third time to pet one of the cats. They skillfully evaded the cigarette-smoking nurse's touch again.

"Dang cat." Stormy laughed and climbed into her pickup. She lit another cigarette and backed down the driveway. With the cigarette dangling between her pursed lips, Stormy waved goodbye to the girls and The Five. The Dodge backfired as she disappeared in a cloud of cigarette smoke and dirt.

"Who was that, Mom?" Kinnah yelled from the front porch.

"Oh, that was a home health nurse, Sweetie. She's not coming back."

I sent Stormy away like a dove from the ark and hoped she would find land somewhere so I would never see her again. That meant

I would be alone on a sinking ship with Jade. But it didn't matter because I was alone even when Stormy was there. I was alone in the presence of the nurse who was sent to turn the tide for Jade. I was alone without Jesus. Even with five daughters gusting around on the front porch with The Five, I was alone.

I left the umbrella of our hospital room for a home that was haunted with memories that tormented me. I wouldn't admit it, but I clung to a thin faith. I waited for Jesus to return and join me on this journey. But my faith was shallow. Barely skin deep. Even though Cousin Rich got me thinking about Jesus again back in the hospital, it was just a sliver. I had faith that really wasn't faith at all.

I didn't feel Jesus with me. I didn't know why He had forgotten us. But I couldn't weather this storm alone. The waters were deep. I was already drowning.

Without help from someone besides Todd, Jade and I wouldn't have enough strength to keep our heads above water for long. The storm was too big. We were both going to drown.

13

The Waiting Room

I dwindled away after two brutal weeks at home with Jade. My new life was complicated. Rigorous. An anchor of uncertainty weighed me down. Lack of sleep disintegrated my stamina. I was knobby bones again. A failure. Despite my best efforts, I couldn't control the uncontrollable. Jade wasn't getting better, and we didn't know what was wrong with her.

I was not the same woman who left my children to rush Jade back to the hospital. I was changed. My body was taxed by the same overwhelming pressure I felt with Jade in The Fishbowl. The tectonic movement beneath my feet. The heat that burned my frail and failing body. A transformation had begun. I was metamorphosing into a woman nobody recognized. Including me.

The only lifeline I was thrown was a home health nurse named Stormy, who was no help. I had to figure everything out on my own. Todd worked so we could pay Jade's mounting medical bills. Then he spent every minute of his free time making the girls feel loved and wanted. His hands were full being both father and mother. I was the only person who could take care of Jade. I was engulfed. Overwhelmed. I wasn't prepared for the marathon endurance of love expected and required of me. I barely settled into the chaos of home and needy children when the parade of visits to the outpatient clinics at The Pediatric Hospital commenced.

I was about to snap again.

We had to find out what was wrong with Jade. Why she couldn't eat. Why her head flopped on her neck like a bobble doll. She had as many specialists as there were reasons for her problems. Genetics.

Metabolics. Gastroenterology. Cardiology. Pediatric Rehabilitation. Infectious Disease. Ophthalmology. Neurology. All intertwined in their quest to isolate the reason Jade was so fragile. There were so many doctors that I forgot their names and departments. All brilliant. But cold. Rushed.

Jade's neurologist was Dr. Allen, and he wasn't like the others. He was passionately intent on finding the reason for Jade's neurological difficulties. Dr. Allen was the smartest man I ever met. He was a humble presence of knowledge and experience we needed. If anyone could tell us what was wrong with Jade, it would be him. He cared. It was a trait I craved after many other specialists left me feeling like Jade was just a crippled calf in a herd.

Todd and I met with Dr. Allen for the first time at his private office when Jade was just over a month old. Her feeding problems and floppy tone were worsening. He wanted to know why. While we sat with him, he called in a favor to get Jade ahead of the two-month wait list for a brain MRI at The Pediatric Hospital. We were finally getting somewhere. I knew nothing about the facility except that the more technical procedures were done there. It was where sick and injured children stayed as inpatients. I envisioned a playground of medical treatments where children ran, jumped, and giggled, just like in the commercials I saw on TV. Where they healed all the little children. The Pediatric Hospital would have the answers we needed.

"OK, she's scheduled tomorrow at 1:30. Don't let the building worry you. It's the best place for Jade to get the brain MRI." I didn't know what Dr. Allen meant. But I would soon.

I clung to the picture I created in my mind of a magical place where we would go to fix all Jade's problems. The elusive mecca of help and answers we needed. The haven that was going to take the uncertainty and anxiety from us. I was relieved. A simple answer. A simple cure. I couldn't wait. It was a picture so fairytale-esque I imagined turnstiles and Disney characters greeting us as we ventured in. It would be an amusement park of hospitals made just for children. "It's a Small World" played in my head. Our problems neared an end at The Pediatric Hospital. It was the only place that could turn this thing around for Jade.

But what I saw when we arrived stunned me. Instead of the fantasy in my head, Todd and I walked up to a battered and bruised, hundred-year-old building. It was scheduled to be demolished when the new hospital opened across town the following month. All attempts at maintenance and upkeep had been abandoned. We had the misfortune of starting our journey at the building nobody wanted anymore.

The fairytale ending I envisioned in my sleep-deprived mind dissipated. We stepped over crumbling sidewalks and concrete steps lined with brown and dying coral bells. The large sliding doors squealed open as we approached. The carpet was soiled with large, dark stains of a substance I couldn't identify. My senses were overwhelmed by the smell of stale diapers. Feces. Clothes soaked in urine. Hardly the Magic Kingdom I visualized the whole drive to Denver and the five weeks preceding that day. I didn't see a single merry-go-round or ferris wheel. Only a run-down building that turned my fairytale hopes into a daytime nightmare.

Todd and I stopped at the reception desk, unsure of where to go for Jade's brain MRI. I had already dismissed the possibility that there was anything wrong with Jade's brain. Something like that would be catastrophic. Unrecoverable. Devastating. There was no such thing as a cerebellar transplant. Jade's brain had to be perfect.

"Hi. I'm checking in my daughter for a brain MRI at 1:30." I stood above a young desk clerk, who was distracted by texts on her phone. She was disheveled. Like the building she worked in. I wondered if she was a mother or understood what I was going through. The torment. The desperation that seeped from my pores. The least she could do was put her phone away and be attentive. Every turn of this journey led me to another place where I felt more alone and ignored.

After rhythmically and unemotionally collecting all the information she needed to check Jade in, the young woman directed us down the hall. "Go down this hall and to the right." She pointed ahead of us. "Then go through the double doors that say Radiology. There's a waiting room you can sit in."

Jade was still asleep in her car seat after the long drive. Todd carried her underneath the safety of her blankets to our waiting room destination. It was peculiar to me that there were no children running around. No screaming babies comforted by their mothers. No parents redirecting their toddlers to stay near them. No sounds of children echoing through the halls. Nothing like the commercial on TV. It didn't feel like we were in a pediatric hospital at all. It reminded me of a nursing home. Not a place where children should be. But we ventured down the hall anyway. A putrid odor became thicker as we got closer to the right turn in the hallway. So thick I could taste it.

"Are we in the right place?" I asked Todd. I was confused. It wasn't what I expected.

I made the dreadful right turn and pushed through the double doors. I stopped. I was standing in quicksand. I couldn't move. I scanned the shocking landscape of the room and felt an invisible fist knock the wind out of me. Todd was only steps behind me. He, too, came to a complete standstill.

The waiting room was full. There was a faint hum of a machine somewhere in a place I couldn't see. No talking. No giggling. No screaming babies. There was a single empty chair beside a fish tank growing green algae-like spores. The fish were sluggish. I couldn't tell if they were dying or just sick. I lowered myself to the chair and tried to breathe.

The view in the room sucked the air from my lungs.

Rows and rows of children in wheelchairs and medical strollers lined the inside of the waiting room. Teenagers. Toddlers. Infants. The diagnoses were diverse. But severe. Diseases that did not discriminate. None of the children responded when their parents smiled and talked to them. Some made sporadic, nonpurposeful movements. Others didn't move at all. There were feeding pumps and feeding bags. Emergency seizure kits and ventilators. Medical supplies and equipment hung from the backs of the wheelchairs. The enormity of Jade's problems heart-punched me. I couldn't handle what I saw. It was too much.

I had to face a shameful, dark place that hid inside my soul telling me every child in the waiting room was repulsive. Retarded. Physically and cognitively inferior to me and my children. I would never accept that Jade was like them. Every disgusting, indeliberate thought I had about them begged me to look away. If I didn't see them, then they didn't exist. Todd's face was pale again. We weren't prepared for The Waiting Room.

My eyes fixated on a little girl who was five or six years old, about the same age as my daughter Faith. She sat across from us in a custom wheelchair. Her name was embroidered on the headrest. Lilly. She mercilessly sucked on her chafed, red hands and indiscriminately thrashed her head from side to side. A woman I assumed was her mother removed Lilly's hands from her mouth. Over and over. She gently and patiently wiped her reddened chin with a cloth. She dried the copious amounts of saliva on Lilly's face every time it got wet. But just as soon as her mother released her hands, Lilly sucked and chewed on them again. I tried not to stare, but I was mesmerized by Lilly. Her dark, chin-length bobbed hair. Her thick, bushy eyebrows. Her stunning green eyes. Her thin, tree-branch arms and legs. I couldn't divert my rude gaze away from her. I was in a disheartened daze. A moment of repugnance. A nauseating, unpurposeful, uninterruptible trance.

Lilly's mother noticed Jade and struck up a conversation with me.

"She's so beautiful. Oh my gosh! Look at her hair! What's her name? How old is she?"

"Thank you so much. Her name is Jade. She's just over a month old. She's getting a brain MRI today." I was honest but nervous. The nasogastric tube in Jade's nose was the only sign to onlookers of the mountainous struggles in her short life. I was grateful Lilly's mother interrupted my catatonic state.

"This is Lilly. Say hello to Jade, Lilly." The woman feigned a prompt to Lilly, who was unable to speak, and waved Lilly's right hand at us. Lilly continued to put her hands deep into her mouth until she gagged and threw up on her shirt and the floor. "Oh, she does this all the time. We're used to cleaning up puke all day. Lilly had an NG tube for a while too." She motioned to the tube in Jade's left nostril while she cleaned vomit off Lilly's hands and face. "But I had enough of her pulling it out, and then I'd have to put it back ten times a day. We finally caved in and got her a G-Tube. Best decision we ever made!"

"I don't think Jade will need a G-Tube. I think she will start eating soon. She just needs to get stronger. Just a little more time to get used to breastfeeding." I was offended that Lilly's mother brought up a G-Tube. A surgical procedure. One that would interrupt the perfection of Jade's abdomen. She implied Jade wouldn't get better.

"Lilly didn't breastfeed. She was my foster daughter. Now she's all ours! We got her when she was seven and the adoption was final last year. She's thirteen now and doing great with her G-Tube!" Lilly's mother was excited to tell me about a surgery I would fight to the bitter end.

"Did you say Lilly is thirteen? Thirteen years old?" I was shocked. She was a sparse girl. The same age as my twins. Not five or six years old. Not the same age as Faith. A teenager who sucked on her hands until they were raw. She still sat in a wheelchair and thrashed about. She still pooped her pants. She hadn't gotten better and was never healed. Lilly was a thirteen-year-old infant. Every fear that invaded my mind during the darkness of my endless nights caring for Jade exploded in my head. I was dizzy. I had to face a reality I couldn't handle. We were sitting in a waiting room surrounded by children who didn't just make me uncomfortable. They made my skin crawl with revulsion. Children who were burdens to their families and society. Children who had disabilities so profound I selfishly and ignorantly assumed they had nothing to offer the world.

Jade isn't like these kids.

I went to the darkest thoughts of my mind. I wanted to run from the room. I was about to release a floodgate of tears I couldn't control. The pressure burned my eyes. I had to get up. I had to find a bathroom. I had to escape. My heart was preparing to explode from the rapid pounding in my chest. Sweat formed on my forehead. My hands shook.

"Do you know where the bathroom is?"

Of course Lilly's mom knew. She pointed down the hall where we came from. I leaned in to Todd.

"I'll be right back. Keep an eye on Jade." The color drained from my face.

"Are you OK?" He looked worried.

"I don't know. I need to go to the bathroom."

I stumbled to the bathroom, pausing only to balance my quivering legs. I pushed the door open and locked it behind me just before I fell on the counter, whole body weeping. I balanced myself by gripping the faucet while I threw up in the sink. I imagined Jade in a wheelchair. Being fed through a feeding tube. Sucking on her hands until they were raw. I wretched again. My body was too heavy for my knees. I slid to the floor of the putrid bathroom. I was surrounded by used paper towels, stray bits of dirty toilet paper, and a bloody tampon near my face. I sobbed deeply into my shirt so no one would hear my bellows. I was hyperventilating and couldn't summon a breath deep enough to fill my lungs or calm my spinning head.

"God! Where are you? Why have you forgotten us?" I screamed into my hands and covered my face and eyes. It was the darkest desperation I ever felt. "Where are you? I need you."

I was alone.

On a bathroom floor.

Again.

Enough minutes passed that Todd came to look for me. He was afraid I was passed out on the bathroom floor. I washed the mascara from my stained cheeks and waited for the red in my eyes and face to dull. I didn't want to explain to Todd or Lilly's mom what happened in the bathroom. That I cried and threw up after being pummeled with the possibility that Jade's brain might not be perfect.

That Jade might be just like Lilly.

"I'll be out in a minute."

I returned to The Waiting Room, where undesirable, repulsive children sat. Lilly and her mother were gone. I didn't have to hold myself together in front of them. I didn't know how to reconcile this abhorrent, dark part of me. A character flaw I wasn't even aware existed somewhere deep within me until that day. I was revolted by myself far more than I was by them. I was ashamed of my visceral reaction to a sweet girl who was stronger and braver than I would ever be. I wanted to apologize to Lilly and her mom for who I was. For things they knew nothing about. Forgiveness wouldn't change the person I didn't know I was. But it would dull the sting of shame an infinitesimal amount.

More than a month of unanswered questions, despair, and desperation gouged at my heart. It was then, sitting next to a dirty fish tank in The Waiting Room of my new hell, that I knew I would never return to the life I had before. I had to confront truths I couldn't bear. The truth that Jade might be like The Waiting Room children. The truth that I had deep, unknown flaws. The truth that I was more monstrous than I could have ever imagined.

Everything was changed. I was changed. Not just by Jade's struggles. Not just by The Waiting Room. But by the children who took me to a dark place I didn't know existed inside me. Their innocence forced me to see the defects of my heart. There wasn't a single thing in my life left intact or untouched. I was a ruin. A wasteland. I was alone with Jade in our own wilderness. I was about to give up on God for good.

I looked at Jade as she slept in Todd's arms. Every one of her features was exceptionally beautiful. A beauty that was interrupted only by a feeding tube dangling from her nose. The only thing that reminded me she wasn't perfect.

Then I scanned the room filled with children and parents who had journeyed much further than us. They had changed me. This was the place where I caught a glimpse of the creosote on my soul for the first time. I could never again see anything in the world or in myself the same. For the rest of my life, there would be nothing that would enter my senses without thinking of the children or passing through the filter of The Waiting Room.

14

The Scream

The smell of The Waiting Room lingered in my nose and on my clothes as Todd drove the two-hour ride home. For the first twenty-five miles, we sat in silence in the smallness of the car. Still stunned by The Waiting Room. Numb from the experience. The only sounds were the hum of my breast pump and the road noise beneath our tires. There was no place for us to hide from each other. There was nothing either of us could say that would change what we had to face. Todd saw me going to a dark place in my head, and he didn't dare follow. He tried to make small talk. He tried to redirect me to a scenario that was more tolerable than an abnormal brain. He bravely broke the awkward silence between us.

"When do you think we will get the results?"

"I really don't know, Todd. It could be a day or so, I guess." I was irritated that he interrupted my momentary peace. "Dr. Allen is really busy."

"You know . . ." Todd was slow and cautious. He knew I was ready to snap again. "I was thinking that, you know, it's probably a good thing that she doesn't have like a hair lip or a club foot."

If I could have slapped stupid out of him, I would have. I couldn't believe how foolish he was. I would make him regret that he had spoken at all.

"What did you just say, Todd?" I twisted at the waist and stared at his face still holding the breast pump cups to my chest. "What did you say to me? Did you say you're glad she doesn't have a club foot or a hair lip? Did you really say that? Because those things, those things are correctable. Those things can be repaired. But a problem with her brain? Now that's a freaking problem. You know that, right? You know there's nothing they can do if she has something wrong with her brain. Right? Are you freaking kidding me right now?"

The look in his eyes told me he wanted to open the door and step onto the interstate just to get away from me. But the speed of the car and the seat belt latched at his right hip restrained him. Otherwise he would have taken his chances and jumped out. Anything to escape.

"Good grief, Todd. I swear. You still don't get it, do you? You still don't grasp the enormity of what's going on with our daughter."

Todd was simply trying to have a conversation with me for the first time in a long time. As usual, I ruined it and made him sorry. He wouldn't speak again if it meant he would get a lashing. I was volatile. Unpredictable. Ruthless. Todd just drove. I turned my back to him and pumped precious milk for Jade. The tension in the car strangled us both like a boa constrictor. In that dark place in my head, I demanded to know where Jesus was and when He was going to step in and fix Jade.

Todd hit every pothole and bump as he drove down the dirt road to our house. *Strategic.* I assumed everything he did was purposeful and carried out with malice. Something to irritate me. Something to cause a fight.

It can't possibly be me who's the problem.

"Damn, Todd. I'm going to spill this milk. Can you slow down, maybe?" Todd slowed the car down like I demanded. He pulled into the driveway, defeated like a spineless wimp. The complete opposite of the man he was.

The girls heard us coming and peeked out the front window. They held their feral cats up for us to see. They were happy Jade was home. Happy I was home. They still weren't used to being left alone so often. The girls didn't like being forced to find independence on their own. They assumed things would return to normal. But normal would never look the same for us after Jade was born. Brooke and Hope were delegated the unwanted task of babysitting the three younger girls. Every time I took Jade into town for an appointment, they were in charge. Even at their young age, they knew I was only one person. They knew something was wrong with their baby sister. They knew they had to be there when I couldn't. Instead of having a fun summer with their friends, they helped me. They did what was asked of them and didn't complain much.

They were forced to learn about sacrifice years before they should have.

"Mommy! You're home!" Even the twins were happy to see me. The girls ran to the garage door to greet us, still holding cats that weren't allowed inside. They were doing what unsupervised children do. Misbehaving. Ignoring rules. Being kids. The girls were painted from a palette of normal that I was grateful for. Xanadu Gray. A color not found in the rainbow but still strikingly beautiful in its own hue. I wished Jade was like her siblings. Just normal. Just Xanadu Gray. The girls did all the things most children do. They giggled and squealed with delight when their Mommy arrived home. They fought and argued over blueberry muffins and the last Dr Pepper. They ran through the house and made messes like cyclones. Jade's problems brought an appreciation of the beauty of normal. A gratefulness for a bland life. I craved to discipline Jade one day for bickering with her sisters and forgetting to flush the toilet and ruining new school shoes in mud puddles. I coveted the mundane. I hungered for Jade to be just like them.

I hugged the girls while they each attempted to be first in line for a quick minute with me. They had been robbed of so much since Jade was born. I knew they felt great loss. Deeper than anything they had ever felt in their short lives. And there was no end in sight. Nobody knew when or if our home would return to predictable chaos. Nobody knew what was wrong with Jade.

We made our way to the living room where Jade and I spent every day and night together. I unpacked the plethora of bags that accompanied us on our trips outside the house. The girls gathered around Jade's car seat and whispered to her how much they loved her while their wild cats meowed for attention. Rules were broken. A lot of rules. The Five were not indoor cats. We all knew it. But the girls had lost so much already.

I could relinquish one thing to them in their grief.

Todd started cooking the dinner he had planned for us the week before. Every week, he posted a meal list on the refrigerator door. A list I was not part of creating. He was organized. Scheduled. Everything we did as a family had an itinerary created by his masterful hands. He prepared our meal list in advance so he knew what to buy and cook. It was one of the rare things he could still control in our new lives. Instead of being grateful for his help, I was resentful that he didn't give us a choice of what we ate every night.

But Todd could cook. It was one of the things that attracted me to him when we were dating. We were polar opposites in the kitchen. But not on the dance floor. As I watched him rumba alone to the sound of U2 playing through the house, I remembered nights when we used to dance together. How we rocked and swayed while tangled up with each other. Moments of reconnection. Moments of hope for our future. But those nights were a lifetime ago. Everything was different. Everything had changed. Everything except one thing. Todd still filled a food void in me.

The aroma of garlic salt and tomato sauce wafted from the kitchen and washed over the odor I carried home from The Waiting Room. Todd's spaghetti was always a hit. And it reminded me of better days.

"Girls, you should put the cats outside. I really don't want them around Jade. Then wash your hands, please." Faith wasn't happy about parting with Snowball but reluctantly followed behind her sisters. Faith, at almost six years old, was sandwiched between Emmie and Kinnah. Were it not for her strong personality, Faith could have easily been lost in the middle. Even at such a young age, she had to grow up too soon, like my other girls. She couldn't possibly understand all that was going on with her baby sister and her mommy. Jade's problems wrecked me. But I was equally disturbed that the girls had been orphaned by their mother. I lived in the home with them, but

I might as well have been somewhere else. Their time with me was scarce. Wafer-thin. Barely existent.

Faith begrudgingly followed the older girls out the back door. Emmie toddled behind them while she wrangled Mattie under her arm. They all went on the deck to play with their cats and look for rattlesnakes.

In the rush of unloading the car, I lost track of time. It was 6:05 p.m. I was five minutes late for Jade's feeding. Jade was on a strict tube-feeding schedule. If I was late, I had to make up the time and missed milk when I was supposed to be asleep.

"Ah dang. I didn't realize what time it was. I'm so sorry, Jadey Bug. Mommy will start your feeding." I scooped Jade up from her car seat and into my arms. I elevated her head and upper body to a 45-degree angle on a pillow on the floor. It was the only way to keep her from throwing up while I fed her. The vomiting had gotten much worse. So had her fragile neurological system. That's why Dr. Allen ordered the brain MRI. We had to find out what was causing Jade's problems. We needed to get some answers. Answers that would tell us how to fix her so she could be Xanadu Gray.

I scrambled to the kitchen to get her milk and tube feeding ready and dabbed drops of milk on my wrist to ensure it was body temperature warm. I did everything I could do to make untraditional feedings more comfortable for Jade. I was startled by the phone ringing deep within my purse. I wasn't expecting any calls. Especially not from Dr. Allen. It was after hours. He would be at home with his family.

Answer the phone, Angie.

I dove to the bottom of the bag and answered just in time. It was a number I didn't recognize.

"Hello, this is Angie."

"Hi, Angie. This is Dr. Allen, Jade's neurologist. I wanted to see what time you and your husband might be able to come to Centennial tomorrow so we can review Jade's MRI results." Centennial was almost two hours from our home. I was confused that Dr. Allen was calling after hours. I was confused that we needed to go to the office to hear the results.

"Well, of course we can come tomorrow. Any time. But what's going on with the MRI results? Why do you need us in the office to discuss the findings?" I was scared. Still reeling from The Waiting Room. I knew he wouldn't call after hours unless it was bad.

"I would like to sit down with you both and go over the actual scans of Jade's brain so I can show you what I'm seeing." Dr. Allen was unwavering. He insisted we travel to his office to meet with him.

"Dr. Allen, we will come anytime you tell us to be there. But I need to know what's going on with Jade's brain. I can't possibly wait until tomorrow if there's something so important that you need us to be there with you." The sting of tears, uncertainty, and despair welled up in my head. He was adamant about us going to his office the next day. I was adamant that I couldn't wait to know what was wrong with Jade. I put the phone on speaker mode. Todd hovered near me holding a spatula and a spaghetti strainer.

"It's a little perplexing, actually. Jade's MRI shows that she has absent myelination of the white matter of her brain. We normally see this with very premature babies. But Jade was full term, so this is not consistent with her gestational age. The only other possibility is an inborn error of metabolism that could have degraded the myelination."

There was nothing Dr. Allen could have said that would be worse than a metabolic storage disorder.

I fell to the floor and dropped the phone at Todd's feet. Todd finished the call with Dr. Allen and scheduled our meeting for the next morning. I had remained as strong as an Olympic athlete over the last four weeks. But this. This would be the mountain I could not climb. The giant I would not conquer. I lay next to Jade and rocked back and forth with my knees in my arms. I held my breath until Todd ended the call. I was a chestnut on the ground being blown around by a tornado. I refused to breathe. I didn't care that my lungs were empty of air and that my heart was so broken that it would surely stop beating. A sound was forming from the bottom of my soul in a place I didn't know existed inside me. I couldn't hold it back any longer.

I screamed.

I screamed deep. Loud. Savage. A sound that permeated the whole house and stuck to the walls. It frightened my children and ravaged my husband. I was a trapped and dying animal.

It was The Scream.

The Scream of death as it settles into a mother's arms.

The Scream that would be remembered as the most horrific sound my daughters had ever heard.

The Scream that had been simmering just below the surface since our time in The Fishbowl.

The Scream that signaled the demise of every good thing in my life.

"Nooooooooo!" It was the only sound I could push past my vocal cords. I writhed on the living room floor with Jade lying next to me completely unfazed. She was asleep and unaware her mama's world had just been destroyed. I loved Jade from a place I couldn't explain. A deep love of fierce protection and raw emotion. If I loved her that much, how could God not love her more? I cursed at Him louder than my shrill death scream just moments before.

"I hate you! She's just a little baby. Why have you forsaken her?" I was broken. Defeated. Forgotten. I stared at Jade, a baby I had not wanted. A baby I did not deserve. Kinnah snuck inside without me noticing. She hovered over my body. She couldn't move. She couldn't speak. She was shocked and frightened. She had just heard a sound that made her wonder in her child's mind if her mother had died. She had never seen me in such a pitiful place.

But she was right. Kinnah had witnessed death. The death of my spirit.

The death of my hope.

The death of my last remnant of faith in God.

The woman writhing on the floor was a shell of who I was before the phone rang. Transformed into the unrecognizable. A dead body with a beating heart.

It was finished. No wrestling with Jesus to rescue us. No bartering to take Jade's place. We were layered with a thick darkness. Lost. Jade could not survive the battle that lay ahead.

Jesus had forsaken us.

A brutal truth embedded itself into my soul. I spent a sleepless night alone on the couch with Jade and waited for our 9 a.m. meeting with Dr. Allen. My faith was stolen. I thought about my words to God when I found out I was pregnant. How I prayed that death would fall upon my baby. How God simply delayed His answer to that unholy prayer. I thought about Kinnah and the trauma from the death scream still ringing through her ears. I thought about Todd and wondered if he was able to sleep or if he finally understood the magnitude of Jade's diagnosis. The morning light peeked through the blinds, but the darkness remained all around and within me. And I didn't have to wonder anymore if Jesus was going to show up to help us.

He had forgotten us.

We made it to Dr. Allen's office early and unprepared to face the most devastating news we had ever received. Dr. Allen's nurse ushered us into his private office where he waited for us. He offered us chairs in line with two large computer screens sitting behind his desk and revisited our conversation from the evening before. Then he turned on the screen to his left.

"I think it will be easier to show you on the computer screens. The brain on the left is a normal newborn brain." The structure on his left was lit with bright features and had elegant folds throughout its surface. It was remarkable. Then he turned on the screen to his right.

"And this is Jade's brain." The structure he described as my daughter's brain was dark, unlit, and dull. "She has no myelination of the central white matter of her brain. Myelination is the insulation that surrounds the nerves. It's what allows the nervous system to conduct signals. We don't know why her central white matter isn't myelinated. It could be degraded, or it could be unformed. We just don't know at this point. It's highly irregular for a full-term baby to have no myelination at all. In fact, I don't think I have ever seen this before in a baby who wasn't very premature." Absent myelination of Jade's white matter meant she would never walk. Never talk. Never eat. But more importantly, it meant she had something so wrong that it had prevented a crucial part of her brain anatomy from forming. Suddenly, The Waiting Room seemed like a haven. A place I coveted. Not because I wished my daughter would be disabled. But because I wished my daughter would live.

No matter how disabled she might be, I just wanted Jesus to save Jade.

I had accepted that the conversation was going to be dreadful. I was stoic in my chair beside Todd while Dr. Allen's words gouged my heart. He said we needed to watch Jade's clinical course and see if she was improving, worsening, or staying the same. A repeat MRI in three months would give us answers about any further degradation of Jade's brain.

"Oh, and this. This thing right here." He pointed to the base of Jade's neck on the MRI. "This is a cervical syrinx. It can cause problems, but this isn't what's causing her low tone and feeding difficulties. We will need to watch this closely too. I am going to directly admit Jade to The Pediatric Hospital in the next few weeks so we can do a full genetic and metabolic workup." He thought the absent myelination was a symptom of something else. Something sinister. Something evil. There was no other explanation for it. He didn't have to say something I already knew. A diagnosis uncovered by a geneticist or metabolic specialist would destroy us all. Jade would never have a normal life. The girls would be abandoned by their mother to take care of Jade. Todd would watch me disintegrate into a darkness that threatened to take my life.

A relentless hell that aimed to scourge me from the inside out was the answer we got in Dr. Allen's office. We left there changed.

Never again would we be the same parents who walked through his doors.

"Well, there you go. Jade just got two diagnoses for the price of one. Lucky us." Something had turned inside me. With The Scream no longer simmering beneath the surface, I was numb. A hollow shell. A thin, cheap version of the woman I thought I once was.

We returned home to the girls down the long road we had traveled four times in twenty-four hours. I broke the news to them that we would be going back to the hospital. I didn't know when. I didn't know for how long. Emmie thrashed on the floor in her usual display. Faith stomped her feet and screamed. Kinnah stood quiet, still in shock from the night before. Brooke and Hope sobbed about how much they missed me. They all felt abandoned again. Everyone living in our home felt abandoned. We had to take Jade to the dilapidated hospital. A place where we would sleep among dying coral bells and crumbling sidewalks. The thought of going back to that place was unbearable. I didn't know how I could leave the girls again.

But I had no choice.

That was the tapestry of my life. Nothing I did was by my own choice or for anyone's benefit anymore except Jade's. We were all hurting. All grieving. All despondent in our own way. The girls had every right to be crushed and to blame me for it. After all, it was my fault.

We spent the next several weeks in deep grief. There was no way to reconcile or accept the results of the brain MRI. I was fragile. Lost. Hopeless. I would have to leave the girls again to help Jade. I felt like I was being ripped in half.

Then the call came. A bed was ready for her. We had to go.

We left the girls early in the morning under the cover of darkness and made the drive to The Pediatric Hospital with Jade. I cried as we drove down the bumpy, dusty road and left the girls behind. Again. I replayed The Scream in my head that still lingered in our home. Still stuck like gaudy wallpaper. Still echoing through my daughter's ears. The pain and desperation it represented found a permanent place inside our family. There was nowhere to run from it. Nowhere to escape what was coming. We were engulfed by things we didn't understand. Consumed by what The Scream brought to our lives.

None of us would be the same again.

15

Grim Reaper

 odd and I arrived with Jade at The Pediatric Hospital in search of more answers as I struggled to understand Jade's mind-numbing diagnosis. We knew the central white matter of her brain wasn't myelinated. But we didn't know why. Only that nothing good ever came from something so sinister. As soon as Jade was admitted, the multitude of specialists and residents began their unabated marches through her room. Each eyed her like bacteria in a petri dish, studying everything about her appearance and behaviors. They said nothing positive about her. Her forehead was long and broad. She had a large space between her toes. Her head was huge. It was degrading to be stared at and evaluated by strangers. I felt like a monkey behind a glass cage at the zoo. The first day was a brutal stream of endless tests. They drew countless tubes of blood, and Jade felt everything. Her screams pierced my ears and my heart. It was overwhelming for her. It was overwhelming for Todd and me too. Jade was worked over and worked up so much in just a few days that she barely opened her eyes. It was more than her fragile nervous system could handle.

Three days passed, and we were no closer to getting the answers we came for. Todd stayed as much as he could at the hospital, but the girls couldn't be alone all the time. Mom took them to her house, and Becky helped watch them while we were at the hospital. It was a team effort to make sure everyone was taken care of.

The experience at The Pediatric Hospital was taxing. Not just on Jade. I was wearing thin too. The inside of the inpatient unit was not unlike the outside of the building or The Waiting Room. Everything was falling apart and in need of maintenance. I dreaded trying to get myself clean in the family shower room down the hall from Jade's room. The drains were clogged, and water filled with other people's filth backed up on my feet and ankles. Black mold crept up the vinyl shower curtain and the sides of the shower pan where my feet soaked. But I had to get clean. I had to start the day free of the previous day's sweat and tears on my skin. I had to have five minutes to myself even if it was in a disgusting shower. I returned to Jade's room after trudging through black water and hovered over her bed. There were more tests and more specialists scheduled. I needed to prepare my heart for what was next. I cracked the blinds in her room, hoping to enjoy a bit of the warm, beautiful June day outside the window.

When I turned around, there was a man standing at the door of Jade's hospital room. It was Dr. Miller. The head of the Clinical Genetics and Metabolism Department. He paused to adjust the crooked black hat resting atop his thin, white hair. One of his fragile hands held a tattered black physician's bag. It reminded me of something I had seen as a child on an episode of *Little House on the Prairie*. His other hand shifted his hat into place before he continued into Jade's room. His face was weathered. Experienced. Wise. Years of heartbreak showed in every groove on his face. Years of bad news. Years of tragic diagnoses. Years and thousands of children born broken that he couldn't fix. A man who would retire soon and live a life not surrounded by profoundly disabled children. I didn't understand how he did it. How he broke the life-changing news of such complicated diagnoses. Diagnoses that never ended in happy endings. Diagnoses that stole babies and broke parents' hearts. Dr. Miller was the only man who challenged Dr. Allen's brilliance. The only man able to destroy my dreams for Jade's future. I couldn't comprehend how he knew without thought what he had to say regardless of how harsh the words would be spoken or heard. We met Dr. Miller several weeks before in the outpatient clinic, and I realized right away that nothing good accompanied him.

He was the Grim Reaper.

The thief of dreams. The mouthpiece of doom. The emotionless face of death.

When Dr. Miller showed up at Jade's door, it was the beginning of the end. Only bad news would follow.

Only pain.

Only darkness.

Only death.

He stepped through the threshold of Jade's door and shuffled his aged feet. He was a towering man who hunched his heavy shoulders. All the life-ending diagnoses he had shared with families for half a century weighed him down. Those years of burdens bent him over at the heart. He was covered from his head to his feet in a deep shade of black I had never seen. His black knee-length trench coat covered a black button-up dress shirt. He wore freshly pressed black trousers and black dress shoes that begged for a shine. I searched his eyes, desperate to know what was coming. I needed to prepare myself for the discussion that would follow. But what I saw didn't matter. If he was there, our world was about to be decimated. There was wisdom in his eyes. But I saw no humanity in them. All I saw was the Grim Reaper standing in front of me. Holding a physician's bag in one hand and a scythe in the other. He was the bearer of the most cruel devastation to lost and hopeless parents.

Dr. Miller approached Jade and me at her bedside and began to speak. I only heard the sound his voice made. I couldn't handle the details in his harsh words. I tried to drown him out. Everything he uttered would change my already-changed life. He was not there to comfort me or soften the blow. He was in our room to identify all the things wrong with Jade. Then he would destroy my future by taking every last bit of hope away from me. As if there was any left to steal.

"Hello, I'm Dr. Miller. I think we met back in May in the Metabolic Clinic. My team got together for care conferences this morning, and we think we know what's causing Jade's feeding problems and low tone."

My heart beat mercilessly just beneath my sternum as a thick bead of sweat formed on my brow. Our fate would be sealed with the next words he said. I nervously played with Jade's thick, dark curls, in awe of how perfect she was.

Dr. Miller sat his physician's bag on Jade's bed and stared at her. He unwrapped the swaddle of her blankets that enveloped her like a cloak of protection. He produced her feet and pointed to her toes.

"You see. She has a large space here between these two toes." I saw a chasm so wide it appeared she was missing a toe on each foot. "And her fingers. Look here. All of her joints are floppy, too flexible, double jointed." He easily contorted Jade's fingers into unnatural positions. She didn't flinch.

Then he looked at her face.

"And her eyes. She has a wide area between her eyes and a flat nasal bridge. She has a bossing forehead, and her ears are low set. But most telling is that she is extraordinarily macrocephalic without hydrocephalus. The clinical findings of her brain MRI and her dysmorphic features have led us to a few potential diagnoses. But one syndrome stands out, in particular. The team agrees that it's most likely the cause of her problems."

I assumed the list of all the things wrong with my beautiful baby would continue if I didn't interrupt him. So I did.

"Yes, I know. I've been told a number of times by the nurses and residents and other doctors and pretty much everyone who comes in here that she has a very large head. But her dad's head is also very big. It's so big that he can't ever find hats to fit him right. And she looks just like her sisters did when they were babies."

"But her sisters don't have low tone and feeding problems." He didn't look up at me. He removed his stethoscope from the physician's bag and placed it over Jade's heart, listening for more abnormal findings to devour her with.

I wanted to delay the inevitable with a hearty conversation about all the reasons he was wrong. That what he was saying had nothing to do with Jade's problems. But I knew I couldn't argue with one of the smartest men I had ever met. He knew far more about these things than I did, so I surrendered to Dr. Miller's knowledge and experience and cowered. I was silent. Passive. Submissive. I just listened.

"We think she may have Niemann Pick Type C Syndrome. This is an unusually rare, inherited disease of inborn metabolism that may be causing the absent myelination of the white matter of her brain. Niemann Pick is always fatal."

I had never heard of Niemann Pick Type C Syndrome. I didn't know what that meant. But I did know what *fatal* meant. My head and my heart spun in a daytime nightmare I was powerless to stop.

Jade had a fatal disease.

I was nauseous. I inhaled fast, shallow breaths that did not fill my lungs and left me dizzy, holding onto the rails of Jade's hospital bed. I didn't know anything about the death sentence we had been handed.

"What does this mean for Jade?"

Dr. Miller took a deep breath. Another tragic prognosis was about to be delivered. I understood why it was easier for him to detach and remain clinical. To not think of Jade as someone's baby. I understood that it was easier to sleep at night if he didn't allow himself to see the humanness in front of him. That she had six sisters and a brother who couldn't wait for her to come home. A mother and father who loved her very much. Grandparents and aunts and uncles who checked on her every day. I also shared heartbreaking news with patients at times. This was the worst part of the job. I understood.

"If this is, in fact, Niemann Pick, Jade will unfortunately never walk. She will never talk. She will never eat on her own. Niemann Pick is a progressively degenerative disease. You understand this, right? It doesn't improve over time." He paused, and then said, "If she has Niemann Pick or any other metabolic storage disorder, she will probably not see her third birthday, definitely not her fourth." He continued with a medical explanation of what a disease of inborn metabolism meant. How I would one day, too soon, be planning my daughter's funeral.

"You should focus on making her life comfortable."

His scythe sliced right through me. I heard nothing else except a pitiful mother somewhere in the room weeping uncontrollably. I could only stare at the unusual space between Jade's toes while I stood over her. I cupped her head in the palm of my hand. She looked up at me, unaware she had just been sentenced to death. Tears flowed from my eyes and fell onto her cheeks. Dr. Miller's trench coat strangely made sense. I understood why he wore it on a sunny June morning. I understood how it protected him mostly from the tears and not the rain. I understood how it insulated his heart from the truth of the profession he had chosen. I understood his coat might be the only way he could perform his job and not drag a day's worth of death to his own family. It wasn't a coat at all. It was a shield. I understood I was not the first parent to hear those words come from his mouth, and I would not be the last.

But there was so much I didn't understand. I didn't understand where God was. I didn't understand why I was still waiting for Jesus to help us. Why He hadn't performed one of those miracles I heard about in Sunday school. Why He wouldn't heal my baby. Why He didn't show up then or any of the days before. All I could do was hover over Jade and protect her from the Grim Reaper and wonder why I was still alone.

"Do you have any questions before I go?" Dr. Miller gathered the physician's bag and returned his stethoscope inside. There were other patients waiting for the Grim Reaper.

I had questions. I had a lot of questions. But none that Dr. Miller would be able to answer. There was a vise on my throat when I responded. I could only produce three intelligible words.

"Not right now."

I was small. Defeated. I stood in a space somewhere between unconscious and almost dead. I wanted to know why. Why would God save Jade when I was pregnant with her just to take her from me? Why would He give her siblings a baby sister they loved so much just so they would have to say goodbye to her? Why would He force me to endure the most painful tragedy a mother could face? Why would I have to watch my daughter die an agonizing, slow death? Why would He give her such a short life with no triumphs?

There would be no first steps. Jade would never tell me she loved me. I would never push her on the swings or teach her to tie her own shoes. She would never be a rebellious teenager and sneak out at night or break curfew. I wouldn't experience the joy of watching her become a woman or a wife or a mother. She would never have children who would call her Mama or me Grandma.

Her destiny was handed to me by a man dressed head to toe in black who held an invisible scythe . . . the Grim Reaper posing as a physician.

I had no screams left in me. I could barely breathe. Dr. Miller turned and walked out the door, a physician's bag in one old, frail hand and a bloody scythe in the other. All I saw was the personification of death. I couldn't see past it. I couldn't see the man who gave the best years of his life to the sickest of children. I couldn't see that his heart hid deep inside his chest, protected from the tragedies of his career. How else could he deliver that kind of news to unsuspecting families day after day?

I stood alone for what seemed like hours stroking Jade's curls— until the silence of my wandering thoughts was abruptly drowned out by screams of agony from a room down the hall. A young father with a new baby boy had also met the Grim Reaper.

"No! No! I don't believe you! You're wrong! You're a liar. That's my son! That's my only son!" The Grim Reaper had struck again. So soon. Even before my own tears stopped falling.

Todd and I joined a constellation of broken, beaten, and battered parents who were handed a fight none of us would win. I was alone in a hospital room with my baby and an interrupted silence. Unable to think any rational thought. Unable to speak a single word. I heard nothing but a screaming father and my own gasps. I was a dying fish flopping around on a desolate shoreline. My heart continued to beat mercilessly while I willed it to simply . . . stop.

There was nothing I could do, and there was nothing I could control.

I had only the power to hold Jade's head in my trembling hand. To run my fingers through her perfect curls. To stare through tears at the deceitfulness of her perfection. To feel the weight of burdens tied around my neck that I carried everywhere I went. To know the evil I had spoken was a curse that followed me everywhere. Stalking me every day until it was time to attack. When it would damage me most. I had done something that was so wrong, so cruel, so unimaginable, and so unforgivable that I would receive exactly what I deserved. And the price I would pay was in a currency I could not fathom or afford.

My daughter's life.

16

A Bird and a Banshee

The Grim Reaper's scythe penetrated my heart and left me for dead. I was alone in a world I didn't know how to navigate with a baby who needed extraordinary care every day until she died. I was terrified. Drenched in blood and fear. The answers we got were life-ending. For both Jade and me. I couldn't live on this earth without her.

Our stay at The Pediatric Hospital wasn't over yet.

I stood guard over Jade while she endured a barrage of tests and evaluations meant to give us a complete diagnosis. Everything Jade was going through was my fault. My unholy, cursed prayer gave her a death sentence. I deserved anything I got. I deserved to sit in the filth of a dilapidated hospital that was about to be torn down. I deserved relentless days and nights with no clear beginning or end. I deserved to bleed to death at the hands of the Grim Reaper.

But she didn't.

No baby did. Especially not Jade. So I stayed there with her. I hovered over her. I fiercely protected her. It was all I could do if the Grim Reaper or his proxies showed up at our door again.

And they did show up. Right on schedule. Every day.

Every morning brought a new round of residents and specialists with a new plan for what would be done next to Jade. They were intent on identifying every last thing wrong with her just like the Grim Reaper. There was no consideration for the pain they put her through. Every day was grueling. More blood tests. Ultrasounds. Tests that brought screams but no answers.

There was a daily discussion about surgery. The bitter end I fought so hard against came far sooner than I expected. Jade couldn't keep the NG tube any longer. It wasn't safe. It was a nuisance. It came out often—just like Lilly's did. She developed an aversion to anything near her face or nose, and the NG tube made it worse. She threw up with the smallest facial threat. She arched her back and gagged when I tried to breastfeed her. She cried and pushed away from me. It broke me more. The heavy burdens of Jade's struggles were mine to carry. They were bigger and more powerful than anything I had ever been faced with. And they were all my fault. Nothing was getting easier or better. Every day was more unbearable. The load was a massive weight to carry for a woman who was skin and bones.

A difficult and dreaded conversation with the surgeon was imminent. I didn't know how to talk about cutting my baby open. I didn't know how to consent to something that would hurt Jade so much. I didn't know how to endure such gut-wrenching anxiety. I had to learn to accept the future and a journey that would be far shorter than I expected.

Jade's nurse let Todd and me know the gastrointestinal surgeon was on his way. There was nothing I could do to stop what was coming next. Dr. Daniel flew into the room with an authoritative presence that intimidated and overwhelmed me. He was sharp and rushed. He moved quickly and purposefully. We were a pit stop on his way to somewhere more important. Dr. Daniel introduced himself to the new family who had just moved into our shared room. When he realized their baby wasn't Jade, he was irritated. Too proud to be embarrassed, he took offense to himself and directed his agitation at us. His words were sharp and frigid.

"Hello, are you Jade's parents?" Dr. Daniel snapped the blue privacy curtain closed that separated us from our new roommate.

"Yes, we are. I'm Todd. This is my wife, Angie. And this is little Jade."

Dr. Daniel poised himself over the three of us like a buzzard. The family sharing our room was within earshot of everything he was about to say. I hadn't even had time to talk to them or get their names or find out why their baby was in the hospital. I looked at the curtain separating our family from theirs. A pair of brown women's sandals stood close to our side. They were listening. They would hear the surgical plan for Jade at the same time we did.

"My name is Dr. Daniel, and I'm a pediatric gastrointestinal surgeon. I received an order to place Jade's G-Tube, and I want to know if this is what you have decided." Dr. Daniel continued to read from a scripted presurgery checklist without pausing to hear my response. "This meeting is a surgery consultation. I will take Jade for surgical placement of a gastrostomy tube tomorrow afternoon at 4 p.m. Dr. Miller has also requested a biopsy of her liver and one of her spleen since they are both enlarged. She can have nothing to eat after 8 a.m. The procedure will last about an hour, and then she will stay overnight here at the hospital to ensure that she tolerates the surgery. One of the surgical residents will follow her case when she gets out of the PACU. She may require pain medicine because some babies have a difficult time with this surgery. Scott, will you be staying at the hospital with Angie and Jade?" Dr. Daniel caught his breath and checked fifteen boxes on the surgical consent.

"Yes, I will be here." Todd didn't correct Dr. Daniel or interrupt his long-winded monologue.

Dr. Daniel continued to discuss the checklist and cover the risks of the surgery and anesthesia. It was all too normal for him. He rattled off the checklist like it was commonplace to put a hole in my baby's abdomen. He didn't skip a beat when he got Todd's name wrong. He was emotionless. Jade would be just another patient. I spoke up above the intimidation I felt.

"I know you've done many, many of these surgeries. But I'm asking you, please. Please treat Jade as if she were your own daughter."

Dr. Daniel rolled his eyes, signed the surgical consent, then shoved the clipboard toward me so I could sign it too. He was offended again.

"I treat every patient the same."

He could have lied and made me feel like Jade was special. Like he would treat her with the same care he'd give his own child. But he didn't. His words were cold. He was in a hurry. Jade was just like every other baby to him. He would puncture her abdomen and place a permanent feeding tube in her stomach like he had thousands of times before. Jade was no different from the others. He snatched the clipboard from my fingers and spun around disgusted by my offensive request. He ignored the family on the other side of the thin blue curtain and walked out. There was no time for questions. No time for anything but anxiety.

"I don't think I like him so much." Todd didn't usually volunteer criticism about doctors.

"Me either, Scott."

We had to prepare for a surgery that would keep Jade alive until her brain and body wore out from the pressure of a metabolic disease that would kill her. The irony was incomprehensible.

The next day came far too soon. From 8 a.m. until 4 p.m., Jade was starved in preparation for surgery. There was no use for the NG tube anymore. So I pulled the long, thin tube out of Jade's left nostril and removed the tape from her cheek. I took a picture of Jade's face without the NG tube. Then I took a picture of her wearing only her diaper. Her abdomen was perfect. No penetrations. No scars. It was the last time I would see my daughter without a reminder of those days for the rest of her life. However long that would be. By noon, the hunger pangs were more than Jade could handle. She wasn't used to an empty belly. By 12:30, I cried with her. I spent the afternoon soothing her as best as I could. Bouncing and rocking her. Distracting her from the hunger pangs. But I was a failure. Again. All my attempts to comfort her were worthless.

A technician dressed in green scrubs and a blue mask and hat appeared at the door an hour late. He pushed a surgical bed through the door. He was ready to take Jade from us.

"I'm sorry. Dr. Daniel is running behind. I'm here to take Jade to surgery."

I couldn't let him take her. I begged him to let us walk beside Jade as far as we could go. I followed alongside her rolling bed and held her tiny hand in my own. Todd looked shaken like I was. I leaned down and whispered in her ear.

"Mommy and Daddy love you, Jadey. Everything is going to be all right. We love you so much. So much, Sweetie."

"This is it, folks. You can't go past that red line."

I kissed Jade on the forehead. She looked at me as if to ask why I wasn't going with her. I promised her in The Fishbowl I wouldn't ever leave her again. My gut ached. Then I gave my daughter to a stranger in surgical scrubs, knowing a callous but competent surgeon would be the next person to have his hands and a scalpel on her. I watched Jade disappear down the long, sterile hall. It was more than I could take. I collapsed in Todd's arms and sobbed, desperate for Jade to return safely to us.

Todd and I were led to the surgical waiting room and told to stay there until someone came for us. Jade hadn't been out of my reach since our time in The Fishbowl, except when I showered in the sludge of the family shower room. I was afraid I would lose her. I couldn't imagine my life without Jade. I didn't know what I would do if she didn't return to me from that operating room. It would be more than I could bear. I paced inside the waiting room like a bird in a cage. Dr. Daniel was cutting into my baby's abdomen and liver just on the other side of the waiting room wall. I was desperate. So desperate that I again turned to God. Even after I had given up on Him like He had given up on me. I didn't know what else to do. I was scared and angry. Lost and alone. So I prayed. And I hoped God hadn't really given up on me.

Two agonizing hours of birdcage pacing passed. I was frantic to get to Jade. It was taking longer than I expected. *Oh God! Is she OK?* I sat in the corner and sobbed while Todd held his face in his hands. Moments later, the same young man in green scrubs appeared at the door and escorted us to the PACU to see Jade. I rushed to her and scooped her up close to me. I climbed into the bed with her and held her in tearful, cleansing gratitude for her life. A large, white surgical dressing covered the imperfection she had in her lower abdomen, and orange betadine solution was still smeared across her torso. She was restless and in pain. She cried a shrill, heartbreaking sound unlike any I had ever heard from her.

"Can you give her something for pain? Please?" Jade's PACU nurse busied herself charting and didn't seem to notice her cries.

"We just gave her some Tylenol, but I will see if I can give her something stronger." She let the door close behind her.

"Tylenol? Freaking Tylenol? They're giving her freaking Tylenol for pain?" I was ready to release wrath on someone.

The nurse returned with a syringe of liquid and pushed it through Jade's IV. Morphine. She immediately calmed down and then fell asleep in my arms.

An hour later, Jade was moved back to her hospital room where a new post-op surgical patient had replaced the family from the day before. He was a two-year-old who had just had a tonsillectomy. And he was in pain.

Todd and I heard his screams from around the corner as we approached the nurse's station with Jade. The staff appeared overwhelmed by the intensity of the cries coming from our room. The room we had stayed in for five days. We weren't offered the option to move into a different room because the unit was full. We had no choice but to stay with a screaming toddler. There was no way to keep Jade comfortable in a shared room. We were separated only by the thin blue curtain. I didn't know how I was supposed to calm my infant when the volume of screams right beside us ricocheted from wall to wall. I didn't know how I was going to keep it together under the worst of circumstances. I pleaded with the charge nurse to move us somewhere else. Anywhere else. But we were confined to a shared space with a two-year-old screech owl for the rest of the night.

Jade whimpered in pain while I sat in her bed holding her. The one dose of morphine wore off. Tylenol didn't work. The nursing staff was reluctant to give her anything else. They tried to convince me she wasn't in much pain despite what I knew as a mother and a pediatric nurse. They refused to help her. I was shocked by their lack of compassion. The screech owl in the room with us continued to scream in sporadic cycles. I had no sympathy for him after four hours of random outbursts.

The cycle went on for hours. Jade would fall asleep. There would be ten minutes of silence. Just enough time for her to relax and feel safe again in my arms. Then from nowhere, the screech owl would scream into the darkness and jolt Jade from sleep. Jade's pain multiplied every time. She would startle awake and writhe in pain again. I tried to comfort and calm her. I covered her ears with my hands to protect her from the unpredictable squeals on the other side of the curtain. But it didn't work. It seemed the cycle would never end.

I couldn't put Jade down. I couldn't pump. I couldn't move. My shirt was soaked with sour breast milk. My rock-hard breasts cried out from the pain of not pumping on schedule. They continued to grow fuller and harder every time Jade cried and moved in my arms. I was wrecked. Jade was wrecked. I felt no compassion for anyone but her. Definitely not the banshee beside us who triggered my daughter's pain. Everything hurt Jade. I called her nurse every hour through the night. Just before sunrise, after no sleep, no pumping, and nerves that were shredded by our roommate, I hit a brick wall.

"I have freaking had it. Give me that nurse button. I am done with this. Someone is going to do something for Jade, or I'm going to lose it." Todd sat straight up. He knew. Todd reluctantly handed over the call light then sunk back into the couch. I held the device in my palm like a hand grenade and pushed the button repeatedly with my thumb. I gently juggled Jade in the crook of my other arm, trying not to cause her any further pain. I could tell Todd knew this was not going to end well and begged me to hold my tongue.

"Don't go off on her, Angie. Don't lose it on that nurse when she comes in. Don't get kicked out of here. Please."

"Oh, don't you worry about anything, Todd. I've got this handled." He could barely hear me over the screams on the other side of the curtain.

A nurse I didn't recognize walked to our side of the room.

"Can I help you?"

"Uh, yes. I hope you can help me. I have been trying for eight hours to get Jade something stronger for her pain. Every time she falls asleep, the little boy on the other side of the curtain starts crying and startles her. See. She has tears running down her cheeks. She's hurting. Why can't someone contact the resident on-call and get another dose of morphine? I don't understand why she is being ignored. Can you help us? Because if you don't, I'm going to call the GI clinic on-call line and wake up Dr. Daniel." I wasn't taking no for an answer. The nurse had better make that call or I would share the hell I was living in with everyone around us. Including the screech owl and his parents.

"Oh, of course. I can call Dr. Bantam. Oh yes, I can see she's in a lot of pain. I'm so sorry. I will get an order and come back with something for her."

I was angry. I had waited too long for Jade to get help. After she suffered through the entire night in extreme pain, a nurse who wasn't assigned to us was finally doing something. Not even fifteen minutes later, the same angel nurse returned to the room and pushed a small amount of morphine through Jade's IV. She settled deep into my arms and closed her eyes. Her body was no longer tense and rigid. I was so grateful that I cried.

"Thank you. Thank you so much for helping my baby." I felt a moment of peace, knowing Jade finally wasn't in pain.

As the nurse turned to leave, the door to our room opened on the other side of the blue curtain. Six loud, assertive thuds walked toward us. A young, disheveled man in army green hospital scrubs appeared in the dim lights at the foot of Jade's bed. He clearly had been woken up by the nurse to get an order for pain medication for Jade. And he was annoyed.

"I'm Dr. Bantam, the surgical resident covering the night shift for Dr. Daniel." He adjusted his glasses, looked at Jade sleeping in a medicated peace in my arms, and then stared back at my face.

"It doesn't look like she's in pain," he cawed. I paused just long enough to organize my thoughts. Todd cocked his head and flinched. He knew what was coming.

You son of a . . . Oh, you did not just say that to me.

This short, almost bald, thirty-something surgical resident at the foot of our bed wasn't even a real surgeon yet. He was not going to get away with speaking to me like that. My hell was about to become a reality for this guy. I teetered between keeping Jade comfortable and making Dr. Bantam extremely uncomfortable. I was a warrior mother. Dr. Bantam would be sorry.

"Um, what did you say? Hold on. Wait. Wait. What did you say to me? Dr. Bantam is it?" My attack started. He lost his opportunity to flee or retreat. Todd took a deep breath. He knew it was too late. Dr. Bantam would not leave the room without wounds. I was ready for a fight. He would regret going into pediatric medicine when I was done with him.

"Did you say, 'It doesn't look like she's in pain'? No, I'm sure you didn't just say that shit to me. Do you know what we have been through the past five days? No, actually you don't because this is the first time I've seen your face in this godforsaken place. You think those letters in front of your name give you the right to walk into our room and talk to me like that? Let me tell you something, you short, bald, piece of trash. If Jade hadn't just gotten comfortable for the first time since her surgery ten hours ago, I would get out of this bed and kick your ass myself. Do you understand me? Take your short legs and your shiny head and get the hell out of this room. And don't come back." I looked over at Todd. His face was buried in his hands again. He knew I could be harsh but had no idea I was capable of that.

"Be sure to send the freaking social worker and security in here so I can have a few words with them as well," I politely told him before he had a chance to turn and leave. I was careful not to wake

Jade up. She was finally resting from the morphine.

Dr. Bantam backed out of the room in shock, terrified I might resume my attack. He learned a hard lesson about warrior parents that day. He would forever see my face perched at the foot of every bed he stood at. He would think twice next time.

Shortly after Dr. Bantam left bruised and humiliated, the screech owl was moved out of our room with no explanation. I was asleep with Jade in my arms when I heard the door close. I probably would have moved my child, too, if I was put in a room with a crazy woman.

Jade slept peacefully on one dose of morphine, and I was able to start feeding her again. But now my freshly pumped breast milk infused through the G-Tube in her abdomen. Eight hours later, Jade was tolerating the pain and her tube feedings. We were discharged from The Pediatric Hospital without even saying hello to the social worker or a security guard. Todd was relieved. I was a little disappointed.

Todd carried Jade in her car seat out the front doors of a hospital we would never return to. A few weeks later, the crumbling building was closed and all the services moved to a brand-new, state-of-the-art building across town. As apprehensive as I was about going home with a baby with extraordinary needs, I couldn't get out of that hell fast enough.

But there was uncertainty for Jade and me. More tests. More pain. More despair that would follow me like the cursed prayer stalking us everywhere we went.

I had to learn how to be the mother of a child with disabilities. I had to learn how to mount an attack again for Jade even when I had no fight left. I had to learn how to walk without stumbling on a road I did not choose.

I had to do the impossible and accept our journey together, no matter how long or how short, before Jade made her way to heaven.

17

Every Beautiful Thing

he girls and The Five waited on the front porch for us as we drove down our bumpy road again. Running as fast as her nubby legs would carry her, Emmie sprinted to the end of the driveway, leaving her sisters in the dust she kicked up beneath her bare feet.

"Baby Jade's home!" Emmie squealed as Todd pulled into the driveway. "Mommy! I missed you, Mommy!" Emmie ran beside the car as we approached the garage. She was wearing her blue gown. Her blonde curls were in a deep mat on the back of her head. She giggled and jumped up and down when I opened the door and let her climb onto my lap.

"I missed you too, Em. I love you, Sweets." I stared at Emmie and how perfect she was with her matted curls and tattered gown. I pulled her in close to me. I didn't want to let go. She was so healthy. So normal. I was grateful for the beautiful Xanadu Gray of almost all my children. But my hug was too long so she pulled away from me and climbed over the console toward Todd. Faith followed Emmie into the car and told me in rapid-fire excitement about her week with Mom and Becky.

"We made cookies, and we went for walks. Then Becky brought us home, and we saw a baby rattlesnake! A baby rattlesnake, Mommy! We stayed up late and watched movies and Nana even braided my hair! Becky's kind of a jerk, but I love Nana so much!" Faith was unfazed by my absence. I was relieved. Especially because she celebrated her sixth birthday while we were away at the hospital. Another day and celebration I missed to take care of Jade. They all got along just fine without me.

The tweens ran to the car behind Emmie and Faith to see Jade. They didn't cry out for me. I was invisible. Their pain changed them. They were feeling what I felt. They, too, were confused and sad. They didn't even know how sick Jade was. They just behaved how children do when a family succumbs to tragedy. When a mother is suddenly distracted by heavy burdens she must carry. When children grow up overnight because everything in their world has gone awry. I was about to break under the weight of the guilt I held on my shoulders. Not just for causing Jade's problems but for being the reason my children were in pain. The tectonic plates continued to collide. I was metamorphosing into someone or something I didn't recognize.

Mom appeared at the front door and made her way to the car behind the girls while The Five trailed close to their feet. She knew I would notice the blue gown.

"I took it off her once while she was asleep so I could wash it, but she woke up mad that she wasn't wearing it. So I had to put it back on her. How are you doing, Honey? How is Jade feeling? You look real tired. Are you OK?"

"I don't know, Mom." I climbed out of the car and put my arms around her. "I don't know how I'm going to do this. I'm in a really bad place." I sobbed in her arms. But I didn't want the girls to see me break down. So I choked back my tears to spare them from what I was hiding.

I was falling apart. Every beautiful thing I treasured was gone. I didn't know how to walk on a road that ended at Jade's grave. I didn't know how to prepare for her death. I didn't know how to live in a world with this kind of grim reality. My life was dark and cruel. The blackness of depression seeped from every pore in my skin. Nothing could stop it. Nothing could change it. Nothing could prepare me for the days that followed the hospital stay from hell.

Todd and I were happy to put The Pediatric Hospital behind us. But we hadn't processed a fatal diagnosis for Jade. We had to focus on getting her through the surgery and keeping her alive. The enormity of our time in the inpatient unit didn't hit us until days later.

Our home was a place I no longer felt even a little comfort. Everything was different. We were all changed. Adjusting to a new life with a medically fragile baby catapulted us into a dark abyss. We coped in our own ways. My way was to hide the truth from my daughters and let depression sink its talons into me. Todd's way was to detach and busy himself with anything he could. The girls didn't have their own ways to cope. They were just angry. Too young to understand what they felt and why. They didn't know I met with the Grim Reaper or that their baby sister was going to die. I couldn't bear to break their hearts like mine had been broken. The evil truth would remain a secret for as long as I could hide it from them.

I had to be strong.

I had to conceal the truth.

I had to wear a mask of bravery to shield them from the same pain that was destroying me.

"Oh, Angie. I'm sorry, Honey. My prayer group at church is praying for you. Everyone I know has been asking about you and Jade. I tell them to pray for healing. To pray for Jade." Mom paused while I wiped my face clean of salty tears that ran down my cheeks. "Are you gonna be OK if I go home now?" Her Southern twang felt like a slice of calm. I didn't want her to leave. But she had to. I was a child again. All I wanted was my mom. I felt a gut punch when I thought about taking care of the girls while I also took care of Jade.

"I'll be OK, Mom. I don't have any choice." I picked Jade up in her car seat. "I just don't understand why God did this to us. Why He did this to Jade."

"Oh, Honey. God didn't do this. He loves you, and He is here with you." Mom tried to reassure me, but I was losing myself to the darkness. Sinking deep into depression.

It didn't feel like God was there with me. I was alone. Overwhelmed. Abandoned. Beat up and beat down. The darkness closed in on me with every breath I took. I didn't remember what it was like to have hope. Everything good was taken from me. I had nothing to look forward to. Jade was going to die. And I was going to die too.

Emmie clung to Mom's legs and cried like she usually did when Mom left. Todd pried Emmie off, and Mom drove away. I missed her before she even got to the stop sign. She didn't want to leave. None of us wanted her to leave. Especially me.

The girls snuggled with The Five on the front porch while we unloaded the car. It was their favorite thing to do. While they comforted themselves with their cats, I carried Jade up the sidewalk and through the front door. Todd carried in all the new medical equipment Jade would need. A feeding pump. A pole to hang it on. Feeding bags and spare parts. Everyone was doing their best. But I was numb. Exhausted. I passed by the girls like a zombie. Then I disappeared through the doorway into the home Jade and I would die in.

I was forced to live a life I didn't want. A life I hated. I tried to settle in, but nothing was the same. Not for me. Not for Todd. Not for my children. Jade had no myelination of the white matter of her brain. It caused her nervous system to misfire constantly, like a spark plug out of sync with its engine. Even the touch of my hand on her bare skin caused her to gag, wretch, and vomit. My arms were a torture chamber for her. I had to prop her on a pillow that deprived us both of requisite human touch. It was the most cruel punishment for a mother who was starving to hold her baby girl.

The endless days in hell passed by like a weeping eternity. One day flowed into the next on repeat. I turned our small office near the living room into a makeshift hospital room so it would be easier to take care of Jade. It was the place that became my dungeon. The room was stocked full of her medical equipment and baby supplies, my breast pump and breast milk bottles. The few hours I slept were on a twin-size bed Todd reluctantly bought me. He wanted things to be normal. He didn't want me to be confined to a self-made dungeon with Jade. I just wanted somewhere to go with Jade where we could die together. I spent every day and every night doing the same thing. Providing extraordinary medical care to a baby who would die.

There were no breaks. Except when I dozed off pumping in the middle of the night. Accidental moments when I closed my eyes and awoke an hour later to the vacuum sound of a breast pump sucking bruises on me. I would fall asleep sitting up as my head cocked sideways on my shoulder while my hands stayed cupped around the funnels extracting milk from my tired breasts. Then I would jerk awake while my eyes popped open to see nothing in the darkness except the hell I lived in. I didn't know when one day ended and the next began. I lost track of which day of the week and which month it was. Every night I laid in the twin bed wishing I could hold Jade close to me. Just once. I wished I would be given one night to cuddle with Jade while she fussed and nursed and then fell back asleep in my arms. I cried over all I was missing out on. All Jade was missing out on. My touch was an enemy to her. One wrong move would make her throw up all the precious milk I carefully fed into her belly. I longed to touch her. Not just to move her from room to room on her pillow. Or change her diaper or clothes. But to touch her. To stroke her skin with my fingers. To relish in her. To bring her close to my chest and marvel at her under the glimmer of the stars peeking into our room. To snuggle with Jade like the girls did with The Five and like I did with each one of my other babies.

But every beautiful thing, no matter how big or how small, was stolen from me. Every. Single. Thing.

I couldn't take much more.

The small reprieves weren't enough to distract me from the truth of our lives. The moments in the middle of the night. The quiet when everyone was asleep but me. The space where I cried for all that was lost in the darkness of our room every night. I cried for the girls. I cried for Becky and AJ. I cried for myself and Todd.

But I wept bitterly for Jade.

I was slipping into a dark dungeon I might never climb out of.

Every morning, I cursed the sun as it rose over a field of dry, yellow stalks of grass and cracked its light into our room. Every passing day was a day closer to losing Jade forever. There was no solace when the sun came up.

It was my battle to fight. Inside me and around me. Relentless. Cruel. Unending. Before I knew it, ninety-two consecutive sunrises had interrupted my darkness. It was the peak of summer. Jade was almost three months old. She wasn't improving. Everything that had happened since she was born was a blur. I remembered only one thing clearly.

Jade was going to die.

Those were the worst days. The ones I could scarcely remember. It was when Becky grew bigger and bigger at the waist. She was due to deliver my grandson in the middle of those days, and she went into labor right on time the third week of July. I missed the last trimester of her pregnancy while I took Jade back and forth to the hospital. I couldn't remember if I even put my hands on Becky's belly or ever felt her baby kick. But I refused to miss his birth. It would be the light in the darkness of my life.

So when the call came that Becky was ready to deliver, I left Jade with Todd for the first time to stand beside my oldest daughter while she made me a grandmother. I was overwhelmed with excitement to be there with Becky. As she pushed her son into the world, I marveled at her strength, and in one breathless instant, I watched a child become a mother. Then I held my grandson in my arms the way I couldn't hold Jade. I was overcome with anxiety when I thought about him being afflicted with the same disorder Jade was born with. But I breathed lighter when he let out a robust cry that reassured me he was healthy. He was strong and loud. Xanadu Gray. He breastfed just like he should, and I cried as I watched him in Becky's arms. Nursing like all my babies did.

All but Jade.

The adrenaline I felt from my grandson's birth didn't last long. I reached the top of the roller coaster just to be plummeted to the bottom again. Jade still had a fatal prognosis. It was a deep plunge this time. All the way to my marrow deep. I went from the highest peak of watching my grandson born to returning to the lowest valley of hell that I lived every day.

Everyone around me saw it. Everyone, including Becky. She should have celebrated her firstborn instead of worrying about me. Every day someone called to check on me. Mom, Becky, Lynel, Mamaw, Cousin Rich. People who meant everything to me. But most of the time, I ignored the phone and put the people I loved to voicemail. I listened to their messages in the middle of the night while I lay in the twin bed alone and cried about all I had lost. I avoided contact with everyone but Jade. It wasn't until the phone rang when my grandson was a few weeks old that I understood how concerned my family was about me.

It was Dr. Warren's office. I had missed my postpartum visit.

"Hello."

"Angie, this is Leslie. I wanted to call and check on you. Becky came in today, and she's really worried about you." A familiar voice was on the other end of the phone. My midwife. The woman who delivered Jade just over three months earlier. The person I disclosed my foreboding fears to while I was pregnant.

"Becky tells me you're really depressed. She says the whole family is worried, actually, and I see that you missed your six-week follow-up visit." I was angry with Leslie. I didn't want to talk to her. I started to sob.

"I told you something was wrong with my baby. The whole pregnancy I told you. I told everyone. But you all thought I was crazy. Paranoid. And here I am. It's all my fault. I did this. I caused this. I am living in a hell I never could have imagined. Do you know they told me that Jade most likely has a fatal prognosis?"

"Yes, Angie. Becky did tell me that. But this is not your fault. You didn't do anything wrong. I think you should come into the office so I can prescribe something for postpartum depression."

"I'm not taking anything." I snapped back at her. "I don't have postpartum depression! I'm sad. I'm grieving that my daughter is going to die. I'm not taking any medication that's going to numb my pain. I'll be OK. I'm fine. I'll be fine."

Leslie continued to insist that Jade's problems were not my fault.

But I knew the truth. The blame was all mine. I convinced Leslie I was OK and didn't need any medication or therapy. We hung up on my promise that I would call if I needed anything to help me get through the hard time. But I was lying. I didn't intend to call her back. I had masterfully manipulated Leslie so the option to end my hell wasn't taken away from me.

Every beautiful thing in my life was gone. I was alone and abandoned. I failed my children. I failed my husband. I failed myself.

I lost all hope. Jesus was nowhere to be found. I teetered on the brink of taking my own life.

I told Leslie I was OK. I told everyone I was OK.

But I wasn't OK.

Minutes after Leslie and I hung up, I did the only thing I could control and pumped more bottles of breast milk. I stored the extra milk in a deep freezer already full of gallons. There was almost enough to get Jade through another nine months without me.

I closed the freezer door and started planning the escape route from my life.

18

Rescue

$\mathcal{I}$ needed to be saved from a cruel fate. One no parent should endure. I needed a rescue. I needed a hero. I didn't have the strength to keep my face above water on my own anymore. Even if I did, I wouldn't have tried. I had almost completely given up. I was lost in an ocean, miles away from the shoreline. Waiting for the next wave to crash down and finally drown me. The only thing that kept me going was Jade. I knew if anything happened to me there would be nobody who would care for her the way I did, keeping her alive every day. One more minute. One more hour. One more day. It was like running a race without a finish line. It was one I would never win. I walked a tightrope alone. One wrong step. One wrong move, and I would fall to the jagged rocks below.

Todd knew I was nearing a breaking point. He had never seen me so lost. He tried to fill in the gaps where I was absent. But there was only so much he could do while he worked full time. We were struggling financially with Jade's medical bills and on the brink of financial collapse. I understood why he was gone so much. We still had to eat. And pay bills. One of us had to work. He was worried about me, but he didn't know what to do. Todd peeked his head in the doorway of Jade's room while I sat on the edge of the bed pumping.

"Hey, come out here when you're done. I want to talk to you about something." I could barely hear him. He didn't want to wake Jade, and he knew I required almost complete silence in her room. We hardly ever talked about anything anymore. So I finished pumping and tiptoed into the kitchen where he waited for me.

"Hey, what's going on? You want to talk about something?" I set the freshly pumped milk on the counter and screwed on the lids.

"Yeah. Hey, I was thinking. I want to take the girls, all of the girls, away this weekend. I was thinking we could stay up in Cheyenne at Little America, and they could go swimming and just get away and have some fun. What do you think?"

I had to take a moment to understand what he said. I wanted to be sure I heard him correctly.

"You want to take all five of the girls to Cheyenne with you? Is that what you're saying?"

"Yeah. I think it would be good for them to get out. Then you could have a little break from all the noise in the house. You good with that?"

Of course I was good with that. Anything to give my children some sense of normalcy. Anything that would let them be kids and be loud and make messes without fear their mother would shush them or get upset with them. It would be a treat for the girls. They deserved it. They had been through so much already, and I wanted them to have some fun. "Yeah. Sure. That's fine with me. I think it will be good for them too."

I was surprised he noticed how difficult my life was. It would be good for me too. I could rest during the day when I was rarely able to nap. I could try to get more than one or two hours of sleep. The moments of silence before rays of sunlight shined into our dungeon could be extended. I would have no other responsibilities but Jade and pumping. I looked forward to the short trip for them. I looked forward to it for me, and I hoped it would reset my psyche. That it might be the rescue I was waiting for. That I might have a clearer head. That my children would go somewhere and have fun instead of watching me fall prey to the darkness of depression.

Friday came quickly, and the girls were wild with excitement to go on their trip with Todd. I helped them pack their bags between pumping and feeding Jade. Emmie pulled her swimming suit out of the dresser. She insisted on wearing it under her blue gown.

"Look, Mommy! I have a Dory svimming suit! I want to wear it NOW." I was hoping to wash her gown while she was gone, but I didn't have the heart to say no. Small things would have to stay small. Todd would have to deal with the dirty gown she'd worn for forty-three consecutive days without being washed. That's what made Emmie happy during the hardest time of her short life. I couldn't take that away from her for the sake of hygiene. It would have to do.

The girls giggled among themselves and gathered their things for the weekend together. They were happy. I hadn't heard them laugh or seen them smile so much for a long time.

"Mommy!" Faith yelled down the hall while I was helping Emmie. "Where are my flip-flops?"

"Oh, Faith, I have no idea. Just keep looking." Except for trips to the hospital, I had only left the dungeon briefly over the previous several months. I barely ventured upstairs. There was a very good chance Faith's flip-flops were buried somewhere in her closet or stuffed under her bed. I couldn't know for sure. I was an absent parent who provided almost no supervision the past three months.

Finally, everyone was packed and ready to go. Even Faith. She found one flip-flop on the deck and one in the bathroom vanity. I stood on the front porch and waved to the girls as Todd pulled out of the garage. Hope leaned out of the car window and yelled to me.

"I love you, Mom! Take care of the cats for us!" I waved again. Then I took a deep breath. The girls were escaping the darkness of their mother and the prison I created inside our home. They were the lucky ones. I turned and walked through the front door. Back to the darkness. Back to the prison. Back to the vacuum pump that jolted me awake when I accidentally fell asleep in the middle of the night.

My first evening alone in the house without my family was eerily quiet. No arguments over the last Dr Pepper. No screaming about which channel to watch on TV. No slamming doors or stomping feet. The quiet was good. I ventured onto the deck alone to watch the sun go down over the tall, yellow grass as it waved to me in the gentle breeze. The Five joined me to watch the sunset. I kneeled down to pet Sasha as she rubbed her full, firm belly across my leg. I hadn't really looked at The Five for several months. A glance here and there, perhaps. But I had bigger things to tend to. Three of our cats were females. And all three of them were pregnant. Big pregnant. Due any moment pregnant. In the midst of my darkness, their expanding abdomens hadn't caught my attention. I didn't know whether to laugh or cry. I couldn't believe we would soon have three litters of kittens to tend to. The girls would be elated. But the thought of having twenty or more cats at one time was overwhelming. I tried to smile, but I didn't have the energy to be moved to emotion by a bunch of cats. I just wanted to enjoy the sunset. Not drown in kittens.

I left The Five on the deck and returned to my dungeon with Jade. She slept peacefully propped on her pillow. I sat on the bed and pumped milk in the fading light of a sun that had gone behind the mountains. My phone buzzed with a message from Todd.

"Made it to Cheyenne. The girls are having a great time. Try to rest." I decided to break the news to him.

"Clear your head while you're gone. I have a surprise for you when you get home. We have three pregnant cats." I waited to see his response and how he would feel about more freaking cats.

"You've got to be kidding me. Unbelievable. Things could be worse." He did it again. Telling me things could be worse.

"Todd! Stop saying that. Every time you do, things do get worse. Just stop already." I shot a quick message chastising him.

I took a deep breath, finished pumping, and poured fresh milk into Jade's feeding bag. I gave myself permission to skip one pumping. I could get almost four straight hours of sleep that way. It would be the longest I had slept in more than three months. I forgot what it felt like to sleep long enough to dream. I set my alarm for 2 a.m. and laid my head on my pillow. Then I closed my eyes in anticipation of a refreshing, deep, four-hour sleep. I just wanted to feel rested again.

Two hours later, I was startled awake when my phone rang. I didn't recognize the number, so I ignored the call and closed my eyes. But the number called again. And again and again. After the fourth call, I answered the phone. It was the deep, gruff voice of a police officer. My heart sank.

"This is Detective Cruz with the Greeley Police Department. Is this Angie, AJ's mother?" I sat straight up in bed then moved into the living room so I wouldn't wake Jade.

"Yes, this is Angie. Is AJ OK? What's going on?" I was shaken.

"Ma'am, AJ is at the downtown station. He was evading a law enforcement officer this evening. I need you to come pick him up since he's a minor."

I hadn't talked to AJ in almost a month. I was overwhelmed with everything going on with Jade. He was a teenage boy. Working. Hanging out with his friends. Doing teenage boy things. He was spared from watching me battle with depression every day. He was able to live a normal life at his dad's house.

But he needed me. Right then. He needed me like when he was a little boy and fell off his bike. It was me whom he ran to when he was hurt. It was me who knelt down to comfort him. It was me who was there for him.

He finally reached out to me for help.

But I couldn't help him this time.

"Detective Cruz, have you called his dad? AJ lives with him now. I'm at home alone with a new baby who is medically fragile. I can't get her out in the middle of the night. I have nobody to help me."

"AJ's father is out of town, apparently. He has no one to come get him. I will let AJ know he will have to stay the night at the station until someone can pick him up."

"No, wait! Can I talk to him? Let me talk to my son. I want to talk to him."

"I'm sorry, Ma'am. You can't talk to him. He's in a holding cell. You can come pick him up. But that's it." The phone disconnected, and I didn't hear my son's voice.

It was midnight. I was alone with Jade. There was no one I could call to help my son. Mom slept with her phone turned off. Todd was in another state with the girls. Becky had a newborn at home. The darkness overcame me again in a dramatic eclipse of reality that plunged deep into my heart.

When my son needed me most, I failed him. I failed him the same way I failed the girls. I failed him the same way I failed Jade. The weight of the darkness returned like an anchor wrapped around my ankles. The waves came crashing down on me. My face slipped under the water. I gave up, and I let myself go under. I couldn't live with letting my only son down like I had everyone else in my life.

It was my breaking point.

There would be no rescue. Nobody showed up to save me. Nobody came to pluck me from a tragedy I never imagined I would be living. Nobody shared the burden of the darkness that penetrated so deep my soul screamed out in agony.

Not even Jesus.

I had thought many times over the previous weeks how my life would end. How I could escape the darkness when it became too much for me to bear.

There was a plan.

I loved Jade too much to take her with me. I had to leave the darkness alone. My family's absence provided my first opportunity to flee from my hell and not be stopped. With this last failure of my life on the tips of my fingers, it was time to execute my well-designed plan.

I dried my eyes and sat calmly on the edge of the bed in Jade's room. I changed my bra and underwear. I put on lipstick and eyeliner. I pumped until there was no milk dripping into the bottles. I pulled my hair up into a tight bun and found the key to the car parked in the garage. Then I hovered over Jade where she lay asleep and filled her feeding bag full of fresh, warm milk.

I was leaving her. She would join me when Niemann Pick or some other evil diagnosis took her. But for now, we would be separated. Separated until it was her time to leave this earth, too. I stared at the perfection of her face and her hands. I ran each of her dark curls through my fingers. They were the only parts of her I could touch without triggering a nervous system reaction. I lowered my face to her head and smelled her. I breathed her in as deeply as I could. Then I whispered into the air.

"I love you, Jadey. Mommy will see you in heaven, my sweet baby girl."

After an aching pause and final look over my shoulder at the beautiful baby Jesus had forgotten, I left Jade and entered the garage just around the corner from her room. I climbed into the driver's seat of my car and put the key in the ignition. My hands trembled on the steering wheel. I remembered my plan.

Start the car. Fall asleep. Wake up in heaven. Ask Jesus why he abandoned me.

I was so lost in my own grief I didn't comprehend that my well-designed plan would end up killing Jade too. It didn't even occur to me that leaving her would be a certain and swift death sentence. She was alone. Todd was gone. The girls were gone. I would soon be gone. Jade wouldn't be able to survive until someone noticed I was dead.

I didn't realize or care to consider I had designed a murder-suicide.

I moved my right hand to the key still in the ignition and grasped it loosely between my thumb and the knuckle of my first finger. All I could think of was Jade. My other seven children. Mom. Todd. The inexplicable pain I would inflict on them if I turned the key. How my last act in the world would devastate them. How they would search until the end of time for the reason I would do such a horrible thing to them. How I would forever alter the course of my children's lives. How I would leave Jade with nobody to care for her. I let go of the key and pounded on the steering wheel. Then I screamed at God again.

"Why? Why have you forsaken me? Why did you leave me? Why are you doing this to me? Why are you doing this to Jade?" I rested my forehead on the steering wheel and started to sob. Big, bellowing sobs that shook my whole body. Then I paused.

"God, please help me," I whispered underneath my breath. "I have nothing left. Nothing."

As I looked up toward the visor, trying to find Jesus in the air above me, something drifted to my lap. It was the photo Becky had taken in the hospital the day Jade was born.

My paper salvation.

Todd tucked it there for me to see every time I drove Jade anywhere. It was taken before The Fishbowl. Before the Grim Reaper. Before Dr. Daniel. It was a picture of innocence stolen. Of the calm before our storm. Of a mother surrounded by children who needed her more than anything. And in the middle of the photo . . . was Jade. She was lying on my chest. Resting her head near my heart as she unknowingly prepared for the fight of her life.

With me.

I was the one who was supposed to carry Jade on this road. To love her. To care for her. To cry for her. To be there for her during her last days. Only me. Nobody would take care of her the way I would. I couldn't leave her.

I snapped back to reality and remembered I left Jade alone in the house. She had never been left without someone in the house for this long. I was frantic.

Jade is alone!

She could be choking or vomiting or crying for me. I was thrown into a panic as I flung the car door wide and hurried to the back door. I fell up the stairs in my rush and sprinted through the living room straight to Jade. I found her awake, squirming and fussing. For me.

"Why did you leave me, Mommy?" If only she could speak, those would be her words.

Tears rained on Jade as I hovered over her. I wanted to pick her up but couldn't. I changed her diaper and made her comfortable on her pillow. I stroked her dark curls again between my fingers. She closed her eyes as I soothed her back to sleep with a lullaby sung in a whisper. Then I promised her that I would be there until the end. I would never leave her again.

I climbed into the bed just as my alarm went off and was reminded that four hours had passed. It was time to pump again. As I gathered my pump supplies, a message beeped on my phone. It was from AJ.

"Mom, I'm sorry. Becky picked me up. It was all a big mistake. I'll call you in the morning. I love you."

I had been rescued just in time. By my children. By God. By a love so strong I could never leave Jade. Not even if it meant returning to the dungeon I tried to escape. I had been rescued. That was all that mattered.

I closed my eyes before the sun permeated Jade's room and reminded me I had barely made it through the night.

19

Bad Things

Morning came, and I was still alive. Nothing had changed. No matter how dark my life became, I still woke up every day. I was confused about why I had been rescued in the garage a few hours earlier, yet Jade had not been. But I was no longer depressed.

Instead, the morning light brought my strongest emotion yet. I didn't even know what to call it. I had been mad before. Mad at Todd. Mad at myself. Mad at God. But this was something else. This wasn't a temporary moment of anger. It was unfettered wrath coiled up inside me like a hissing snake. I was furious that I was alive.

Just over two months had passed since discovering that Jade had no myelination of her white matter. I was angry my life had taken an involuntary detour down a road less traveled on a journey I despised. I was angry about days and nights of endless pumping, tube feedings, vomit, and tears that carved a chasm around my heart so deep no one could get in. I was angry for all the life I had lost. I was a young woman growing old right before everyone's eyes. An exponentially rapid aging that could only be attributed to the hell I was living. Just a few hours had passed since I almost succumbed to one of the darkest moments of my life. When I tried to manage a perfect suicide in my garage. I no longer felt sorry for myself. Instead, I was seething with anger that I had to maneuver in the darkness alone. That I was breathing just enough to experience all the bad things that came with a life God wasn't willing to change.

I sat on the edge of the bed and pumped as the sun glared through the open slats of the blinds. I shielded my face from a ray of sunshine reflecting off the window as it pierced my eyes. Just one more thing to aggravate me first thing in the morning. Jade was content to be in her bassinet propped on a pillow where I tried to protect her from the world. I stared at her beautiful dark curls. I ran them between my fingers as I had done only hours before when I said what I was sure would be my final goodbye to her. I felt a tug of emotions. I was wound tight with anger. But I was also captivated by a baby whom I loved so much. My heart bounced around like a Ping-Pong ball. I had fallen asleep crying. I awoke unnerved. I was angry that my hell resumed in the light of my dungeon. Angry that the sun was so presumptuous to rise on my day. Angry that I was stalked by darkness everywhere I went no matter what I did.

But I wasn't angry at Jade.

Jade was the only person who never made me angry. I was mad at everyone and everything else in my life. But she was the innocent. Unlike me. I had an unusual strength that was shameful but powerful. I could bench-press thousands of pounds of guilt all on my own. I could handle the weight of any shameful strength. So I wondered why God saved me, the guilty, if He wasn't going to save Jade, the innocent. It made no sense. Nothing God did made any sense.

My phone vibrated on the bed next to me. It was a text from AJ. "I just woke up at Becky's. Everything is OK. No charges. Just a misunderstanding. Different blue truck. They thought it was me. I hope you're OK. I love you."

I hadn't even answered his middle-of-the-night text. I didn't know what to say. I didn't want to pummel him with a mood he wasn't responsible for. I didn't go into the garage in the darkness of night because of him. None of it was his fault. Nobody knew my life had almost ended in the garage. I would keep that secret hidden for as long as I could in the abyss within me where all the painful things lived.

"I was worried, Son. I'm glad you're OK. Please, please stay at your dad's tonight and don't go anywhere. Nothing good happens when you're out late on the weekend. Play it safe. I'm sorry I couldn't come last night. I'm so sorry. I love you too."

I didn't get another message from AJ. I was hurt that he didn't respond and got mad again.

I finished pumping and went to the kitchen to put my milk in the refrigerator. There was a thin paperback book on the counter. I hadn't noticed it before Todd and the girls left for Cheyenne. *When Bad Things Happen to Good People*. I didn't know how it had gotten there, but I assumed Todd left it for me to read during the downtime I never got. I read the summary on the back cover and immediately felt my cheeks burn with provocation. The book was about a Jewish rabbi. The father of a young boy who was diagnosed with a degenerative disease and died in his teenage years. I skimmed the first chapter and wondered if Todd thought this would be a good read while he was gone.

Does he think Rabbi Kushner and I have something in common?

I was furious.

I was furious Todd may have thought a book like this would make me feel better about Jade's prognosis. I was furious he was so ignorant and thought I wanted anything to do with accepting my daughter's death. I was furious because Rabbi Kushner actually thought God was not omnipotent to stop evil. The God I learned about from Mom and Sunday school could do anything. Anything. He *chose* to abandon Jade and me. That book and God's choice fueled a rage that was devouring me from the inside out.

The faint sound of Jade fussing in the other room distracted me from my anger and the stupid book Todd left for me. It was about that time of day when her stomach revolted against her G-Tube feeding. When she would throw up everything in her stomach if I didn't intervene fast enough. I returned to the dungeon with a taste of disgust on my lips and a chip on my shoulder.

Why did Todd leave that book for me? Is he just trying to piss me off again?

Jade was writhing in pain when I got to her. I needed to vent her G-Tube and release the built-up gas. I did this many times every day. Most of the time it relieved the pressure and her pain. Sometimes I was too late, and her pain was excruciating. Other times I would attach the syringe and open the stopper on her G-Tube just in time for a volcanic eruption to spew partially digested breast milk all over me.

This day was an *other times* day.

Jade's knees were drawn up tight to her chest. She arched her back and turned her head sharp to her left side. She cried as loud as her weak, floppy vocal cords would allow. Her pain was at its peak. All I wanted was to pick her up and comfort her. To bounce her or rock her like I did all of my other babies. To pat her on the back so she could work the gas up on her own. But I couldn't intervene like a real mother would. If I did, Jade would suffer the most unabated cyclic vomiting episode, and her throat and nose would be scorched by stomach acid. I could only do the one thing that gave her relief. I had to vent the pressure from her stomach. So I hovered over Jade and attached the syringe to her G-Tube while I sang in a whisper over her and tried to console her. I leaned in close to adjust the syringe and unclamp her G-Tube. The pressure inside her stomach released an explosion that splashed my face with sour milk. I could taste her stomach contents in my mouth. I started gagging just as Jade stopped crying.

One day. I just wanted one easy day. That's all.

I was still gagging as I wiped my own breast milk from my face with a blanket. The taste was almost as bad as the taste left in my mouth by the book left to torment me. I got angry again.

Jade was no longer in pain and fell back asleep. I stood over her a while longer and sang her a soft lullaby. Her feeding would have to be restarted and replaced. Most of it was on me. The schedule was disrupted every time she lost a feeding this way. I had stopped crying about these episodes and all the lost milk after the first month. This was just my life. I knew at least half of what I pumped would end up on the floor. Or in a towel. Or on me. It was a cycle I was far too familiar with. It happened every day. Too many times a day.

I reset the feeding pump and decided to take a quick shower for the first time in six days. I looked forward to stepping into the steam to calm the war inside my heart and turn my skin pink. I waited for the water to get hot and looked at myself in the mirror above the sink. Staring back at me was the monster I had tried to escape for months. It had found me in the garage in the middle of the night and was once again tethered securely to my soul. Dueling streaks of silver grew on each side of its head like Lily Munster. Deep-black rings circled its eyes. There wouldn't be enough soap and water to clean the monster from my memory. I craved the chance to spend more than five minutes in a hot shower. I wanted to shave the hair on my legs that had been growing since April. Condition my tangled hair. Feel the water pour over me until I drained every last drop from the hot water heater. Just get clean. But as I grabbed the shaver from the soap dish and made one pass through the jungle of my right leg, I heard Jade's feeding pump alarm. I dashed naked across the house into the dungeon before Jade woke up. My shower was over. I wouldn't wear shorts in the heat of the summer just yet.

I towel dried my hair in the living room and noticed the thin paperback still sitting on the kitchen counter. I skimmed another chapter. Perhaps there was hope lingering somewhere in its pages. But still nothing. Nothing but more rationale for why bad things happen to good people. I was so angry that this book had made its way into my home. I stopped reading and threw it across the living room. It flew through the room and skidded across the kitchen floor. There was no book ever written that would console me about Jade's prognosis. Not a single one. There was nothing anyone could say to dull the sting. There was nobody who could repair Jade's brain. The end would come. It was a certainty. I would have to pick out a casket the size of a dresser drawer, and then I would have to put my baby in it. It was a brutal, uncontrollable truth. Evil at its worst.

There was no peace in the ending we faced. There never would be. God could have turned this thing around any time. But He abandoned us and let us go through hell in a dungeon where I fought to keep my daughter alive just so she would die anyway.

It was cruel.

Resentment flooded my mind, and I found myself in the kitchen. I tore pages out of the book. One by one. Ripping them into tiny pieces. Before I was done, I had violently shredded every page of a book that tried to convince me it was normal for babies to die and that it was normal for God not to help.

I would not accept the lies of a paperback book left for me to read by a fool who was enjoying his weekend away from my hell.

A hailstorm of tiny white pieces of paper lay strewn about the room. I inhaled a satisfaction that strengthened me. My anger gave me muscle. It was all I had to get through every bad thing happening and this cruel fate that Jade and I lived with. I stepped over the pieces of the book and returned to the dungeon to check on Jade. As I sat down on the edge of the bed, my phone buzzed with a message from Todd.

"Hey. The girls are having a blast. I hope you slept good last night. How is Jade?" His text message infuriated me. He had no idea his wife's life almost ended just hours before.

"That's awesome, Todd. I found the stupid book you left on the counter. What were you thinking? Bad idea."

He didn't respond. The battle was better fought when he returned home. For now it was best to leave well enough alone. He was wise when he chose to be.

I spent the rest of the weekend doing what I did every day. The only difference was the darkness of the dungeon didn't feel so depressing anymore. It just made me angry. I was fueled by that anger. A banging drum of hostility. I was pushed forward by a new force. The heat and pressure and tectonic movement ravaged me. The metamorphosis changed my heart again. I used to be beautiful. Like a butterfly. Now I was an ugly brown pupa. I didn't care about anything or anyone anymore except my children. I didn't care who thought I was ugly, mean, or angry.

I found my superpower.

I left the torn-up pieces of a remnant paperback book scattered throughout the kitchen for Todd to clean up. He had a penchant for cleanliness and an organized house. This would sting.

My quiet weekend with Jade vaporized into an inventory of bad things written by an angry woman. Two days that should have been my solace were nothing more than a distraction from the inevitable. I didn't sleep more. I didn't take a long, hot shower. I didn't shave my legs. And Jade was still going to die.

But there was justice in the mess I left for Todd to clean up. A superpower dig. He drove home rejuvenated after a long, fun weekend with the girls and came home to three million pieces of a torn up paperback book he would regret bringing into our home.

The playing field of bad things was level again.

20

Filthy Hands

The grapevine that entwined through my extended family was well meaning, but I wanted to be left alone. After Cousin Rich heard about Jade's brain MRI and the lethal words of the Grim Reaper, he called every day. But I didn't answer. I didn't want to see him or talk to him. I had treated him horribly when he visited us at the hospital a few months before. I was still ashamed of myself. Rich was a blameless bystander caught in the crossfire of a room I called Hostile Territory. He showed up just in time to catch a glimpse of a world out of control. I was spinning from confusion. Pain. Darkness. Nothing was the same for me after we rushed Jade back to the hospital. The tectonic plate transformation had begun. I would never again be the woman Rich once knew.

My harsh words didn't chase him away for good, though. He stood in the shadows waiting. He prayed for us. He rallied his friends to pray for us. He told anyone he could about Jade and solicited them to pray for us too. When he found out how bleak things were for Jade, he tried to get through to me again. But I was unreachable. Distant from everyone who cared about me. Distant from Mom, who helped me as often as she could. Distant from Lynel, who made sure I knew she was there if I needed her. Distant from Rich, who would just make me mad again. So there was never a good time to take his call, but Rich didn't care. Jade and I were on his mind even as I did my best to ignore him. He wouldn't stop until I answered his call. He was on a quest to help us. To step in when I was weak and crumbling. To do the only thing he knew to do.

Rich rode motorcycles with a group of leather-wearing, Harley-riding, cigarette-smoking Christian men who selflessly volunteered their time with the community and told others about Jesus. I called them Rich's Christian biker gang. They called themselves the Eternal Brothers Ministry. Rich wanted to get us all together and pray over Jade. I just wanted to be left alone in the hell of my life. But Rich was relentless, an annoyance that punctuated my grueling days. I didn't want to talk to him. I didn't answer the phone when he called. I was still angry with Jesus for not showing up to save me from the daily, repeating hell of my life, and I was exhausted with Rich's bothersome attempts to reunite Jesus and me. Most of the time, I easily avoided Rich. But one Sunday afternoon I answered a call from an unknown number, and it was him. I knew immediately I had made a huge mistake.

"Hey, Ang. So I have to hide my number so you'll answer?" He laughed. "The Brothers have been asking about getting together to pray over Jade. We were thinking we could meet at Ray's house in Wellington Saturday since it's not far from you."

I was annoyed. Triggered. I didn't want to be nice, but I tried.

"Hey. Yeah, I'm having a hard time, Richard. I don't know. Jade is so fragile right now, and this whole brain MRI thing has me pretty messed up. We don't know if she's going to start having seizures, and she just got over being sick on top of everything else. I really don't know if it's a good idea to take her out." I hoped Rich would drop it and leave me alone. But that wasn't his personality. He wouldn't stop asking until I gave in. But I really didn't want to waste our time or take any unnecessary chances with Jade.

"Oh, well, that's OK. The Brothers said they could come to your house if you can't make it to Ray's." An awkward silence followed. I didn't know these people. I didn't want them at my house. I didn't know what other motives they might have. But Rich wasn't going to give up.

"It's OK, Richard. We will just come to Wellington Saturday. I'll see you at Ray's." It was the only way I could get him off my back. I relinquished all common sense and conceded. Maybe Rich and his friends knew something none of Jade's specialists did.

Todd cleaned puke off Jade and the couch while I was on the phone. He overheard the call and asked me where we were going Saturday.

"We're going to Ray's. In Wellington. He's one of Richard's friends. I don't want to talk about it. We're going. Maybe he will leave me alone about it now."

Rich finally forced a commitment I wasn't ready to make. We were going to join him and his Christian biker friends and their wives to pray over Jade. Todd shook his head. I understood. I felt the same way. We were thinking the same thing. It was a monumental waste of time. Todd and I found common ground in our doubt. But if it meant Rich would leave me alone, then we would meet him at Ray's. It would be a brief, useless meeting to ask God for a miracle and to get Rich off my back.

Saturday came far sooner than I was ready for. Jade threw up almost every G-Tube feeding that day. She didn't feel good, and she was difficult to settle. I vented her more often to relieve her excruciating stomach pain. Whatever was going on was different. It was new. It was frightening. Dr. Allen told us any changes in her behavior or ability to keep her feedings down should be addressed. But I didn't want to bother Jade's pediatricians on a weekend unless it was urgent. I had the biker group prayer party to attend anyway. So I waited to see if she would get better.

It was one of our hardest days at home yet. One of those days I didn't get a shower. I neglected everyone but Jade, as usual. Including myself. I ate little more than a sandwich and drank a few sips of soda. My clothes hung off me. I was a bag lady in droopy sweatpants. Lost somewhere inside a transformation I had no control over. There was always something to worry about. Always something to fear. Always some new struggle I wasn't prepared for. I didn't know when Jade would take that final turn for the worse. Everything was a threat. Everything was a loss. Loss of freshly pumped milk as it launched like a missile across the room. Loss of months of my life spent pumping I would never get back. Loss of sleep I craved like a drug addict looking for a high. Loss of an unextraordinary life with a typical baby who would grow into a remarkably normal adult. I was disgusted by it all.

We were running late. We had to meet Rich's buddies. I smelled like spoiled breast milk and vomit in clothes I had worn for two days. It was a typical August afternoon in Colorado. More than 100 degrees. I didn't need to dress up. But I didn't want to smell sour around Rich's friends. There was no time to change, and the whole thing was just one more irritation in my burdensome life.

Todd pulled in front of a modular home on a small corner lot lined with tall, mature trees. A chain-link fence surrounded the modular and was guarded by a stocky pitbull on the prowl. A large cottonwood grew in the middle of the small front yard. Underneath the canopy of deep green leaves stood a group of Rich's friends shading themselves from the scorching heat. They were dressed in black leather jackets and boots. Chain smoking. Laughing. A group of cigarette-smoking Christian biker dudes. We were at the right place.

"Are they smoking weed?" I was aggravated. Todd made a U-turn and parked across the street from Ray's modular. At least fifteen Harley Davidson motorcycles were lined up in an impeccable row next to one another. I wasn't impressed.

"I think it's just cigarettes. But what the hell are we doing here? I thought these people were in a Christian group. I didn't know we were coming to a damn biker rally." Todd was frustrated we were there. I was frustrated too. I was angry we left our air-conditioned home to drag Jade out to something so unworthy of our time. She was asleep in her car seat, so I left her in it, and Todd carried it from the car. The day had already been hard. There was no way I could hold Jade without making her throw up again. I hesitated when I stepped out of the car. The pitbull stared at us while it paced back and forth. I wondered which one of us it would eat first. My vote was for Todd.

We walked up to the chain-link fence and waited, trying to decide if we should go through the gate or wait for Rich. I scanned the area for potential dangers for Jade. There were too many to count.

"Maybe this was a bad idea. Let's go back home." It was hot. I was nervous. But as we turned to go to the car, a man walked toward us holding an American Spirit between his fingers. Cigarette smoke wafted in our direction. There was no turning back. The pitbull approached us at the gate, wagging its tail and smiling at us.

"What the? Since when do pitbulls smile?" Todd reached out to unlatch the gate.

"Her name is Connie." Ray perched the cigarette in the corner of his lips and held out his hand for Todd. "You must be Rich's family. This must be Baby Jade. We've heard a lot about you, Peanut."

"Hi. Yes, I'm Angie, and this is my husband, Todd." No last names. Better to keep it simple. I was angry I brought Jade out. Angry I was walking through a plume of cigarette smoke to get to Jesus. Angry He was nowhere to be found in my own air-conditioned home. Shocked that anyone would think He was in a modular house owned by a biker dude named Ray and guarded by his dog, Connie.

Rich roared up on his motorcycle late as usual and parked with the others. He was dressed in all black with that long, thick impressive braid down the middle of his back. I was jealous. I had lost handfuls of my long, curly locks from the stress of Jade's diagnosis and postpartum hormones. There was no fairness in his abundance of hair. I was irritated with Rich. Irritated we were there tiptoeing through cigarette butts and smoke to get to Jesus. It was beneath me. These were not my people.

"Hey, Cousin." Rich greeted us with a smile just below his crooked nose and bushy mustache. Rich and his friends were rough. Their faces were imprinted with hints of the experiences that surrendered them to Jesus. Scars. Deep grooves from years of smoking cigarettes or something else. Tattoos hidden under their leather jackets. Even Rich had a road map of a sordid life on his face. His nose was broken by thieves when he was much younger. He was beaten across the head so brutally with a baseball bat that his jaw was broken and his mouth wired shut for months after. He was left for dead in the middle of a street somewhere in Louisiana. We almost lost him that time. But that was Rich's life before he found Jesus.

"You ready to go in?" Ray motioned toward the modular.

"As ready as we'll ever be." I wanted to turn and run. But we proceeded up the four, splintered, wobbling, wooden steps and went into the living room, leaving the cigarette smokers outside to finish up their last few drags. Connie led us into a small but welcoming home. The kitchen was packed with women who were cooking side dishes for an impromptu barbecue they planned after everyone showed up. The house was filled with the smell of good food. The living room walls were lined with unusually normal family photos and crosses. Nobody in black. Nobody in leather. No Harleys in the pictures. Common folks. Motorcycles were a way of life for them. The crosses and devotionals on the walls told me Jesus was their passion. But I was skeptical of it all.

More men and women clad in black leather greeted us in the living room. The women in the kitchen gushed over Jade and how beautiful she was. The space was small. Crowded. No one else could fit after the cigarette-smoking group came inside. I took Jade from Todd and held her in her car seat close to me while we stood in the middle of the living room. The bullseye of their target. Jade was still asleep and surprisingly peaceful with all the noise in the house. I kept her safe from the crowd that surrounded us.

"Brothers and Sisters! Can I have you join us in the living room please?" Rich raised his voice to get everyone's attention. "I want to introduce you to my cousin Angie, her husband, Todd, and Baby Jade, who we have gathered here today to pray for and lay hands on."

I knew we were there for prayer. I didn't know Rich or anyone else was planning to touch Jade. I cringed. Jade was medically fragile. I didn't want anyone touching her. I was scared she would get sick again.

I froze. I was surrounded by people I didn't know, who intimidated me. Todd stood on the periphery like I did in The Fishbowl. He had never seen anything like this before. Neither had I. This kind of thing didn't go on in the Baptist-like church Rich and I grew up in. I was paralyzed with fear for what the bikers were about to do. I was rigid. Still in the center of the room. Ready to posture myself for a fight. I intently watched the movements of all the people encircling us. I moved Jade's car seat and held it with both of my arms tight to my chest. She woke up and looked around at the predicament I had gotten us into. Her head and neck were still floppy. She was neurologically unstable and couldn't be touched. But her eyes were wide with awe and strangely comfortable with the attention she garnered in the center of Ray's living room.

Rich started to pray. Twenty or more pairs of hands raised up above our heads. Some straight to the ceiling. Some toward Jade and me.

"Ah, Lord. We know You are here today. We have gathered in Your name to ask for complete healing of Baby Jade. You are the Great Healer, Lord. Jehovah-Rapha. Send Your Holy Spirit, Father, to intervene in her body. Let our words and our hands cover her with Your love. With Your healing power. With Your strength, Jesus! We declare in Jesus's mighty name that Baby Jade is healed, Lord. We believe it! We declare complete healing."

When Rich was quiet, everyone in the room prayed loudly. Each asked God in their own way to heal Jade. Some spoke "in tongues." Some cried. Some sang. I had never heard so many "Praise Gods!" "Hallelujahs," and "Amens." My head was spinning. I didn't know what was happening. While prayers continued in the room, several women came close to us.

Then they put their hands on Jade.

One on her stomach. One on the top of her head. A tall man with a cross tattoo on his neck moved in close to us. He put his fingers on Jade's cheek and lips.

"Hey, someone get me Tank's oil," he said. Tank was a beloved brother of the group. A towering man of God who loved Jesus and his family deeply. He carried his anointing oil with him until the day he was in a tragic head-on collision that took his life. His oil was entrusted to the group when he died, and Ray kept it with him for a time such as this.

Someone passed Tank's oil to the man, then he dabbed it on Jade's forehead and massaged it into her scalp. I could still smell the cigarette he smoked just minutes earlier. I was overwhelmed. Disgusted. Afraid Jade was going to get sick again. Everyone made their way to Jade and touched her head. There was no consideration for hygiene. Or cleanliness. Or the sterile environment I created for her at home. I was fully engulfed by the "fire of the Holy Spirit" in a Christian biker group and lost sight of my escape route. Todd stood to the side. He was stunned. All three of us were imprisoned. We weren't going anywhere. Not until the prayers ended and every person in the room had put their hands on Jade.

Thirty minutes passed, and the unceasing prayer came to a close. I signaled for Todd to rescue us. I had never stood so long for a prayer. I wanted to escape. I was overcome with worry for Jade. I feigned gratitude to Rich's friends while we found our way to the door. I had to leave. I had to sterilize Jade somehow. We made it to the car, and Rich came up behind me while I was putting Jade in the back seat.

"I'm glad you were able to come today. The Brothers were looking forward to getting everyone together to pray over Jade." He was humble and gracious but proud of what happened in Ray's modular. I was offended and angry.

"Richard, this is not what I expected. Jade is medically fragile. She's sick all the time. I didn't know they were going to touch her. Not a single person washed their hands. They all smell like cigarettes. Why would you and your friends put your filthy hands on Jade like that? After I already told you how sick she has been. We're leaving, Richard. I'm sorry. This was a big mistake. Please pray again for her that she doesn't get sick from today." I shut the car door and sat in the back with her. I didn't want to talk to anyone. I didn't want to hear Todd tell me I was a hateful, mean woman. I already knew who I was.

We pulled away from Ray's modular while Connie stood at the fence wagging her tail for Rich. I hurt him. Again. But I didn't care. I was too worried about Jade.

"Let's go. I need to get Jade home and sterilize her." I looked at Jade in her car seat next to me. "I'm sorry, Jadey Bug. I'm sorry Mommy just put you through all of that nonsense."

With Tank's oil still glistening in her hair, Jade looked back at me and smiled. A tender, sweet smile from lips that had been downturned since she was born. Then she made a noise. A deliberate sound she was never supposed to make. A quiet but audible coo from somewhere in her I had never heard before. Jade locked eyes with me and smiled again. Deliberately. I didn't understand what was happening. I didn't believe what I had just seen. I didn't let myself accept the truth. It simply wasn't possible.

Despite the peace that cascaded over me.

Despite the calm that pulsed through my veins.

Despite the hope that erupted inside of me.

Something I couldn't explain had just happened in a crowded modular home surrounded by a group of Christian bikers and a pitbull named Connie. Not just to Jade but also to me. I felt it. Those filthy hands had given us far more than germs. Those hands had given us a miracle.

It would only be a few short weeks before I was able to understand what happened in the most unlikely of places with the most unlikely of people.

I would have to find a way to explain the unexplainable. A supernatural metamorphosis. A holy transformation. A miracle that could only be accomplished by Jesus and the anointed hands of a Christian biker group.

21

Smile

Something remarkable happened at Ray's modular. I couldn't explain it. I didn't understand it. But it was there. Almost palpable. It made the hairs on my arms stand at attention. Something moved through me. Like a gentle windstorm that rushed through every cell of my body. But more importantly, something moved through Jade. Whatever it was, it changed us both.

For the first time in her short life, Jade looked up at me and purposefully smiled. The first time she had the strength to form her droopy mouth into a perfect upturned quarter moon shape. The first time she made a perfect baby sound across her vocal cords when she locked eyes with me. The first time I felt hope infuse into my soul like a waterfall pouring into a river.

It was the most beautiful sound I ever heard.

It was a ray of hope shining on our dark world.

It was something I could not explain.

A transformation was happening in front of my eyes. Not just in Jade but also in me. Even though everything at home was the same, the anxiety and fear became bearable. Tolerable. I wasn't chased into the garage in the middle of the night anymore. I didn't cling to anxiety as my crutch. I didn't feel hidden or lost anymore. Not angry. Not depressed.

I was strong.

I was changed.

I was a warrior.

I found a level path to walk on. One that gave me confidence and allowed me to take Jade out of the dungeon more. One that grounded me and helped me organize my time. One that removed the rush to get out the door with Jade and my breast pump and her feeding pump and diaper bag and medical paraphernalia. One that offered an even road of stability that had been lacking for months.

A Bible made its way to the table beside my bed in the dungeon. Maybe I could lure Jesus back. Or maybe He was already there with us. After our meeting at Ray's, I started to wonder if maybe we were back on God's radar. I wasn't entirely certain, but maybe.

I found tools to make my life manageable. Hurried mornings filled with anxiety were easier. I carried towels in the car and diaper bag to catch puke everywhere I went with Jade. I scoped out every location we went to and found the closest sink or bathroom in case Jade threw up. My hands-free breast pump attachment allowed me to multitask safely on our many trips in the car. A game changer.

It worked like a charm.

Until the morning I drove Jade to one of her many therapy sessions and swerved into the left lane of the interstate while clearing Jade's feeding pump alarm. In front of a Colorado State Patrol Trooper.

Red-and-blue flashing lights immediately appeared in my rearview mirror as the trooper drove up close behind to pull me over. I guided the car to the shoulder of the highway and mumbled under my breath.

"Well, here we go. How am I going to get out of this?" Jade sat behind me making more deliberate noises. She enjoyed using her new voice to delight me. "OK, Jadey. Mommy's getting pulled over. Put on your sweetest smile." I had a talent for getting out of tickets. I had to decide quickly what my strategy would be this time. Tears? Play dumb? I wasn't yet sure. Something brilliant would come to me exactly when I needed it to.

The trooper left his cruiser and walked toward my car in a purposeful stride of authority. His left hand rested on his holstered gun when he approached my window. He was a tall, beefy, handsome man with a chiseled jawline and hands the size of baseball mitts. I lowered the glass. The rhythmic sound of my breast pump echoed in the car as the hands-free device remained securely suctioned to my breasts. There was no time to remove it. I had no place to set full bottles of milk. The car was full of kid trash and medical equipment, old sippy cups of curdled milk, fast food sacks, backpacks, and dirty diapers. I was embarrassed.

"Hello, ma'am. Can I see your license and registration, please?" I awkwardly fumbled through the purse sitting on my knees for the documents he requested. "Ma'am, do you know why I stopped you?"

I kept searching through my wallet as the hum of the breast pump sucked in and out.

"Um, no. I'm not sure. I mean, did I swerve a little back there? I may have. My daughter's feeding pump alarmed, so I had to clear it." I handed him my license and registration.

"Yes, ma'am, you did swerve. Have you consumed any alcohol today?"

I burst into laughter.

"Have I been drinking?" I laughed some more. "You think I've been drinking? I have slept about fourteen hours in the past three months. But no, sir. I definitely have not been drinking." I kept laughing. He didn't seem to think I was funny.

"Ma'am, I saw you swerve into the left lane, and that's why I pulled you over. Ma'am, can you please exit your vehicle?" If I didn't get a ticket for the unsafe lane change, I would definitely get one for not following a police officer's orders.

"Um, well that may be difficult. I don't know if you can see, but I have a hands-free breast pump going right now." The pump continued to suck in and out just under the bottom of my shirt. "I have a medically fragile baby in the back seat who I'm trying to get to a therapy appointment. And it was time to pump." I paused and looked down at the bottles dangling just above my legs. "So, I'm pumping." I shifted my head and smiled up at him. His eyes widened when he looked at my lap. There were two breasts peeking out the bottom of my pulled-up shirt and two full bottles of milk hanging over my legs. I removed the funnels from my breasts so I could get out of the car as requested.

"Here, can you hold these for me? I don't have anywhere to set them, and I don't want to lose this milk. Liquid gold, you know?" I smiled a cheesy grin at him again.

He backed away from the bottles of freshly expressed breast milk.

"Uh, ma'am, it's OK. Just stay in your vehicle. I'm going to run your license and registration, and then I'll be back." Jade and I waited on the side of the interstate for the handsome trooper to come back.

"What do you think, Jadey? You think Officer Good Looking will arrest Mommy?" I could only hope.

The trooper returned to the car and handed my documents through the window. "I'm going to give you a warning today. I appreciate you being honest with me. Just be careful. Your baby needs you." He drove off before I even got my seat belt back on. His red-and-blue lights blazed in hot pursuit of the next lawbreaker to pull over.

I laughed at how brilliant I was. It was a huge win. I got a warning. His thought of having to hold two bottles of breast milk had gotten me out of a roadside sobriety test. He couldn't leave fast enough when faced with such an unnerving experience.

I shot a quick message to Lynel. "My boobs just got me out of a ticket."

"Pumping and driving again? I warned you about that hot state patrolman I saw the other day," she reminded.

I was laughing.

I was laughing hard.

I couldn't remember the last time I had laughed.

When I got home, I laughed even more when I told Todd about what happened on the side of the road.

"Are you serious, Angie? Did he actually hold the bottles for you?"

"No, Todd. He didn't hold the bottles. That's the funny part. I know the sight of breast milk makes men cringe, but at least I got out of a ticket. Five points for my boobs."

I sat in my favorite brown recliner, stained with breast milk and peanut butter. I was still laughing. It was time to pump again. It was always time to pump. I had just settled into a good flow when there was a scream from the deck. The back door flew open, and Faith ran into the house with a look of terror on her face. She was so upset she could barely speak.

"Mommy! Mommy! Sasha! Something's wrong! Sasha!" I scrambled to my feet and turned off the pump. Breast milk sprayed in streams across the coffee table and onto Todd's arm. He jumped up and sprinted to the kitchen, gagging as he ran to the sink.

"Faith, what's wrong? Are you OK?" I ran toward her at the back door.

"Mommy!" Faith was crying. "Mommy! Sasha! It's Sasha. She has a bubble coming out of her butt!"

Sasha scampered into the house through the sliding door and ran straight to the kitchen toward Todd. He was still disgusted that he had been sprayed with breast milk and was wiping himself clean at the sink. Sasha stopped at Todd's feet, let out a loud meow, and deposited a small yellow kitten directly on top of his foot. Faith was right. Sasha did have a bubble coming out of her butt. A large transparent bubble filled with amniotic fluid and a kitten. The sac broke as it landed on Todd's foot.

"What the . . .? What the hell is going on?" Sasha scooped up her new baby and moved it away from Todd under the dining room table. She delivered two more kittens just a few minutes later.

Todd ran up the stairs to shower, still gagging from the breast milk. He sounded like a newborn calf straining a loud bellow for its mother. He hadn't thrown up since that one time he got drunk in college. His streak ended that day.

"Girls, go get a cardboard box and put an old blanket in it for Sasha. Let's give her a place to take care of her new babies and let them nurse. We will put them in the garage for now."

The cat fandango had started. We were soon inundated with kittens. I instructed the girls to find Star and Matt the Girl Cat and make cardboard labor rooms for them in the garage next to Sasha.

The last thing I wanted was for them to deliver their kittens in a window well or the neighbor's barn. The girls were in heaven. They were given a sweet distraction from their prison lives in our house. They were ecstatic about the kitten farm in our garage.

"Can we sleep with them tonight, Mom?" Brooke begged. "We want to be with them if they have their babies or if Sasha has any more."

"No, girls. You can't sleep in the garage. There are mice out there and probably snakes. You will be so uncomfortable. You can stay up late and get up early to check on them, but you absolutely cannot sleep in the garage."

The girls were disappointed. "Aw, Mom. That's not fair." Kinnah argued. "What if they need us? Please, Mom. Please."

But the cats didn't need guests for the night. We stayed up later than usual, and I shuffled the girls off to bed after my midnight pumping. They absolutely were not going to sleep in the garage that night or any other night. I hugged the girls and sent them upstairs to bed.

"Get some sleep so you have some energy for tomorrow. You're going to be busy taking care of cats."

I laid down for a short nap and woke up around 2 a.m. I needed to pump again, refill Jade's feeding bag, and change her diaper. My internal alarm woke me up right on time. Even if I overslept by fifteen minutes, my shirt would be drenched with milk and wake me up anyway. I hovered over Jade and stared at her like I often did. She made me smile. She was such a beautiful baby. Were it not for her problems or the tube in her stomach, no one would know that her prognosis was so dark.

I wasn't angry anymore. In the absence of gut-wrenching rage, I was able to enjoy these middle-of-the-night moments. I was able to drench myself in every second I had with Jade. I no longer dreaded the darkness of the night because it was my time with just her. I looked forward to standing over her and imagining her as a teenager even though those days would never come. I wrote stories in my head about how she would sneak out her window in the middle of the night to go see her boyfriend. How she would yell at her sisters over the last Dr Pepper. How she would bring home a report card with four A's and one F. How I would watch Todd walk her down the aisle.

I loved to create those stories. I loved imagining what Jade would become were it not for this thing she was born with. I loved going to a place that did not exist so I could linger there with older Jade. It was the only place I got to spend that time with her. I didn't know how much time she had left. How much time I would be given to stand over her. To soak her in. To remember her scent. To write beautiful stories in my mind about the Jade I longed to know some day.

But those were just stories to tide me over and pass the time at night.

I was interrupted by a noise in the garage. I was sure we had another litter of kittens to welcome to the family. I went to investigate. As I turned the doorknob to the garage, I heard giggles from a group of girls who were supposed to be asleep. All five of my young daughters were huddled in front of the boxes in our garage turned *caternity* ward.

"Girls! What are you doing? I told you that you were not to go back in the garage. You need to go to bed. Right now. It's 2 o'clock in the morning!"

"Look, Mommy! Star already had ten kittens!" Kinnah exclaimed. "And we watched them all be born!"

"Oh, good Lord. Are you kidding me?" I was shocked and concerned at the same time because Star only had seven nipples to feed her ten babies with. When I crouched to look at Star's babies, she stood up and screeched out a labored "meow." Kitten number eleven was born. The girls were mesmerized. They had just experienced birth. Eleven times. They were soaking in those babies the way I soaked in Jade every night.

"Girls, Star can't feed all these babies. Some of them probably aren't going to make it." They would soon learn more about death.

"Mom, we can't let them die." Hope pleaded with me. "We will have to try to bottle-feed them." The girls were crying. They couldn't stand the thought of even one of the kittens dying.

"Girls, you can't keep them alive with bottles. But," I paused, "did Sasha have any more babies?"

Sasha only had three huge kittens. She was done. We could give five of Star's babies to Sasha and see if she would accept them as her own. She was fully equipped to nurse more than the three she had. Sasha was bigger than Star. Healthier and stronger. Star was a gypsy who wandered away frequently like Emmie did. We chose the smallest five of Star's litter and placed them in the box with Sasha. Star didn't care. She was overwhelmed with the six that were left and exhausted from delivering eleven babies in less than two hours. I stepped back from the box to give Sasha time to smell and lick the five new babies squirming in front of her. I wasn't sure what she would do. But as her adopted babies started to cry, Sasha held out her mama paw and scooped them all in. She moved them near her other kittens where they lay nursing. Sasha's five new kittens began to nurse while she licked and cleaned them. The girls were learning so many lessons in the middle of a dirty garage.

They couldn't believe what they had just seen. They were exhausted. Emotional. I insisted we all go to bed and leave the mamas to tend to their new babies. Matt the Girl Cat was lying in the corner of her own bed writhing. She wanted some privacy. All was well in the garage. It was time for us to sleep. I leaned over Sasha and her eight kittens.

"Good girl, Sasha." I stroked the top of her head. "You're a good mama."

I left Mattie to deliver alone and lay down in my bed next to Jade, where she was still sleeping in her bassinet. I was experiencing life outside the dungeon again. First when I was pulled over by Officer Good Looking. Then when the deliveries of new life started and the girls repeatedly disobeyed. I was a mother again to all of my daughters who needed me. I was finding my way home.

Jade was smiling. The girls were smiling. I was smiling. I could get used to micro victories like this.

The only person in our home who wasn't smiling was Todd. He was traumatized by the assault of fluids that made him throw up for the first time in twenty years. He didn't even hear five young girls sneak past his bedroom door and go into the garage in the middle of the night.

But the rest of us were smiling.

Finally.

It was a long time coming.

22

Normal

The night was interrupted by the excitement of new life and mischievous children. It was short, and the sun rose too early. I was tired. More tired than usual. But I awoke with a smile when I remembered Sasha and her eight babies. Safe and resting in the garage. Despite being an exhausted mother, she hovered over her kittens and cared for them like a good mama does. Even the ones Star didn't care about. I smiled again. My girls were acting like kids. Sneaking past Todd's room and down to the garage at midnight. Disobeying me. Elevating the volume of their voices in the house. I welcomed the return of their laughter.

The girls were up with the first sunbeam that pierced through the blinds in their rooms. I found them in the garage cuddled up with our new mamas and their babies. The girls simply couldn't resist the temptation to lie on the garage floor surrounded by kittens. Jade didn't notice things were changing and slept through the clamor of happy children. Most mornings I hovered over her bassinet as long as I could and admired her until I awoke her with my stare. But this day I wandered into the garage to look in on our new babies and my daughters.

As expected, Matt the Girl Cat delivered in the peace and darkness of the garage without help from anyone. We awoke to eight more babies. Mattie's were beautiful calico and tortoiseshell kittens. They looked like their mother and their uncle Storm. I was certain they were all fathered by their uncle-dad, and I was amazed every one of them was normal. They all lived through the night. Star didn't miss her five stolen babies. They nuzzled into Sasha and nursed with their new litter mates. Star lay almost motionless in her bed while nursing the six she had left. She was lazy. She didn't even try to take back her own babies from Sasha. Star was a vagabond cat. She stayed with her remaining kittens because of instinct and a full dish of cat food beside her bed. I stared at the excess in the garage. We had The Five plus twenty-two littles. My mind returned to what Todd said a few months before.

"I freaking hate cats."

I stood over my daughters in the garage while they named twenty-two kittens. Just like they had done with The Five. Todd was still reeling from the delivery of a kitten on his foot. But he stood beside me. Arms crossed and a smile on my face, I waited for him to announce how we would be getting rid of every freaking cat as soon as they were weaned. That we would not be keeping a single one. That the girls would be responsible for feeding twenty-seven cats. But he didn't. He said nothing. He just stood in the garage with us, smiling too. I knew he was grateful. I could see it on his face. Grateful the girls had a new distraction. Grateful a cloud of anger mysteriously lifted from our home. Grateful things were ordinary again. Even as he counted kittens, he let the girls delight in the newness of far too many cats he freaking hated.

The garage was full of an irony that made our lives stunningly normal again. Xanadu Gray. A colorless departure from the darkness of charcoal black. I welcomed a life of stable instability and commonness more than two dozen cats gave us.

But I didn't forget we really weren't a normal family. I also didn't forget that in three days we had to take Jade to the new Pediatric Hospital campus and repeat the brain MRI. Three days. Another reminder of how not normal we were. The first MRI sent my world spiraling to hell and evoked The Scream that shook our home and my children's hearts. It introduced me to death and the Grim Reaper and sent me down a quicksand road I almost drowned in.

Three days. It was written in bright red Expo marker on the calendar hanging on the refrigerator. Every time I pumped. Every time I opened the door to store my milk, ten or twelve times a day, the reminder slapped me across the face. Another brain MRI was coming. I couldn't escape the evil truth. I had to face it despite the pleasant distractions living in our garage and the smiles on my girls' faces.

I was terrified of what another brain MRI would do to me. I didn't want to be catapulted back to the darkness. I wasn't strong enough yet to handle more tragic news or the worsening of Jade's brain images. I had started to claw my way out of the dungeon, and I couldn't afford to be engulfed by it again. I dreaded another trip to the hospital. Another brain scan. Another reason to sink back into depression. But it was inevitable. It would happen. I had no choice. I had to take her in and find out how deep in the mire we were. And how close to the end Jade was.

Very soon my daughter's prognosis would be confirmed. I would be given a projected lifespan of not more than a year or two. The *normal* in the garage and under the roof of our home wouldn't feel so normal anymore. I would have a battle for peace to fight again.

I would have to learn how a mother buries her child.

Todd and I had gotten used to traveling to the new Pediatric Hospital campus in Denver. It was a shiny building. Inviting. Welcoming. Not like its predecessor. The waiting room outside the MRI room was fresh. It smelled like new paint. It was clean. No stains on the carpet. There were children and teenagers waiting in wheelchairs just like those we met months before. Everyone had a medical bag or a feeding pump or a ventilator. Including us.

But the room no longer debilitated me. I didn't throw up in the bathroom or sob uncontrollably. There were beautiful children who would live beyond the years Jade would. There were mothers and fathers who were warriors just like us. Mothers and fathers who had felt the tectonic plate movement of their souls like I had. The heat. The extreme pressure. These were the mothers and fathers with brutal struggles like ours. But their journeys didn't end in a premature death sentence like ours would.

I was jealous of the other warriors.

They made it through the muck and were steady on their feet. They battled through the trenches of darkness, depression, and their own dungeons. They trudged to this place in their lives where The Waiting Room wasn't frightening. They sat with us in a shiny, new place with their children doing exactly what we were.

Waiting.

Waiting for the next battle. Waiting for another procedure. Waiting in steady patience for their next plan of attack. Something I hadn't experienced yet.

These were my people now. I had found a tribe to walk the distance with me, however short or long it would be for Jade. They were professionals at the warrior life. I was an amateur. My grief was still immature. But I was more like these strangers than I was just a few months before. We had one thing in common.

We were warriors for our children.

I would not allow myself to get sucked back into the hell I escaped. I would not succumb to depression. I would never find myself behind the wheel of a car in the darkness of the night in my garage again. Jade needed me. I made a promise to her that I would never leave her again. I would be with her until the end, and I would be her greatest warrior. Just like the room full of parents I sat with who fought for their children. I would fight like that for Jade.

A nurse appeared at the door and scanned the waiting room.

"Jade? We're ready for Jade." I picked Jade up in her car seat, and we followed the nurse to the imaging room. The MRI took only minutes. Then it was over. I prepared myself for the battle that was coming. We passed by the warriors in the waiting room on our way out. I tried to absorb the strength I felt in the room. I knew it had taken them years to get that way. And I didn't know if I had that kind of time with Jade.

The next day, we were back in the car and driving the long road to Dr. Allen's office. Only this time, it would be so he could explain the second brain MRI results and talk to us about the rest of Jade's life. Todd and I sat next to each other in silence as he drove almost two hours from our home. There was nothing Dr. Allen could say that we hadn't already heard or researched. The worst scenario was already on the table. It couldn't get any more desolate than what we had already gone through. Todd zipped into a parking spot and braked hard. He didn't want to be there. I didn't want to be there either. It was a necessary evil neither of us wanted to face. But we had to. That's what warriors do.

Todd and I had a routine down. We each had a job when we traveled for appointments. I carried Jade in her car seat, and Todd carried everything else. The medical bag and feeding pump. My breast pump bag and the diaper bag. It was a routine we had perfected. We didn't even have to ask who was doing what anymore.

Todd and I were greeted at the front desk by Lindsey, Dr. Allen's nurse.

"We already have you checked in." She smiled a big, awkward side smile. She knew something I didn't. "I saw you pull into the parking lot." Lindsey led us to Dr. Allen's private office the same way she did the first time we visited him. It seemed like a lifetime ago. It was too familiar. I didn't like that we were repeating the same steps. Being led by the same nurse. Sitting in the same office. It felt like another ending. My heart was boggy. The results would be devastating. Again. I couldn't handle it.

"Have a seat and Dr. Allen will be with you in a few minutes. He will be right in." She smiled at me again as she walked out of the room. I thought I saw her wink.

"What's she so freaking happy about?" Todd asked. He was nervous. Being flippant was how he coped.

I paused and deeply exhaled two lungs full of thick anxiety.

"You know this isn't going to go well," I said to Todd. "You remember what happened the last time we sat in his private office, right?"

Todd scoffed and refused to reply. He didn't want to discuss anything negative anymore. He just wanted data and facts. Better not to talk. Instead, I sat next to Jade in her car seat and scanned the walls of Dr. Allen's office. There were degrees and awards he received when I was only a child. The entire wall behind his desk was covered like wallpaper in his accolades. He was the neurologist I wanted Jade to see. Even if he didn't have the power to save her life. He was the one I wanted to care for her brain until she died.

Dr. Allen entered the room with a humility that made him human. Unlike most of the other specialists Jade had seen. It was his calling card. Somehow his presence calmed me. Even though I knew he was about to share the results of a brain MRI that would steal my daughter. Todd stood up and shook his hand as he passed in front of his neatly organized desk.

"Hello, Dr. Allen. It's good to see you again," Todd said.

"Hello, Todd. Angie, how are you doing? And how is little Jade doing?"

"Hello, Dr. Allen. It's been pretty rough actually. Jade's not eating at all anymore. Every feeding goes through the tube. She had been puking probably eight or ten times a day, but now it's only four or five times a day. She's not holding her head up, and she's still very floppy. But she did start smiling, and she's making some purposeful noises." I paused. "We try to have hope, but we are aware that absent myelination of her white matter is probably a metabolic storage disorder or a leukodystrophy. We know what to expect if it's Niemann Pick. Most of the metabolic tests aren't back yet. They said the really bad ones are going to take a few more months. We are trying to prepare ourselves."

"OK, yes. Let's talk about the brain MRI Jade had yesterday." He invited Todd and me to join him directly in front of the two computer screens he used to show us the first MRI results. I sat in the same chair as before when Dr. Allen explained the abnormalities of Jade's brain. My hands began to tremble as I remembered his words.

"She has no myelination of the central white matter of her brain. We don't know why it isn't myelinated. We just know she lacks myelination. This is an extremely concerning problem for a newborn." I hadn't forgotten his words after three months of hell in a dungeon I didn't want to return to. I waited for Dr. Allen to turn on the computer screens as he did before, and I braced myself for the dark spiral down a black hole of despair I had already escaped once. The screen on the left side would be the normal newborn brain. It would be lit up with bright features and elegant folds throughout its surface. Just like before. The screen on the right would be Jade's brain. I knew what to expect. I knew we were only there to find out how much more degradation had occurred and how much time we had left with her.

Todd was perched on the front of his seat, still edgy about being there. I sat closest to Dr. Allen while he explained the newest results.

"I think it would be easier to just show you like I did last time on the computer screen." As before, Dr. Allen turned on the screen to our left. As before, it was a remarkable sight. It was perfect. The most beautiful thing I had ever seen. I was jealous of the parents of that newborn because theirs was a perfect baby with a perfect brain. I shifted my gaze to the computer screen to our right and waited for Jade's brain image to appear just as it did before.

But the screen remained dark.

Dr. Allen paused and shook his head. He stared at the computer screen to our left with a puzzled look.

"I don't know how to explain this, but this. This right here is your daughter's brain MRI from yesterday. It is completely normal. The white matter of her brain is completely myelinated. The syrinx in her cervical spine has disappeared. I have reviewed this MRI multiple times and even had a colleague review it." He paused and rubbed his forehead. "In all my years of being a pediatric neurologist, I have never seen such a dramatic change in such a short amount of time in white matter myelination. I can't explain it."

I couldn't speak. The darkness of a fatal diagnosis had just been lifted from Jade's life like a storm cloud blown away with one heavenly breath.

"So, you're telling us that Jade's brain is normal?" Todd leaned in closer to the screen. He tried to examine every part of the perfection he was staring at. "Completely normal? You don't see anything wrong anymore?" Todd stammered his words, hardly able to form his sentences.

"No. In fact, I do not. Her white matter is completely myelinated. The syrinx is gone. She has a perfectly formed, age-appropriate brain in the images we got yesterday. Like I said, I have seen a lot. But never have I seen unmyelinated white matter completely restored in such a short time. It's truly remarkable."

I felt a rush of tears fall around me like a cleansing waterfall rain. I still couldn't speak. I didn't even try to dry my face. I was staring at Jade's perfect brain on the computer screen. Wondering how this miracle unfolded in the darkness of a dungeon and a garage that almost took my life.

Then I remembered a pitbull named Connie and the filthy hands of a Christian biker group.

I was paralyzed with the realization that something extraordinary had happened.

It was then that I knew Jesus had been there all along. Fighting for us. Reaching down into the raging waters to pull us out of the storm.

He was with us through the hemorrhages. He was with us in The Fishbowl. He was with us in the dungeon. He rescued me in the garage. He heard me cry out to Him and scream at Him and ask Him why He had forsaken us.

Jesus never left me. And He never left Jade.

I stopped staring at the image of my daughter's brain on the computer screen and turned to Jade in her car seat where she sat looking at me. She was a beautiful porcelain doll. Perfect in every obvious way. She was angelic. Flawless. Breathtaking. For the first time in more than three months, the darkness was extinguished. Everything was going to be OK. Jade was going to be OK.

Only Jesus could have done this.

The screen on the right remained dark as we gathered our things and Jade to leave Dr. Allen's office. When I got close to the door, I turned back and looked at the screen on the left one last time. Just to make sure I wasn't dreaming.

It was perfect.

It was Jade.

It was . . . normal.

23

Mountains and Giants

The mountains just beyond Todd's shoulder and the driver's side window were massive. Majestic. Commanding of my respect. The heavy winter snow was gone from their peaks, leaving behind a lush landscape I marveled at. The changing seasons always brought new beauty to their slopes. I had seen them thousands of times in my periphery. But I hadn't seen them that way. Not until then. They were even more spectacular than on the drive to Dr. Allen's office just two hours before. I admired them like it was the first time. Because it was. They were extraordinary.

Despite the ruggedness concealed beneath their emerald slopes. Despite the threat of flooding the rivers below them any time they chose. Despite what lay beneath their alluring terrain.

They were beautiful. Deceitful. Their threats were hidden.

Just like the baby with a normal brain asleep in our back seat.

We had so much to celebrate. Everything was within our reach. Even the magnificent Rocky Mountains ten miles away were close enough to touch. Jade was going to be OK. The crystal-clear morning brought with it a new day. A new way of seeing everything in the world. Todd wiped his cheeks of tears I seldom saw him cry. I stared at Jade in her car seat and marveled at the gift of life she was given. I cried with Todd. Tears of disbelief. Tears of shock. Tears of gratitude. Neither of us knew what to say. We basked in the miracle in our own ways.

Jade's brain was normal. The cloak of death lifted. Many tomorrows awaited Jade. The finite days of her life were extended. The dungeon was a temporary space, and we would persevere beyond its darkness. Jade had a future that didn't exist the day before.

The house was still when we came through the garage door. The girls were with Mom enjoying their last days of summer away from the monotony of a fragile baby, medical equipment, and breast pumps. I stood in the same spot where I had lain the night Dr. Allen called just three months before. The place where I fell to the floor and screamed at God for forsaking us. Where I told Him I hated Him. Where The Scream shook the inside of our home and altered the course of my children's lives. In that same place, I fell to my knees again. This time in gratitude for something I couldn't explain. Something nobody could explain. Not Jade's doctors. Or science. Or anyone. Except Jesus and a Christian biker group, who prayed over Jade and laid their hands on her. I sobbed deep, body-shaking bellows. Then I did what Rich and his friends did at Ray's modular. I reached my hands high into the air. And I praised God with a gratitude that comes from a broken mother whose baby has escaped death. I thanked God for healing Jade. I thanked Him for loving me more than I ever knew. I thanked Him for fighting for us every step of the way.

I thanked Him for sending an unlikely group of Christian men and women into my life to cast light on the darkest areas of my soul. I hoped one day Cousin Rich and his friends would understand the broken woman they selflessly helped. The monster who saw them as wretched. Less than. Filthy. I hoped they would understand who I was. Before them. Before Jesus. I hoped that I could thank them all one day for having enough faith to make up for what I lacked. Even though the mountains and giants were still there, still threatening, the difference was that Rich and his friends showed me that Jesus was still there too.

But even with a miraculous metamorphosis of Jade's brain, there was no spontaneous change in the care she needed. She still struggled. But we faced those struggles together. There were still battles. But they were battles we could win. She wasn't going to succumb to degradation of the white matter of her brain. But her problems persisted. Jade's G-Tube was still her lifeline. She still cringed when I tried to hug her. I still pumped and fed her every two hours. I still craved long, hot showers and legs that were shaved. I still longed to hold her close enough to feel her warmth. To run my fingers across her skin. To play with her toes in a game of "This Little Piggy."

A miracle healing had occurred. But there was still much work that would require years of patience. Perseverance. Faith. There were still many mountains to climb and giants to slay. But Jade was going to live.

That was all that mattered.

A painfully slow transformation was starting in Jade. The collision of tectonic plates was changing her again. It was a long, agonizing wait of many months and many tears to see those changes. She made gradual progress. Tiny steps only. Slower than other babies. She was significantly delayed. Still fragile. But I was grateful for even the minute changes. The inches forward that were miles for Jade. Eight months slipped away to the grind of daily therapies and tube feedings. Before I knew it, Jade's first full spring was upon us. It was time to celebrate a day we thought would never come. Another rainy April day. The first birthday of our Jewel of Heaven.

Jade had graduated from the small bassinet in the dungeon a few months before she turned a year old, and we moved into a queen-size bed just down the hall from Todd's room. I awoke on her first birthday and stared at her sleeping next to me. She was sideways. Tangled up in the feeding pump tubing that hung from the metal IV pole beside our bed. Her head was pushed tight in the mesh bed rail that kept her from rolling to the floor. She was a thrasher when she slept. I untangled her many times every night to keep her from pulling her G-Tube out. I didn't want to wake her yet. I just wanted to look at her. Her chubby arms and legs. Her shoulder-length dark curls. Her porcelain doll face. Jesus and a miracle gave her back to me. Without either, I wouldn't be lying next to her. I wouldn't be smiling and anticipating the life ahead of her. Appreciating the life almost stolen from us. I couldn't resist. I ran my finger across her forehead. Her eyes popped open.

"Good morning, Jadey Bug! Happy Birthday! Mommy loves

you!" She smiled and rolled herself into another tangle to get closer to me. She couldn't say a single word yet, but her face said everything.

I love you, too, Mommy! I heard her thoughts though she had no words.

I unhooked the overnight feeding, untangled Jade, and carried her to the living room. The house was quiet. Todd was at work. The girls were at school. I perched Jade upright on a pink pillow on the living room floor. Her Princess Throne. The place she lay every morning. Jade lived on her Princess Throne. It kept her safe. Safe from choking on her own vomit. Safe from a living room of threats. Safe from a great big world she would have to learn to live in. Jade was still floppy. But physical therapy helped make up for her low tone with muscle strength. Jade had taught herself to fold her body at her waist and position her knees over her shoulders. An Olympic-level gymnastics move. Her favorite position. Surprisingly, it didn't make her throw up like almost everything else did.

Jade was joined on the floor by her favorite cat. Matt the Girl Cat. One of only a few of The Five left after a harsh predatory winter in the country that stole them from my daughters. Jade loved Mattie. She loved to watch Mattie stalk her toys and pounce on her feet. She loved to track Mattie with her eyes from across the room. The other cats still weren't allowed in the house. But Mattie was. Mattie had a new job. She helped Jade. She motivated Jade to move and do hard work. Jade giggled at her. Loud. She clapped her hands when Mattie pounced on a toy. But she didn't move from her Princess Throne. She could effortlessly roll in the oblivion of sleep. But when confronted with a room full of the harsh realities of scariness, Jade lay still on her pillow. That's where everything happened in Jade's life. Therapies. Feedings. Stretches. Diaper changes. Jade was safe there.

While she was distracted by Mattie, I got on my hands and knees and crept around the corner out of her sight.

"Jadey Bug!" I popped my head around so she could see me. "Happy Birthday, Jadey Bug!" She was startled and turned her head toward me. I rounded the corner on all fours like Mattie and removed her legs from above her head. I kissed each of her toes and put her feet to my mouth while I blew against her high arches. She laughed again.

"This little piggy went to market." I held the big toe on her right foot. "And this little piggy stayed home." Jade was giddy with excitement. She knew what came next. "And this little piggy ate roast beef. But this little piggy had none." Jade began to squeal. The littlest piggy was about to have its turn. It was her favorite. "This little piggy . . ." I held her foot above the floor and dangled it by the littlest piggy. "This little piggy right here . . . Jadey, it went . . ." Jade shook with happiness. She knew what was coming. "This little piggy went, 'Wee, wee, wee,' all the way home!" I squealed like a mother sow and snorted into the sole of Jade's foot as I released my grasp on her perfect piggy. Jade quickly drew her foot from me and burst into a breathless giggle.

I loved our hints of Xanadu Gray.

The most beautiful color unworthy of the rainbow. At least it was to me.

Moments like this brought clarity. I understood the dungeon. I understood its darkness. I understood why I had to live in it. Our victories were so much grander because of it.

The mountains and giants were conquerable. But not without work, tears, and faith.

Jade's first birthday came and went with few changes in her progress. But she was alive. Happy. Giggling like a one-year-old. She could hold her head up most of the time. But she still needed support to sit, and she still hadn't learned to use her mouth to eat. Jade's physical therapist ordered a toddler wheelchair. Jade would need it since she wasn't crawling or walking. No signs indicated she would do either any time soon. I gave in and agreed to an adaptive stroller that would accommodate Jade for the next few years. One like Lilly's with Jade's name embroidered on the back.

Then it happened.

Jade was one month past her first birthday when the tectonic plates collided again. Something changed in her. Sudden but unintentional. An extraordinary accident.

Jade and I were working on her therapy exercises as we did every morning. Most days Jade cried and struggled. Everything was hard for her. Physical therapy made her uncomfortable. So uncomfortable she threw up. Things were different this morning, though. Safe on her Princess Throne, Jade clapped the bottoms of her feet together and swiped at the toys I dangled above her. Mattie distracted Jade and pounced on a toy near her foot. Jade laughed. Mattie's tail brushed across Jade's face. That was it. Jade wanted her. She wanted her hands around Mattie's tail and to teach that cat a lesson. Jade reached hard across her chest to the right to grab a handful of Mattie. A sideways twist moved her close enough to grab Mattie by the tail. Mattie jerked, and Jade rolled off her Princess Throne onto her hands and knees. She let go. She was shocked. Shaken. She looked at me in disbelief. She was still alive. The four-inch fall didn't kill her like she expected. She stayed on all fours for a few minutes then lost her confidence and dropped to her belly.

"Oh, come on, Jadey. You can do this." But she was done. She didn't want to try any more. Everything in Jade's life was in her time. I applauded her bravery but didn't push her. If I did, she might not ever try again.

The next day brought more acts of heroism. Jade was enamored with her newfound ability to roll over to a crawling stance. So, she rolled off her Princess Throne onto her hands and knees again. But this time it was on purpose. This time it was her choice. Her confidence soared. She knew from her success the day before that she wouldn't die so she held her position and grinned. She knew she was brilliant. She shuffled her right hand and left knee forward one pace. That was far enough. Frightened and confused by her ability to move on her own, Jade dropped to her stomach.

"Wow, Jadey Bug! Good job! You almost crawled! Let's try again!" Jade started to fuss when I held her on all fours, so I put her back on her Princess Throne. She was more interested in her toes and played with them the rest of the day. She was still leery of another roll off her Princess Throne. Still cautious of the world around her. But she had not forgotten her two days of greatness. She was proud of herself. I was proud of her too.

Another day came, and I wondered what it would bring. I could tell Jade did too. I sat next to her while I pumped and chatted with her about how stunning she was in her periwinkle stretch pants. I reminded her of her excellence. I encouraged her to be bold and brave again. I looked away to turn off my breast pump, and Jade rolled herself to the floor again. Perched on her hands and knees, she scanned the horizon of the living room in front of her. Looking for threats. Searching for hazards. Contemplating her next move. Then the most beautiful and unexpected thing happened.

Jade moved her hands and knees in perfect timing. Like she had been crawling for months. Like it was easy. Like she wouldn't die if she moved.

Then Jade crawled across the entire living room without stopping.

I couldn't believe what she had just done. She couldn't believe what she had just done. She was crawling. Jade was crawling! After more than a year of excruciating work for few and small victories, she taught herself to crawl. In three days. She was no longer a fragile baby tethered to the safety of her Princess Throne. She was a toddler exploring the immediate space around her. My life got beautifully complicated with her ability to move anywhere and get into anything she wanted.

"Jadey! You're crawling! Baby girl, I'm so proud of you!" It was an epic victory. Only one of many mountains Jade would have to climb.

I called her physical therapist and canceled the stroller. Jade didn't need it.

But the work wasn't over, and life still wasn't easy. Jade cried every time we worked on her exercises. But eventually, she developed both the strength and the confidence to pull up and stand by the couch. Six more long months of intense work standing, pulling up, and balancing passed. But Jade still couldn't walk. She refused to try. She stood at the side of the couch and held on for safety. She wouldn't let go. That was too dangerous. Too scary. Even if I coaxed her, she would plop to the floor. She finally had the strength, but she was afraid. Everything was accomplished in Jade's time. I couldn't push her. It would set her back, and we would lose precious time. I had to be patient. I had to wait for her to be ready.

Months of therapies and doctor visits passed, and before I knew it Jade was nineteen months old and still wasn't walking. I hadn't given up on her. I would never give up on Jade. She could stand and balance herself with the couch, but there had been little more progress since Jade started crawling six months before. She was content to get around on all fours on the floor. A brisk Colorado winter was settling in, and a thin layer of snow covered the grass. Jade's second Thanksgiving was in three days, and I would need to carry her everywhere we went for the holiday. Not the end of the world. But I was hoping she would have started walking by then after her impressive strides with crawling. Not yet.

I sat cross-legged on the living room floor beside Jade while I pumped and watched TV. We were getting ready to work on physical therapy exercises like we did every morning. Jade pulled herself up to the couch beside me as she often did and watched Maury Povich with me. It was one of her favorite shows. I was distracted by the breast pump and the young man on the TV as he protested the paternity claims of a woman he had spent one night with.

"That is not his baby, Jadey. What do you think? You think that's his baby?" She smiled. "You think that kid is his baby? No way, Jadey." I turned back to the drama unfolding in front of us. I didn't even pay attention to Jade. She was still standing beside me. Playing with a toy. Not watching our show. Jade was solid on her feet. But not brave enough to let go. Not brave enough to let her feet carry her anywhere she wanted to travel.

"You are . . . *not* the father." Maury broke the unfortunate but expected news to the woman as she ran from the stage with her hands covering her face.

216

"I told you, Jadey. That baby doesn't look a thing like that guy." She didn't like being wrong and didn't respond. I continued to stare ahead. But a movement grazed the periphery of my left eye. Barely. Nothing to divert my attention from Maury or my breast pump. Probably Mattie. Seconds later, the movement made its way toward the television in front of me. Whatever it was, it was bigger than Mattie. I jerked my head to the left and saw Jade. She had released her hold on the couch.

She was walking. By herself. Across the living room.

For the first time in her life, the girl who was never supposed to walk took her first steps. All by herself. Without prompting. Without fear. I dropped the bottles of milk I held in my hands and stood in disbelief. Liquid gold spilled on the carpet below me. Nineteen months of therapy, practice, tears, and work were moving across the living room in front of me. Jade was a toddler. She was walking!

She conquered another mountain, and nothing would stop her now.

"You did it! Jadey Bug, you did it! Mommy is so proud of you, Jadey!" I scooped her in my arms and cried happiness over her. Jade knew she was amazing. Her long, dark curls bobbed up and down below her shoulders while I bounced with her in my arms. Her crystal-blue eyes glistened with pride and confidence. I had to see if she would do it again. I stood her in front of the couch. She released her grasp again. Then she walked across the living room to me. She slayed the giant.

Todd and the girls were visiting his parents in Nebraska. I had to call them. I couldn't get to the phone fast enough.

"Yo," Todd answered the phone on the first ring. I started to talk before he could even say hello.

"Todd, you're not going to believe this." I was hyperventilating. "Jade is walking! She's walking everywhere. I can't keep her still. Oh my gosh, Jadey Bug. Look at you!" Todd's phone slipped to the floor. He screamed like a fan at a Nebraska Husker football game. Then he started to cry.

"Yes! Yes! Yes! She's walking! Girls! Jade is walking!" He yelled. He was more excited than I had ever heard him before. I could hear the girls and Todd's parents celebrating with him. It was a monumental day for Jade. It was a monumental day for all of us.

One more mountain climbed. One more giant slain.

We could move to the next conquest. Jade was crawling and walking anywhere she wanted. There was so much to be grateful for. But she still didn't talk. And she still wouldn't eat. Not a bite. Even after extensive feeding therapy, Jade was completely G-Tube fed.

But I knew that in her time and in God's time, Jade would defy every bad thing that was spoken over her as a baby. Every mountain would crumble and every giant would fall in front of her one day. Jade would talk someday. She would eat someday. We just had to have patience. And we had to wait for her to decide when she was ready to conquer those mountains and giants, like she did all the others.

That night, Jade and I lay in our bed. I started Jade's night tube feeding and rubbed her back until she fell asleep. I stared at her in the dim light cast from the feeding pump. I was mesmerized. She was my perfect porcelain doll. I couldn't take my eyes off her. She was magnificent. I ran my fingers through her dark curls and sang a hushed tune over her.

"Jesus loves you. This I know. For the Bible tells me so." Jesus loved all the little children. But especially Jade and her Waiting Room friends.

I rested my head on the pillow next to her and thought about all the mountains she had climbed in her life and all that were waiting for her. I thought about all the giants she would battle and all the battles she would win. I thought about our days in the dungeon and how far she had come in our escape from the darkness. I thought about the future and what it held for her. I imagined the heavens rejoicing as Jesus smiled down on His perfect Jewel of Heaven.

Then I leaned in close to where she lay asleep and whispered softly in her ear, "You did it, Jadey Bug. You did it."

24

Tender Hearts

s time passed, the mountains and giants fell before Jade in unhurried succession. The life we lived after the dungeon transformed again. Three years had passed since that rainy April day in 2007 when my Jewel of Heaven entered the world following a breathless grunt and an unsettled push. After all that time, I still labored over G-Tube feedings, and I still cleaned up vomit. It became clear that Jade's last mountain to climb would be steeper and higher than almost any she had experienced. Eating was her nemesis. Her fourteener. Her Goliath. But the evil that had come for her three years before was defeated, and the sharp edge of fear that held a blade to my throat was gone. I was no longer controlled by anxiety. I was no longer afraid every day that I would lose Jade to some dark and sinister plan. I was no longer held captive to a life of uncertainty. In her time, Jade learned to walk. She learned to run. Then she learned to talk. Jade did everything that was impossible for a baby who had been visited by the Grim Reaper.

Everything but eat.

The freedom of being untethered from fear allowed an unexpected door to crack open when Jade was almost three years old, and I returned to work as a pediatric nurse. But the position wasn't like my dance floor at the hospital where I was John Travolta good. No job would ever replace the magic I performed on the postpartum floor or my dynamic duo partnership with Lynel. But it was a job that helped me contribute substantially to our family's income. Something that gave me a reprieve from the constant routine of keeping Jade alive. Something that gave me a taste of freedom again. Something that reopened my eyes to a world outside the walls of my home. Becky and Mom swooped in to help with Jade when I worked, and I quickly proceeded up each rung of the ladder of a company I would grow to loathe.

Within two short years of working for a home health agency that provided care for more than two hundred patients with disabilities, I was promoted from an entry-level pediatric nurse position to the director of nursing. I started at the bottom of the company, providing in-home care for a baby girl named Harper and ended at the top, handling professional responsibilities unlike any I ever had as a nurse.

But never would I forget Sweet Harper.

I met Harper when she was a seven-month-old infant who spent every day of her life as a resident of The Children's Hospital of Colorado before she was released to go home with around-the-clock nursing care. Harper was born two years to the day after Jade. She was a resilient girl who came into the world with overwhelming physical anomalies. Her care was beyond any I had ever given at the hospital. She defied odds that most babies couldn't and persevered through too many surgeries during a life that was still counted in months. A hole in the center of her windpipe was filled with a tracheostomy cannula and a tube connecting her to a ventilator that moved oxygen through her lungs. Her abdomen was littered with a road map of surgical scars and a G-Tube just like Jade's. The nursing care I gave Jade was overwhelming, but Harper's medical needs frightened me. I was afraid I was going to break her. Hurt her. Fail her. But I showed up to my 6 a.m. shifts anyway, and Sweet Harper smiled just enough above her absent mandible to remind me that she missed me while I was gone. Mornings came too early after pumping for Jade every three hours through the night, and my early start with Harper was a brutal reminder that I had aged rapidly since Jade was born. Only Harper could make an exhausting drive in the dark something I looked forward to.

Every morning I snuck through the front door of Harper's bilevel home, crept up the stairs, and sat my nurse travel bag beside a medical crib in the living room. "Good morning, my Sweet Harper," I whispered to her. The blankets covering Harper's feet bounced as she turned her head toward the woman she had come to recognize as her day nurse. I scooped her medically fragile body into my arms, mindful of the plethora of tubes and wires that sustained her life every second of the day. Then I held her close as I sang "Jesus Loves Me" to a baby who was unable to hear through small nubs of ears that had grown on her cheeks. She watched my lips move and smiled back at me, never the wiser that my tune was always off-key.

My time with Harper was short, though. Just a few precious months. And before I knew it, I exchanged an in-home nursing position for a management position. The owners of the company recognized early on that I had leadership potential, and they rushed me through myriad vacant nursing positions to push me to their peak. They needed more and more of what they deemed my expertise, which fueled my rapid ascent to the top of a company that would betray me in the end. When Jade was five years old, I was at the pinnacle of my nursing career with a salary, a title, and respect that I earned at the expense of time with Jade, the girls, and my husband. In that order.

Two years into my expeditious climb, I understood why I was catapulted so quickly to the top. The professional climate was unbearable. Nobody stayed long. I served faithfully under three different directors of nursing in those two years. Three highly experienced registered nurses. Three hard-working women with families to support. Three wise supervisors who saw things I did not. Had I not been so consumed with establishing my own professional dominance, I would have realized early on that the ladder climb was dangerous. It proved to be perilous to both my position and my ego.

The morning of my last day with the company, I drove toward the office with a gnawing in my gut. I gripped the steering wheel and remembered something Mom said many times. *Thy will be done, Lord.* The gnawing continued even after I whispered Mom's words to

Jesus. I couldn't explain it. I was reminded of the ominous foreboding I had felt five years before when I was pregnant with Jade. Something was off. Something was wrong. Something was about to happen that would once again change the trajectory of my life. Another one of those things I knew without knowing how.

"Angie, we need to see you in Jeff's office." I was greeted by the poker face of one of the owners as soon as I walked into work. I followed him to Jeff's office and sat in front of two men who strong-armed most people but didn't scare me. After all, I had beat the Grim Reaper. Nothing could happen in my life to buckle my knees again the way a fatal diagnosis for my baby had. And nothing they said would change the miracle that rescued Jade from the grave. I had already persevered past the worst pain I would ever experience. Those two guys were merely a sneeze on the Richter scale of my life.

"Angie, we have made a decision that all management-level employees will be required to sign a No Compete Agreement in order to remain employed with the company. That basically means that you agree not to work within a fifty-mile radius as a professional nurse if you separate from us. It is a condition of employment." I stared blankly at them as I remembered the three previous directors of nursing I had come to respect but who no longer worked for the company. I understood precisely what was happening. I was not the first, nor would I be the last, to sit in an uncomfortable hot seat waiting for life to change. I paused only long enough to take one solitary breath.

"I'm not signing anything." Words spoken beyond that were superfluous and redundant. Nothing more mattered after I had the nerve to so bluntly state my position.

The last thing I heard before I was handed a final check dated the day before was "Then you are no longer employed here."

Fifteen minutes earlier I walked into a place that gave me purpose again, promoted me from staff nurse to leader of the organization, and forced me to cultivate professional abilities I never even wanted. Just as quickly and for the first time in my life, I walk-of-shamed out of that place as I carried a box of personal items and donned a pink slip on my forehead for everyone to see. Blindsided by my own ignorance, I drove home knowing I had made a fatal mistake. I thought I was more valuable than the three directors before me. Instead, I was humiliated by a termination I didn't deserve.

Salary gone. Title gone. Respect gone.

But I still had Jade, and I still had my other children and Mom. I thought about those most important parts of my life on the drive home. The company could steal my dignity, but they couldn't take away the people I loved most.

Absent from my thoughts was Todd. I didn't even consider calling him. Our frail marriage had not gotten stronger over the years, and despite bonding over the necessity of keeping Jade alive, neither of us was truly invested in the other. The gap between Todd and me had grown to a chasm so wide that we didn't even try to bridge the distance. I was certain the need for love and affection he craved from me had been found somewhere else. Nothing he could say would change my mind. I had no proof. It was just a truth I created in my head. I was crazy again.

Not unlike when I was pregnant with Jade.

My emotions were raw and exposed the rest of the day as I lived with this newest transformation of my life. I was sharp, then weepy. Angry, then confused. By the time Todd arrived home from work, I had experienced the grief cycle on repeat for ten hours. I sent the girls to the living room and put on a Disney movie for Jade. I had to break the news to Todd that I was no longer employed. But I didn't know how. Divorce had hovered around my life and stalked me for more than five years. I would be such a disappointment to Todd again. That was hardly the worst of it though. The thought of being a single mother again was daunting. But the thought of being an unemployed single mother was overwhelming.

"Why are you home so early?" Todd asked as he entered through the garage door carrying a gym bag and briefcase. Sitting at the dining room table in a haze of self-pity and humiliation, I ignored his nonchalant stroll into the house. I quietly strategized how to drop the bomb on him without starting a nuclear war. But everything about him made me angry. How he played U2 so loud I couldn't think. How he screamed at the TV during Nebraska Huskers football games. How he cut off the bottom half of his old T-shirts and sported belly shirts on his days off. Things that I once found tolerable in Todd had become sources of instant irritation. I couldn't even look at him without shuddering in disgust. Todd and I had slept in separate beds since Jade was born. Five full years. There was no couple time. No rekindling of lost passion. No connection to each other physically or emotionally. I didn't even like his cooking anymore.

There was nothing left to save.

I was on the precipice of becoming a single parent again long before the morning's events. But the magnitude of being unemployed coupled with the demise of my marriage had come to a head at the same time. Unbeknownst to me, both would be dealt with in a single conversation. I didn't mean to surprise Todd with a sneak attack when he simply went through his day's motions of work, gym, and then home. It just sort of happened.

"Hey. Why are you home so early?" He repeated.

I looked up from my haze and stared at him. I shuddered again. My head dropped, and my eyes shifted to the table in front of me. "I was fired this morning," I whispered. Before he could inhale enough air to cross his vocal cords he responded to my revelation in a volume that felt like a freight train running through my ears.

"You what? You were fired this morning? What the hell are you talking about, and why didn't you call me?" His cheeks grew red, and the look on his face told the story of where the discussion was headed.

"What were you going to do about it? Yell at me like you're doing now? Because I definitely didn't need that after what I went through this morning. Don't worry, I saved almost all of my income from the past year. I'll figure this out." I looked back down. I was humiliated. With trembling fingers, I traced scratches on the table from years of family dinners.

"What the hell happened, Ang?" He said as he dropped his gym bag and briefcase hard to the floor and walked toward me.

"I got fired, Todd. Did you not hear me? I got freaking fired. I no longer have a job. I'm no longer employed. I'm no longer making money. So that means I'm no longer valuable to you. As if I have been anyway for the past five years."

"What are you talking about?" He bellowed even louder. "Don't you put this on me. I didn't even know about this until five seconds ago. What did you do to get fired?"

A sparring of words ensued over the next two hours in which we equally and cruelly pointed out everything wrong with the other and hurled insults like javelins. When the shuddering didn't stop, I knew the time was at hand. The time to disconnect completely from my husband. The time to start a healing process. The time for my third marriage to end. It wasn't ideal or convenient, but it was a conversation that was more than five years in the making.

"I'm done, Todd. I can't do this anymore. We don't have a marriage. You and I both know what's been going on for years now, and I'm just done. Even if I'm wrong. Even if I'm wrong about everything, I am done."

"What are you talking about, Ang? You want to get a divorce? Are you kidding me right now? You want to end our marriage after almost thirteen years over what? An argument?" He paused then attacked again. "You really are a three-time loser, aren't you?" I had taught him well over the years how to use his tongue to do the most damage.

If I had any hope for reconciliation left, it was stolen with those words. Todd didn't understand that it wasn't about just one argument. It wasn't even about fifty arguments. It was about an accumulation of years of mistrust, bitterness, and resentment. Losing my job was merely a catalyst for change that had been gusting around in my head like a tornado for years. I was done this time. There was no going back. There was no repairing the damage. There was no longer a future together. Even if I was just crazy again.

"Don't do this, Ang. Please don't do this. I just want my wife back. You don't touch me anymore. You don't say, 'I love you,' anymore. We don't even sleep in the same bed anymore. I don't want a divorce, Angie. I just want my wife back." Todd wept so hard I could feel his sorrow across the room.

"You want your wife back?" I paused before my final attack. "Did you say you want your wife back? I spent the first two years of Jade's life alone in a freaking dungeon keeping her alive while you did things I still don't even know about. You want your wife back now? I'm sorry, but you can't have her back. You lost her years ago. I can't do this anymore." My heart was numb from too much trauma over the previous five years. Trauma that wasn't brought on solely by Jade's extraordinary medical care. "I'm done, Todd. I don't love you anymore."

My words broke him. I broke him. He fell to his knees and sobbed the same way I had when Dr. Allen delivered Jade's first brain MRI results. Todd surrendered his desire to keep our marriage intact there on the floor, then packed two suitcases for the journey that started for both of us that night. I didn't watch him walk out the front door because I was afraid I would change my mind. He didn't look back because he didn't want me or the girls to see how broken he was.

After he drove down the road, for the first time in years, I crawled into a king-size bed in the master bedroom with Jade and closed my eyes with peace in my cold and hardened heart. I was relieved. I was free. But I was a failure again.

Todd was right. I really was a three-time loser. And I might even be crazy.

I awoke the next morning curled up next to Jade, aching with sadness for all that was lost. I no longer had a job. I no longer had a husband. I no longer had my dignity. I slid out of bed into the darkness of a day that had not yet dawned while Jade snored like Emmie and Todd. I crept down the stairs to the unfinished basement, a place I had not visited for some time. I needed to be far enough away from the girls and Jade so they wouldn't hear the cry of a three-time loser and the sound of failure coming from their mother. I stood at the bottom of the stairs and closed the door behind me as I looked around at boxes of memories I wouldn't soon forget.

Wedding photos.

The first box I saw was labeled with a red Sharpie in Todd's handwriting. I wasn't ready to open it or look at all I had lost. All Todd had lost. All the girls had lost. Then I remembered not only was I about to be divorced again, but I was also unemployed. A cataclysmic emotion I had never experienced swirled around me like a Tasmanian devil. I began kicking boxes, throwing picture frames, and cussing loudly until I found myself crying on the cold, concrete floor where I was reminded of other floors Jesus had joined me on in the past five years.

"What now, God? What am I supposed to do now?" Even though Jade's miracle had brought me closer to Jesus, I was still a broken mess of a woman. I wasn't back in the dungeon, but I was in a basement. A cold, dim, unfinished basement where I was surrounded by boxes of my life, stored for another day. But that was before another day had taken on a new meaning. That was before another day would be faced as a single mother with six children at home. That was before another day would come with no prospects for a job to buy food for those children.

I was still crying when I felt my phone vibrate in my pajama pants pocket.

"I heard what happened. Don't let this get you down. You are an amazing nurse, and we love you. Harper misses you." Jill was Sweet Harper's mother and the fiercest Warrior Mama I had ever known. She sent a message that would jar me back to my place in this world, make me look around at where I was lying, and open my eyes to a possibility I had not considered until that moment. It was as if God heard me and responded with a message I couldn't ignore. Suddenly, the unfinished basement I was staring at metamorphosed in my imagination into an office with desks and computers. Employees bustled about as we discussed our patients. Home health patients.

All children with disabilities. A company where I could take care of more babies like Sweet Harper and grow a team that would also be like family. A company that would bring my life full circle from the woman I was in The Waiting Room to the woman I had become since then. A company that would give me freedom to do the right thing in all that I did simply because it was the right thing to do.

My company.

I sprung to my feet with a vision of a future where I could care for Jade at home, pay the bills, and discover a new level of professional success. A future where others mattered more than me. A future where I was surrounded by Harpers and Lillys and Jades.

I ran up the stairs with a genesis brewing inside. Jade was awake in a bed she was unfamiliar with and whimpered as I entered the room.

"Jadey, it's OK. Mommy was just downstairs," I said. Tears I cried in the basement were not yet dry on my cheeks, and Jade started to cry for me.

"Mommy sad?" Jade was wise beyond any predictions of the experts.

"Oh Jadey, you have such a tender heart, my sweet girl. Don't cry. Mommy's OK." I gently pulled Jade toward me and then realized what I had said. *Tender Heart*. Jade had a tender heart. It was the perfect name for a company that would take care of children with disabilities. *Tender Hearts Home Healthcare*. Jade's sweetness led me to the name of the company that had just been born in the cold basement of my home.

"Bravo, Jadey Bug. You are brilliant." A dream was blossoming. I had to call Lynel even though it wasn't light out yet. I couldn't wait to tell her about Tender Hearts and to ask her to join my company.

"Hello, Angie? Are you OK?" Lynel was groggy but awake enough to know it was me.

"Lynel, I just had to tell you. I got fired yesterday, and I'm getting a divorce, and I just decided to start my own home health agency!" I spoke so fast Lynel asked me to repeat what I said.

"You're starting a home health agency? Todd's gone? You got fired? What's going on?" Lynel was fully awake at this point but confused by my rapid-fire life updates that machine-gunned her through the phone.

"Lynel, I want you to come work with me once I get everything in place. We can be the dynamic duo again!" I was giddy to work with Lynel again. Starting my own company would be sweeter if Lynel and I were back together.

But Lynel wasn't excited like I was.

"Oh girl, I didn't want to say anything yet. But we're moving. Lance took a job in Oklahoma, and we're going there to be closer to my family."

I couldn't believe it. Lynel was leaving me. We wouldn't work together again. I was terrified to do life without Lynel close enough to cover for me when I was drowning. And the trifecta of life events of the previous twenty-four hours certainly was enough to sink me. But instead of letting myself slip under the water again, I started a G-Tube feeding for Jade and pondered all the uncertainty that came with being fired, getting divorced, and starting my own company.

All in less than a day.

When the girls woke up later that morning, I gathered them together and broke their hearts with the news that Todd was gone. For good this time. Even though sadness permeated our home, a sense of relief overshadowed our pain. A hard marriage hadn't just been difficult for Todd and me. My daughters were also enmeshed in the dysfunction. I could wear the brand of Three-Time Loser. But I didn't want the girls to be affected any longer by a marriage that was doomed to fail long before the last baby was born into it. I looked around at our home, the girls, and a future that overwhelmed me. I took a deep breath. I prayed. And I trusted that I could handle whatever would come next.

Then I remembered Mom's words. *Thy will be done, Lord.* The same words I uttered without knowing the magnitude of what they meant or what they could do. The power of surrender had taken over my life, and I was about to watch God's plan unfold for all His glory. I didn't know how, but I knew I had to trust Him in a way I never had before. All that Jade suffered and all that I struggled through were about to make sense in a way I couldn't have planned or scheduled on my own.

The days that followed were long and exhausting as I feverishly built my company from the basement up. Kinnah helped with filing and phone calls. Brooke and Hope helped with babysitting Faith, Emmie, and Jade. Five months after naming a company that was no more than a vision in my head, Tender Hearts Home Healthcare admitted its first pediatric patient. The month after my divorce was final, I received my first paycheck. Five additional months later, I had eight patients and ten waiting for me to find time in my busy schedule to admit them. My life had metamorphosed again.

From the basement of my home where I started a company for the Harpers and the Lillys and the Jades of Northern Colorado, there was also a redemption of the creosote on my soul I first noticed in The Waiting Room. Never could I imagine from the pit of my professional career and personal life that I would emerge in a place only God could have designed. Never did I expect the redemption of my brokenness. Never did I dream I would one day become the owner of a tremendously successful home health agency. It was there, on a cold concrete floor in the basement of my home, that I found beauty from the ashes and my place in this world . . . with Jade and her Waiting Room friends.

25

I Know Heaven

Two more years passed in what felt like a moment in time. Tender Hearts afforded me the opportunity to laser-focus on Jade again, and she made strides she was never supposed to make. I was in awe of her and the life she was given. Consumed by all she accomplished. More than seven years of intense heat and pressure of the tectonic plates had changed Jade. It had changed me too. I was strong. I was faithful. I was different.

I rested my head on a mound of pillows and watched Jade climb to the top of the king-size mountain in my bedroom. It was an exhilarating climb for Jade. The *Rocky* theme song played in my mind while Jade pulled her body over the footboard and landed with a smile and a sigh at my feet. Every time she scored a triumph like this, I was reminded of the dungeon. The days I feared she would never accomplish a feat so great. She scaled the bed by herself just to join me in evening cuddles. It was a microvictory to others but a championship ring to us. I was as proud of Jade as she was of herself. She arrived at the top of her Mount Everest smiling big enough to show off the gap left by her missing front teeth. This was but another milestone I was naively assured Jade would never meet.

Jade knew the trophy awaiting her would be coveted time alone with Mommy at the end of our long day. It was a welcome escape from the chaos that ensued outside the doors of my bedroom. The girls were downstairs arguing with one another over the TV, a boyfriend, the last Dr Pepper. Some meaningless aggravation. Not much had changed over the previous seven years except that everyone was older, taller, and louder.

Jade and I rested together on the bed as we often did. We curled up and giggled while my fingers chased her and begged to play with her beautiful dark curls. My fingers weren't merely an annoyance to Jade. They were a menace. They were relentless. They were the enemy.

I grabbed at Jade unforgivingly while she giggled then yelled at me in a voice she had found years before at Ray's modular.

"No, Mommy! Top, top! Pwease, pwease." Jade couldn't stand for me to play with her curls anymore. They were hers, after all. I loved her expressive opinions that emerged when she started talking.

During times of rambunctious play, it was easy to forget the internal struggles Jade had. Her fragile nervous system still misfired and got confused. Anything near her face was a threat. Food. Drink. Kisses. She hadn't had a haircut since she was born, and the ends of her hair had grown with her since our very first rainy April day together. The day I met my Jewel of Heaven. If I touched the ends, I would touch a time from seven years before. A time I would never forget.

When I could get close enough to Jade, I ran each strand of her hair through the tips of my fingers. I thought about when she was a baby with a head full of dark, curly hair. I remembered the times I would gently stroke her curls with my fingers. When I was anxious or one of us was crying, which was often. One of the only ways I could comfort myself in our darkest days was to play with Jade's hair. To feel part of her that I might not be able to touch someday. I longed for the days I could touch her hair when she was too little to pull away from me. But then I was grateful that she was able to pull away from me.

The little girl who was never supposed to crawl or walk got onto all fours and dove in to kiss my cheek. Soft like a butterfly but stealthy like an owl. With one awkward leap onto my chest, Jade dissolved the presumption that her life would be short and tragic. I relished in her ability to crawl atop me. To elude my fingers like a professional boxer in the ring while I reached for another tickle or lock of hair. She giggled and squirmed even more. She tried to get far away from me. Jade was strong. Jade was brave.

"Read a me, Mommy!" Jade knee-jumped on the bed next to me. "Read a me fwom my book! Pweaaaase, Mama!" That was the white-flag ending to our pretend battle. I returned my fingers to their holsters and reached for the book on the table beside my bed that Jade wanted me to read. It was a children's Bible storybook. A present to Jade from my grandmother. Mom's mom. The grandkids and great-grandkids called her Mamaw. The book was Jade's favorite. We read it every night. There was one story we hadn't yet read, so I turned to that chapter, chapter 18.

"*Dancing in Heaven*. That's the name of the chapter, Jade. Heaven is where Mamaw and Mattie live now." Jade raised her eyebrows high. She remembered Mamaw, who had passed away a few years earlier. She remembered Mattie, our tortoiseshell cat, who taught Jade to crawl.

"Mamaw still wuv me?" Jade asked with a sad little-girl face. Jade was close to Mamaw before she died. She still didn't understand why ninety-year-old mamaws left their great-grandchildren. Especially ones as sweet as Jade. Jade often spoke of the time she ate her first bites of real food when she was three-and-a-half years old. The night Mamaw and Mom were there beside her cheering her on at the kitchen table and gushing over how brave she was. A plate of spaghetti prepared by Todd became the gateway to Jade eating everything by mouth. She never forgot Mamaw was there when she was so brave. When she climbed one of her hardest mountains.

"Jadey Bug, of course Mamaw loves you." I gave her a deep hug and brought her in close for the few seconds she allowed. "So does Mommy, Jadey. Sooooo much." Jade had more questions.

"Mattie's in heaven with Mamaw?" We had already gone over this many times since Mattie was struck by a car in front of our house. But Jade struggled with remembering. She had to be told the same story over and over until it found its place deep inside her memory. Jade hadn't forgotten the day we found Mattie lying in the road outside our house. She would never forget such a loss. She just didn't remember the heart-crafted story I made up about Mamaw and Mattie together in heaven. She missed them both terribly.

"Yes, Jadey. Mamaw is taking care of Mattie for us since they are both in heaven now. Mamaw feeds her and plays with her and loves all over her for us. Isn't that sweet, Jadey? Mamaw is taking such good care of Mattie." It was at least the twentieth time I told Jade the story about Mamaw and Mattie in heaven. It gave Jade peace to hear about them being together.

Jade took a moment to think about what I said. She stopped crawling on me, and her arms fell still at her sides. She paused to find the path that would lead to the memory garden under her curls. Her eyes scrolled up and to the left. She was looking somewhere far, far away to recall the story I had already told her many times.

"Remember, Jadey? Remember what I told you about Mamaw? And when Mattie went to be with Mamaw in heaven? Remember how I told you we'll get to see Mamaw and Mattie again some . . ."

Jade interrupted me before I could finish. She found the memory she was looking for. But it wasn't about Mamaw or Mattie.

"Ohhh!" Jade tilted her head and curls toward the ceiling and pointed up with her index finger. She was knee-jumping again beside me, excited to tell me all she knew about heaven.

"I know heaven, Mommy!" I readied myself for a beautiful story. "That's where I met Jesus!"

I pulled Jade onto my chest. I held her close and squinted my face at her.

"You met Jesus, Jadey?" I wasn't sure I understood what she said.

Then Jade told me a story so grand it had to be true. Only a seven-year-old with the cognitive abilities of a four-year-old could so truthfully and stunningly describe a meeting with Jesus in heaven.

When she was still a fetus in my uterus.

Jade was so anxious to tell me about when she met Jesus that her little hands danced wildly above her face. She continued to point to a place and a person above us that neither of us could see.

"Yes, Mommy. When He was making me, I met Jesus. I couldn't find you, so I asked Jesus, 'Where's my Mommy?' And then He put me back in your tummy."

The clarity and profoundness of Jade's words left me stunned. I cradled the daughter I almost lost eight years earlier in my grateful arms. She knew nothing about the day I found myself covered in blood. Experiencing a "catastrophic hemorrhage" in front of the toilet on the bathroom floor. On my knees in complete agony before God. Begging Him not to take the tiny life inside my body. I had only been pregnant for thirteen weeks and two days. It was a pregnancy-ending event. I remembered my words. My shrill screams. My heartbreak. My petition for another chance to be my baby's mommy.

"Oh God, please don't take my baby! Father! Father! Hear me, please, Father! Please let me raise this baby!" I sobbed while on my knees in front of a toilet full of blood and clots. There was no way a baby so small could survive a blood loss so great. There was no way my baby would make it to my arms. My pregnancy was over.

But then, it wasn't.

I sat on the bed still holding Jade close to me and remembering my cries for help all those years before. I imagined my sweet cherub baby wearing her angel wings. Frolicking in heaven. Searching for her mommy.

Mama! Mama! Where awwww you, Mama?

In my mind I saw Jesus appear from a white, marshmallow cloud in front of Jade. Arms stretched out and smiling beneath his bearded cheeks. Ready to receive this newest citizen of heaven with all the other miscarried, stillborn, and aborted babies who hadn't met their mommies yet.

Where's my Mommy? The only words spoken between them.

Agonal cries and desperate prayers interrupted the celestial meeting in heaven. Jesus heard me. Then He saved Jade, and He gave her back to me.

He put me back in your tummy.

Just like that, everything was changed. There was no further conversation between Jade and Jesus. I was no longer alone on the bathroom floor. Jesus joined us there, cradling me in His arms while I lay in a mess of blood and tears. Such a merciful Father that He met me right where I was. Despite the location.

Then I realized Jade loved me so much that while dancing in heaven in front of Jesus, she was looking for me. That my prayer permeated heaven's gates and filled the heart of Jesus. That He came down from His place in heaven to hold me and to give Jade back to me. That He loved us that much.

There was no making up a story like that. I wondered how Jade knew what happened to us that day on the bathroom floor. I had never mentioned it to her. Even if I had, she simply didn't have the cognitive abilities to understand any of it or weave a story so brilliant on her own.

I didn't know what to say to Jade. I lay on the bed with her favorite book still in my hand and chapter 18 unread. I was stunned. I held Jade closer than ever before. I stared at her in all the perfection Jesus made her in as she gazed up at me, utterly delighted in herself. She remembered her meeting with Jesus and told me all about it.

It was astounding.

Jade knew all about heaven. Not because of a story I made up about Mamaw and Mattie. But because that's where she met Jesus. My little storyteller, who was never a storyteller before and hasn't been one since, rested her head on my chest. I caught my breath, ran my fingers through her perfect curls, and let my heart baste in the revelation of our very first miracle. One of many we would experience in Jade's life. A miracle I didn't even know we were the recipients of until that day. The day Jade declared, "I know heaven."

26

Beauty Under Pressure

$\mathcal{J}$ ade wasn't a diamond in the rough anymore. In her thirteen years, she conquered many mountains and giants. She learned to crawl. Then walk. Then eat. Her G-Tube was merely a placeholder these days. A nuisance. A constant reminder of a difficult time gone by and necessary only if she became ill. We still had to visit The Pediatric Hospital every few years for evaluations so the specialists could glean more data and try to steal our hope. Every time I took Jade there, I was reminded of the darkness of our dungeon when she was a baby. Not because I was still that shameful woman who threw up in the bathroom sink of The Waiting Room. But because the specialists who evaluated Jade pounced on anything that would classify her as a disabled child.

But Jade was Jade. Beauty Under Pressure. A jewel formed from a lifetime of intense heat, massive pressure, and tectonic plate movement. She could handle almost anything after all she had been through. So even an evaluation at The Pediatric Hospital was just another day for the girl who did everything the experts said she never would.

For the third time since Jade was born, a team of residents, psychologists, and medical specialists observed and studied Jade, like bacteria in a petri dish. The day was an agonizing succession of appointments and assessments aimed to define Jade and her future. We were on a merciless march from room to room. Evaluator to evaluator. Critic to critic. Everyone had questions. Everyone had opinions. Everyone had Jade in their crosshairs. They stared at her over tilted glasses and through postdoctoral filters, intent that she would not escape unscathed.

I made sure she did.

We trudged through the day, stopping only to use the bathroom and take a lunch break. Rooms full of experts gathered updates about Jade. How she walked. How she pronounced words. How she built LEGOs. How she reasoned through questions even I didn't understand. How she would have lifelong struggles. How she was different from my other children.

At the end of the merciless day, we were invited to a crescendo meeting where I would be told everything they found wrong with Jade. As usual. The team tried to be cordial but were disconnected and sterile. Factual. Data driven. Their voices repeated relentlessly. Like nails on a chalkboard. They had done this many times before. With many other children and families. They naively expected that I would accept everything we were told. Like I did when Jade was a baby. But they didn't know the mother sitting in front of them. I was changed. I was a warrior. Like Lilly's mom. And Harper's mom. Nothing they said was so shocking that I would be thrust back to the dungeon. They wouldn't break me this time.

"Jade has made significant progress. Far more than anyone could have anticipated. She is such a pleasant girl and easy to work with. And so beautiful. These are things that will be strengths for her as she grows into her potential, but . . ."

But.

There was always a "but" when the specialists talked about Jade.

They were boringly predictable. They always forgot where our journey started and the obstacles we overcame to get here. They forgot it was the doctors at The Pediatric Hospital who spoke words of death over Jade thirteen years before. With predictions of genetic syndromes and metabolic storage disorders. With Niemann Pick and every other fatal disease they could think of. With inaccurate prophecies of Jade's death that almost killed me in the garage. With promises of nothing more than a tiny casket and a funeral.

No hope. No joy. No future.

But I was changed. I wasn't falling for it again. They wouldn't steal my hope this time. I knew who Jade was better than anyone else. Especially strangers.

Nobody in the room wanted to talk about the miraculous healing of Jade's brain except me. Or the normal MRI that perplexed so many. Or the complete restoration of the myelin of her central white matter in three short months. There was no scientific explanation for it. So they didn't talk about it.

But that's the way it is with miracles. They are unexplainable except by faith.

"But Jade's IQ has remained unchanged since she was evaluated five years ago and also ten years ago. Her trajectory is the same." The first examiner was a hefty woman with a round face and deep, coarse voice. I stared at the thick red lipstick smeared on her tight lips and front tooth while she talked. She told me things about IQ I already knew. Fairly constant. Unchanging. Jade's was 58. Below normal. Below the IQ of some kids with Down syndrome. This was no surprise to me. I was reassured Jade would be able to have a full and rich life in one of the many wonderful programs for the intellectually disabled.

"Look at the bright side. She could be the captain of the ARC softball team some day."

They had no idea what a bright side looked like. But Jade would.

There was no discussion that day about the monumental strides Jade made in her short life. The accomplishments. The feats of strength and bravery. The mountains she climbed and the giants she slayed. There was no time spent on those accolades. Her monumental victories were insignificant details to the experts. Unworthy of even a second-place trophy or honorable mention. Her miracle was ignored. The team focused on tests and benchmarks. Scores and numbers. Scales and grids that told them Jade wasn't like other kids her age. That she wasn't Xanadu Gray. That she never would be. They recommended special programs for special kids who needed special help. They assumed I would just go along with what they thought was best for Jade.

But they didn't know the mother sitting in front of them. I was transformed into a person who put my faith in Jesus instead of them. Metamorphosed by extreme pressure and tectonic plate movements of stress, anxiety, and lack of sleep. I trusted that God had a purpose and a plan for Jade's life. Just like Mom said. The journey was long. It was hard. We never escaped the struggles or the trouble. But we weren't alone. That made all the difference. I had strength. I had hope. I had Jesus. Nobody would steal my joy again or speak anything negative over my daughter. I wouldn't stand for it. Not ever again. I looked forward to watching Jade prove them wrong. Just like she had done so well on so many occasions.

They shuffled papers and closed their briefcases signaling they were done with their evaluation and report of Jade's limitations.

"Well, that's pretty much it. Do you have any questions for the team?"

I waited. Then I posed a question to the seven men and women staring at us.

"Yes, actually, I do have a question for you all. Do you know how jade is formed?" I stuttered then clarified my question.

"Not Jade. Not my daughter. I mean the gemstone. Jade." They looked at one another puzzled. They didn't know.

"It's actually very interesting. Jade is formed by intense heat and tectonic plate movement. When ocean basalt rock sustains extremely high pressures, it's transformed into something beautiful. It's a metamorphic rock. Jade wasn't always jade." The team didn't understand why I was telling them how dark, crusty rocks become beauty.

"I didn't know how jade was formed when I named my daughter. I was still pregnant with her when I chose her name. I had no idea before she was born what we would go through these past thirteen years. But I want you to know, and I'm asking you to hear me. Really listen to me, please." I paused so they could focus. "Just like the gemstone is formed by pressure, so was my Jade. So was I. So are all my warrior friends who have children with disabilities. And so are their children. I don't want you to ever forget this. Every time you sit in front of a family like us. Don't lose sight of the beauty these children bring the world. Don't discount it. Celebrate it. Jade is beauty under pressure. I am beauty under pressure. This girl sitting in front of you, my daughter . . . she wasn't always Jade. She was transformed by the miracle that healed her brain and the journey we've traveled. So it doesn't matter to me if her IQ is 58 or 98. God has a purpose for her life and never would have left her crusty basalt." Jade and I stood and walked toward the door. "Thank you for your time today."

They got it. They understood. If only one person in that room changed the way they viewed us in our world, then I made a difference that day for a family who would follow behind us on a road they did not choose.

I stepped into the hall and looked at Jade. She was my Jewel of Heaven. The one Jesus left the ninety-nine to find. She was made exactly how God intended for her to be. Perfectly loved.

I was used to walking away from these appointments with a heavy heart, but not anymore. I would never again be choked by people who didn't know Jade. They didn't intend to lessen Jade's value. But they didn't see who she really was. Who she was beyond the graphs and statistics. Who she was made in the image of. We would never return to sit in front of this team again. It was time to step into the future untethered by false predictions. Jade would have more mountains to climb. I was certain of this. I saw her struggles every day. Long before they did. But we would conquer every one of them. Together.

We walked out of the office gleaming with pride after slam-dunking thirteen years of transformation at them. I wasn't hobbled. I didn't limp out. I held Jade's perfect hand and summoned a lion's strength to fight every battle headed our way. Even if the battles paled in comparison to all the others we had already fought and won. Jade skipped out of the building beside me remarkably full of energy after such a long, exhausting day. I would not allow her to be reduced to a statistic. She was beauty under pressure. A miracle. The flesh-and-blood result of a massive tectonic plate collision. Not a disabled teenager with an IQ that would prevent her from mundane tasks like driving a car. She was so much more than that.

I looked at Jade. She smiled and laughed at everything. Her curly, waist-length hair flowed behind her. She was a bursting balloon of happiness. Content just to be with me and hold my hand. She had something I did not and might not ever have. An innocence that protected her heart from the darkness of the world.

I thought I wanted to be like Jade. Oblivious. Unaware of the certainty that more struggles would come. But then I might not understand the awesomeness of the journey ahead of us. A spectacular chapter of new life about to unfold. I couldn't possibly miss out on that.

Jade sprung into the front passenger seat. She snapped her seat belt in place, flipped down the visor mirror, and admired herself.

"Mommy, I have my dad's blue eyes, don't I?"

"Ah yes, Jadey. You have beautiful blue eyes. You definitely got your dad's eyes." I stared back at her through my old and faded brown eyes.

"And I have your big butt, right?" Jade laughed. It was an energizing jab, reminding me Jade was a teenager. We were a team. Just alike. She was mine, and I was hers. Despite being on a journey I wouldn't have chosen, I was grateful for the one we were on.

When we arrived home, I made my way to the haven of my room where I usually retreated when I was overwhelmed. I needed to unwind. To rest. To think about all the blessings and miracles the doctors at The Pediatric Hospital ignored. I forgot how easy it was to let a room full of experts crawl under my skin. I shuffled through a playlist on my phone and listened with my earbuds. I absorbed the words of songs that meant so much to me. Songs that played in the background of my life after I dug myself out of the dungeon. Songs that yanked the faith out of me when I was faithless. I played one of my recent favorites on repeat. "Beautiful Story." A song that lulled me to sleep so many nights I could sing it backward.

The hot caramel voice of Michael Tait and the Newsboys soothed my soul while I sat with Jesus and talked to Him about our day. I refused to let anyone steal Jade's victories from us. I refused to look at her life as anything but a series of miracles. There was a time when I lost heart. When I lost faith. When I had no idea the plans God had for us. But that was all changed. Once I saw the miracles, they couldn't be unseen.

I heard a thump from the living room. A loud thud that sounded like Jade had taken a fall. I looked at the table beside my bed to garner a quick view of the security video screen that captured every movement in the room below me. Jade hadn't fallen. She was dancing. Twirling and jumping like I had never seen her before. An unlikely dance unfolded on the screen in front of me while "Beautiful Story" continued to play in my ear.

You work all things together for good.

Jade was dancing to a tune on the television that I couldn't hear in my earbuds.

But she wasn't just dancing. She was twirling round and round in the exact rhythm of the song playing in my ear. Her arms were outstretched beside her as she leaned her head way back. "Beautiful Story" played while Jade danced in perfect rhythm to its beat.

While I watched her dance, I remembered something spoken over Jade when she was a baby. Words that were painfully seared onto my heart. Words that I carried with me for thirteen years.

"She will never walk. She will never talk. She will never eat. You should begin to plan for a short life of many challenges."

I watched Jade on the video screen continue her perfect dance. They were so wrong. I proclaimed out loud, "BUT they never said she wouldn't dance!" It was one of the most beautiful days of my life. The day when everything became so clear. I watched the girl who was never supposed to walk, talk, or eat perform a dance so perfect she could have been mistaken for a trained dancer. Jade spun around like Clara in the *Nutcracker* ballet. This was what beauty under pressure looked like.

I covered my face with my hands while tears of gratitude flowed.

I delighted in Jade's dance. Her outstretched arms seared a new memory onto my heart and extinguished the words spoken over us thirteen years before. I marveled at her magnificence. I loved every square inch of Jade exactly how she was made. She was perfect. Perfect to me and perfect to Jesus. She was perfect in all her imperfections. An extraordinary human being with a heart bigger than anyone else I had ever known. A life Jesus orchestrated before she was born. One only He could so intricately design. Hers was a *beautiful story* of transformation, metamorphosis, and miracle healing.

The past thirteen years finally made sense.

Unasked questions were answered. Tears were turned into sweet, drenching peace. Jesus had an exquisite plan for Jade's life all along. Her unexpected dance brought us full circle. From the Grim Reaper's visit in her hospital room to the Filthy Hands of a Christian biker group to that exact moment where Beauty Under Pressure danced in the living room.

He works all things together for good.

Jade was proof of that.

I was full. Rested. Healed and restored. I looked at the video screen again to catch another glimpse. She was still dancing in all her glory on the stage she commanded in our living room. Her platform was far bigger and her purpose far greater than the smallness of my home.

As she twirled around, I sang along with the words of the song. I praised God that He has a plan. That He always knows best. That He works all things together for good. Especially during the pressure, heat, and collision of tectonic plates meant to change crusty basalt into gemstones.

We had celebrated thirteen unpromised years of struggles and triumphs. Some days were more difficult on my heart than others. This one, however, was an extraordinary day in the life of my Jewel of Heaven. I wouldn't trade Jade, or our beautiful story, for anything.

Not for Xanadu Gray.

Not for a life void of hardships.

Not even for a road more traveled.

27

Gratitude

I stood near the bottom of the stairs in a crowd of family and friends. Becky and AJ, Brooke, Hope and Kinnah, Faith and Emmie, Mom and my grandchildren gathered near me. They all moved in close as I dabbed my eyes dry with a tissue. Tears fell again when I thought about the last sixteen years of my life and how the days were blown away like waves upon the ocean. It wasn't supposed to be this way. We weren't supposed to be standing there together in my home that April afternoon.

Every specialist warned that Jade would not survive beyond a few years of life. And I believed them.

Until I didn't.

A miracle healing had saved Jade all those years before. The day at hand arrived upon the fragile wings of faith. A day none of us thought would come sixteen years earlier. A day that was almost stolen from us.

Almost.

As we waited impatiently at the bottom of the stairs for Jade to finish dressing, a black stretch limousine pulled in front of our house. The words "Happy 16th Birthday Jade!" decorated the rear window of the limousine. It was right on time to pick up Jade and her friends. We were excited for Jade to join us for her sweet sixteen party.

Surrounded by people who loved Jade, my mind was taken back to a place many years before. The place where I laid my head every night. Where I cried alone in the dark and wondered what Jade would have been like as a teenager. Where I dreamed of the mischief she would have gotten herself into. How she would have snuck out her window to meet a boy I didn't like. How she would have left her dirty clothes strewn about her room.

But I didn't have to dream about Jade's life. Soon my sixteen-year-old daughter would emerge from her bedroom and grace us with her presence on this extraordinary day. Wearing a dress she chose on her own. With her hair combed and styled all by herself. Walking gingerly down each stair in one inch heels she had never worn before. The suspense was thick among the crowd gathered to honor and celebrate Jade. In typical Jade style, she kept us all waiting.

"Jade! Your driver is here," I yelled up the stairs to her.

"OK, Mom. I'm almost done." Seconds later, the door to Jade's room opened. She stood in all her beauty at the top of the stairs. Truly magnificent. Her long, light-brown hair lay soft across her shoulders. The curls that survived her childhood were weighed down by the length of hair falling past her waist. Her crystal-blue eyes glistened in the late-afternoon sun. She wore a soft-white dress with pink flowers that stopped just above her knees and size 8 cream-colored women's heels. A rose-gold sash hung across her chest that read "Sweet 16," and she wore a tiara with the number 16 decorated in faux diamonds. Jade made her way down the stairs to the applause of a house full of guests. It was her day. The gratitude in our home was rich, like a chocolate cake on a sixteenth birthday that was never supposed to be.

This day that was almost stolen from us imprinted a memory on my heart that I would never forget.

Jade continued to the bottom of the stairs and reached out her arms to hug me. She was taller than me in her new shoes, and she smelled of sweet Calvin Klein perfume dabbed on her wrists and behind her ears. She smiled big enough for all of us to see a sliver of space between her two front teeth that she loved to display. Jade held me tight, and I began to weep as I remembered all she and I and Jesus had been through together. The Fishbowl and the dungeon. Bad Things and Normal Things. Doctor appointments and therapies.

Even Dr. Williams, Jade's trusted pediatrician for the past thirteen years, was left without words during her annual health checkup the day before. He was there when she vomited ten times a day. He was there to offer a voice of calm when Jade was sick. He was there to quiet my fears and reassure me. When I asked how many babies he had seen in his career born like Jade, who had their myelination fully restored, he answered by pointing at Jade. There was only one. Only Jade.

We had come so far.

I couldn't help thinking about all the extraordinary things Jade had done in her life. Things most children never get to experience. Just four years earlier, Jade and I climbed Lenawee Mountain in Colorado with Emmie and some friends. All the way to the summit. We were in the company of other individuals with disabilities and volunteers who helped them along. We claimed title that day to conquering our own Mount Everest. There were tears most of the way up the mountain. But in the end there was a triumph waiting for us at the peak. Another mountain climbed.

We did it together.

Later on, when a pandemic shut down the world and people locked themselves inside their own dungeons, Jade traveled with Emmie and me twenty-four times to Tijuana, Mexico, where we served as missionaries in the dirtiest, poorest areas of the Baja region. We built houses with other servants of the Lord. Then we established a mobile medical clinic and provided free healthcare to some of the sickest patients I have ever taken care of. It's where Jade learned to be a friend to strangers in a place that wasn't our home. Where I often saw Jade and little girls, whose language she didn't understand, walking down the dusty, dirt roads holding hands. Or braiding one another's hair while I tended to my patients. She learned to give and receive love in a way only Jesus and Tijuana, Mexico, could teach her.

Jade accomplished all of this before she was sixteen years old.

The baby who was supposed to die early in her life had climbed a mountain and become a missionary in Mexico. Only God could compose a symphony of life so perfect. Only Jesus could make beauty from ashes like He did with Jade's life.

I was lost in our memories, so Jade pulled loose from a hug I didn't want to end. Then everyone around us hugged Jade too. Including Mom, who took her turn and then looked at me with tears in her eyes.

"Angie, I told you God had a plan for your baby all those years ago. He knew this day would come, even when everyone told you it never would." I put my arms around Mom and held her tight.

"I never would have made it through the early days without you and Becky, Mom. Thank you for not giving up on me. And thank you for not giving up on Jade. Even when I did."

Jade made her way through a crowd of hugs, eager to go on her birthday limousine ride. A quick "Happy Birthday" song and photos with the family would have to do. It was her day. I let her write this story any way she wanted to.

I placed a long red runner outside the limousine as Jade requested, and she and her friends spent extra time on the "Red Carpet" while they were photographed by "paparazzi." She bedazzled us with her smile and charm as she posed for photos and inhaled a pretend life she dreamed of. Then Jade, Emmie, a few of my grandchildren, and Jade's friends climbed into the limo, laughing and giggling like teenage girls do. I stood back and stared at Jade in awe. I absorbed every bit of her I could get to soak into me. I basked in the miracles that saved Jade's life, and I wept again in gratitude for all we had been given. Instead of putting Jade into a coffin as I was assured I would someday, I was putting her into a limo for a birthday that was never supposed to be. Jade rode off with her friends and Emmie as the sun began to go down over the Rocky Mountains. I stood a while longer and watched the limo drive down the street with my miracle daughter while I marveled at the remarkable person she had become in those sixteen years.

As the limo drove away under the setting of the sun, I was reminded of the evening I stood on our deck alone. When I looked out over the tall, yellow grass while Jade rested in her bassinet in the dungeon, being fed through her G-Tube by a machine. The same evening I realized three of The Five were pregnant. The same evening my life almost ended in the garage. Sixteen years later, Jade no longer had a tube in her stomach. The cats were no longer alive to comfort my children when they were sad. And my life had been spared by a rescue so profound I would never be able to adequately explain it. So many tragedies had occurred since Jade was born. But so many tragedies were also averted. So many losses. But also so many victories.

We were just like every other person in the world.

We had a Xanadu Gray life.

Exactly what I prayed for.

One person in Jade's story was noticeably absent at Jade's party. A man who deserved to share in the triumph we were celebrating. In the years of Jade's feats of greatness, as she conquered many mountains and giants, much happened in our lives. Many deeply personal experiences and some unclimbable mountains that changed the tapestry of our future. Todd was not there. The person whom Jade loved more than anyone but me. Years of struggle with Jade had forged Todd and me together with a common bond but also created a chasm between us that we ultimately could not cross together. I was sad he wasn't there to see Jade come down the stairs or celebrate our daughter on a day we both fought so hard for.

As I lamented lost things, Jade's limo disappeared from my sight. The guests returned to their homes, but this evening wouldn't leave my heart for at least an eternity. Several hours later, Jade's friends were safely delivered to their own homes, and Jade and Emmie arrived back at our house. It was late, and Jade was exhausted from her evening of celebration. She and I walked up the stairs together, just the two of us. She went to her room, and I walked toward mine. I turned to look at her again before she closed her door.

"Jadey Bug . . ." I paused while I studied her and sixteen years of beauty under pressure. "Happy Birthday, Jadey Bug." She turned her head toward me as I rounded the corner to my room. Just like she had done fifteen years earlier while lying on her Princess Throne on her first birthday. I remembered the feeling of her feet on my lips as I blew against her high arches and how she giggled when I played "This Little Piggy" with her.

"Jadey," my voice cracked, "do you want to play 'This Little Piggy' with Mom?"

"What, Mom? Do I want to play what?"

"Never mind, Sweetheart. I love you. Sweet dreams." I shut the door to my room.

I couldn't explain the gratitude I felt knowing Jade had become a princess without a throne.

I crawled into my king-size bed and lay alone thinking again about sixteen years of mountains and giants. Dungeons and darkness. Miracles and Gratitude. I remembered all the people along the way whom I would forever be indebted to. Loved ones and strangers who had selflessly given or prayed or just been there in the shadows while I tried to drown myself in the sludge along the way. They were all placed on this journey with us for a reason. Each one of them a piece of a fantastical puzzle that could never have come together if just one of the pieces was missing. I thought about each of them and all they had given Jade and me.

Mom, who finally settled into retirement and was enjoying the quiet that came with age.

Each of The Five plus our sweet Twenty Two, who were surely being taken care of by Mamaw in heaven.

My children, who were all grown. Some who were married and some who had children of their own.

Becky, whom I owed my life and sanity to. She had two boys and worked as a speech-language pathologist with children like Jade.

Lynel, who still worked as a lactation consultant but hadn't met a woman yet who pumped for almost four years like I did.

Todd, who was remarried and happy with a wonderful woman God chose just for him.

Dr. Allen, who closed his practice and worked for a university imparting his brilliance to neurology students like only he could.

Cousin Rich and his friend Ray, who still rode their Harleys, volunteered their time feeding the homeless, and told anyone they could about Jesus.

But most of all, I thought about Jesus and how much He had done for us. How He was there with us all along. There on the bloody bathroom floor. There in The Fishbowl. There when the Grim Reaper showed up to steal Jade from me. There to Rescue me from myself in the garage. There to anoint the hands of a group of Christian bikers. There when Jade's brain was healed. There when she found the courage and the strength to take her first steps. There through all the Mountains and Giants.

He never left us. He was always there.

He sent all the right people at the exact right times, designing a road map so complex only Jesus could have charted our course.

The transformations that happened to both Jade and me in those sixteen years were astounding. Beauty Under Pressure. Jade metamorphosed into a beautiful butterfly just waiting to spread her wings and conquer more mountains and giants. And me . . . I was transformed from a lukewarm Christian who accepted Jesus Christ as my Savior at the age of eight to a Christ follower at the age of thirty-eight.

First, He saved me from my sins. Then He saved me from myself.

Sixteen years and a lifetime of miracles led me to find what was missing in my life. Freedom was right beside me all along. Nothing would ever again fill me like Jesus did.

I couldn't let the night end without one more look at Jade on this, her sweet sixteen birthday. A day I once thought would never come. One that would never come again. I tiptoed into her room where she lay sleeping, still wearing her birthday dress and sash. I laid my head on the pillow next to her head and thought about our days and months and years together. How we fought so hard and how I kept my promise to never leave her. I basked in the warmth of her skin as I lay next to her and thanked God I was not visiting her on this sixteenth birthday at a graveside. I had spent her first few years distracted by the dungeon as I struggled to claw my way out. But I found myself wishing I could go back there for just a moment and play "This Little Piggy" with her tiny toes and sing her a lullaby again. If only I could lie next to her like I did when she was little.

Just once more.

I stared at Jade through the dim nightlight that shined in her room with the most profound gratitude I had ever felt. I ran my fingers through her curls once more like I did when she was a baby. Then I stood and hovered over her like I had done so many times throughout the last sixteen years. I didn't want to leave her side. Not ever. I leaned over and kissed her on the forehead one more time, in awe of a life that was almost stolen from me.

Then I brushed my cheek against hers and whispered softly in her ear as she slept.

"We did it, Jadey Bug. We did it."

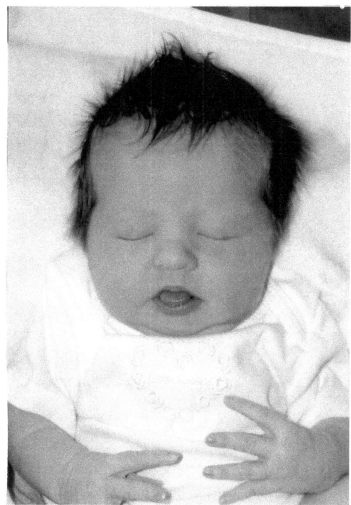

Jade's first photo

Brooke and Jade

Hope and Jade

Kinnah and Jade

  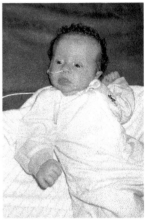

Faith and Jade   Emmie (in her favorite   Jade with her NG tube
                        blue gown) and Jade

Brooke, Hope, Todd, Jade, and Kinnah

Left: Ray and Tank

Far left: Mamaw and cousin Rich

Left: Grandma, Grandpa, and Jade

Jade with Mommy and Daddy

Jade's first
fish

Jade at two and a half

Jade at three

Emmie and Faith

Jade at four

Jade and Angie

Jade with a large jade stone

Jade at fifteen

Angie and Lynel

Jade on Kauai

Russ, Rich, Jade, Ray, and Bill

Rich, Ray, Bill, and Russ

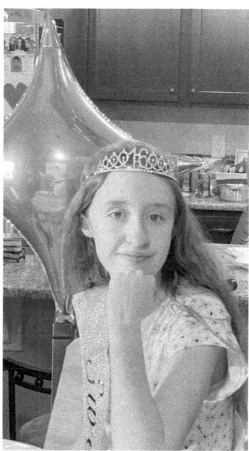

Nana and Jade

Jade's Sweet Sixteen

AJ, Jade, and Nana

Jade's high school graduation

Jade at seventeen

Jade and Angie

Invitation

YOU ARE BEING INVITED TO ACCEPT THE GREATEST
GIFT YOU COULD EVER IMAGINE!

The power of this compelling story is the redemption and transformation that Jesus offers to EVERYONE, no matter who you are and no matter what the circumstances may be in your life! Jesus gave Angie a testimony to share with the world, and she wants EVERYONE who touches this book to receive the power, hope, joy, redemption, and NEW LIFE that Jesus offers.

The transaction is simple. It's all about the greatest news ever! It goes like this:

- We give to Jesus all that we are . . . our brokenness, failure, discouragement, pain—all the shortcomings of our life.
- He offers us an abundant life now and eternal life for the future!
- AND this is a gift that is offered to everyone! That's the GOOD NEWS! And it is as simple as A, B, C.

A—ADMIT that we need a power greater than ourselves!

For everyone has sinned; we all fall short of God's glorious standard. (Romans 3:23 NLT)

B—BELIEVE that Jesus offers us NEW LIFE.

For the wages of sin is death, but the free gift of God is eternal life through Christ Jesus our Lord. (Romans 6:23 NLT)

C—COMMIT our lives to Jesus.

> *Don't copy the behavior and customs of this*
> *world, but let God transform you into a new*
> *person by changing the way you think. Then you*
> *will learn to know God's will for you, which is*
> *good and pleasing and perfect.*
> (Romans 12:2 NLT)

If you want to start a new life and experience all that God wants for you—all you need to do is ask! Here's a prayer to God that will begin your new journey.

Heavenly Father, thank you for your abundant and unfailing love for me. I admit I need You. Thank you for sending Jesus to die on the cross and to offer me forgiveness and eternal life. Today I receive all that Jesus offers me and I receive Him as my Savior. I receive Your love and grace and confidently believe my life is forever changed. Help me live for You. My heart and life are open to what you have for me! I want to love You with all my heart and love others as You love me. Thank You for your grace, mercy, love, and forgiveness! Thank you that through Jesus I am a new person. Use me to bless others. In the name of Jesus, I pray. Amen.

Blessings to you on your journey!

Carl Sutter
Founding Pastor
Foundations Church
Loveland, Colorado

About the Author

*A*ngie Howell is a pediatric registered nurse, former International Board Certified Lactation Consultant, CEO, Christian entrepreneur, inspirational speaker, and author. With more than twenty-five years of experience in the medical field, Angie is uniquely positioned to share her complex and deeply personal life-and-death journey of having a baby with a fatal diagnosis and extraordinary medical needs.

Angie has spent the past fifteen years working with children and adults with disabilities and has grown her company, Tender Hearts Home Healthcare, to a thriving agency in Northern Colorado.

Angie has a bachelor of arts degree in communication and English and a degree in nursing. She loves volunteering her time to help others and founded a nonprofit organization, Baja Blessing. While spending the better part of two years in Tijuana, Mexico, during the pandemic, Angie worked as a medical missionary with her two youngest daughters where they all learned how to love in a language they didn't speak or understand.

Angie is a faithful follower of Jesus, an avid traveler, and a lover of contemporary Christian music. She has seven daughters, one son, and thirteen grandchildren. Angie and her youngest daughter, Jade, travel frequently between their homes in Colorado and Tennessee with their two fiercely loved but obnoxious labradoodles.

www.ingramcontent.com/pod-product-compliance
Lightning Source LLC
Jackson TN
JSHW012040030325
79977JS00008B/21